For the Beauty of the Earth

DAILY DEVOTIONS
EXPLORING CREATION

Featuring Original Watercolors
by Kathrin Burleson

i

© 2018 Forward Movement

Forward Movement
412 Sycamore Street
Cincinnati, Ohio 45202-4194
800.543.1813
www.forwardmovement.org

ISBN 978-0-88028-453-0

Printed in the USA

FOR THE
Beauty
OF THE
Earth

DAILY DEVOTIONS
EXPLORING CREATION

Forward Movement
Cincinnati, Ohio

For the Beauty of the Earth

For the beauty of the earth,
for the beauty of the skies,
for the love which from our birth
over and around us lies;
Christ our God, to thee we raise
this our hymn of grateful praise.

For the beauty of each hour
of the day and of the night,
hill and vale, and tree and flower,
sun and moon, and stars of light;
Christ our God, to thee we raise
this our hymn of grateful praise.

Words by Folliot Sandford Pierpont (1835-1917)
The 1982 Hymnal, #416

Table of Contents

Foreword

The watercolor paintings by Kathrin Burleson and the soul-deep meditations by talented and faithful writers from across the country serve as guides through the wonder of creation. We become witnesses to love in action—flowing colors, winking stars, myriad beasts and blooms, and a garden full of flowers, fruit, trees, and a new miracle under every leaf. This is more than just a book of devotions and pretty paintings—this book is a companion as you rediscover the wonder of creation in God's garden and in your own heart.

Kathrin's watercolors begin each month, along with a short explanation of her process of artistic creation. We asked authors to be inspired by scripture, by the paintings, and by the marvelous and miraculous sights and sounds of the earth and skies.

A labor of love, our daybooks provide a daily devotional practice much in keeping with the voice and rhythm of other offerings from Forward Movement, including our flagship resource, *Forward Day by Day*. Our annual daybooks allow us to share the voices of more writers and provide an opportunity to sit with a particular biblical story or concept for a longer period of time. We could think of no better place to spend the next year than with God and in the garden—to fall in love with creation and the Creator.

Rachel Jones & Richelle Thompson
Editors, Cincinnati, Ohio

Introduction
Artist's Note

Creation is a big subject—huge. Not surprisingly, people approach the story of how the world and all of us came to be from many directions—scientifically, scripturally, literally, mystically. Regardless of which perspective we use to try to understand creation, we are an integral part of it. Odds are that if you are reading this book and embarking on a journey through a new year with these devotions as a companion, you probably figure God into your attempts to glimpse the wonder of creation. I know I do, even when I'm not consciously aware of it.

The paintings featured in this book were completed over the span of a couple of years. I had just finished a series of paintings based on the I Am statements of Jesus as found in the Gospel of John. In those statements we see Jesus through the lens of metaphor, where the ordinary stuff of life is amplified and points to something beyond. After immersing myself in those images over several months, I took a break from watercolors to let ideas simmer without any particular direction or prompting. It wasn't long before Genesis spoke to me and became my primary focus and interest. In retrospect, I see this was the logical next step. In both cases, something knowable and tangible leads us to the ineffable.

There are two creation stories in the Bible; both are found in the first two chapters of Genesis and amount to just a few pages. Who would have thought the expanse of creation could be conveyed in so few words?

My relationship to the creation story isn't hinged to a literal understanding. Like much of my reading of the Bible, I see the stories of creation as true in their very deepest senses—they are true as revelations of the divine to humankind, not scientific or empirically provable, but absolutely true nevertheless. The relationship of the creation story to science is fascinating and worthy of study, but that is a topic for other writers and other books. This book is an exploration of the relationship of the story of creation to the lives of each of us who take time to ponder and wonder, or as *The Book of Common Prayer* implores us, to read, mark, learn, and inwardly digest.

Initially, I thought I would do a painting for each day of creation, but I soon realized that wasn't going to be enough. The description of the first day alone inspired six paintings—and this was just a hint of the richness of inspiration that lay ahead. Painting the early, abstract concepts of creation was both challenging and enjoyable. It was a time to let the watercolor do much of the work—in other words, to let go of control, allow the pigment to react with water and paper, and see what would happen. I wonder if that's what God did—or does: Put elements together and see what happens.

Much of this process of artistic creation has been a dance between observing, letting things happen, and taking control—making choices and then letting the results of those choices play out. The choices have been big and small, from deciding which pigments to use or how much water to add (this sounds pretty elementary, but it really does matter) to resisting the urge to control the paint. Ultimately these paintings developed in a detached yet fully committed relationship with the process. In that respect, this project is a lot like life.

When I started to paint the third day of creation, I faced another big challenge. How could I possibly choose which plants or animals to paint? Creation is, to put it mildly, vast. I needed a strategy. As I leaned against the door of my studio, gazing out on the bluff and pondering (I do this a lot when I am stuck on a painting), an approach came to me. And it was so obvious. I would paint creation in my little corner of the world, the ecosystem where I live.

I took some artistic liberties with this strategy—I couldn't resist including animals encountered during my travels to Africa, but the bulk of this body of work features plants and animals found in coastal Northern California. The blessing in this approach was being able to really see and appreciate some of these animals for the first time—and in many cases, do a bit of a reframe in order to see them in a different light. Mice are an ongoing problem in my basement, raccoons desecrate my potted plants and raid my apple orchard, and the deer dine (uninvited) in my garden. Ditto the rabbits. But I made an effort to see them from a new perspective. It is a bit of a stretch to say that I now see all of them as God's precious creatures *all of the time*—the battle over territory still rages, but in painting and spending time understanding them, I warmed up to these creatures. And I've given up on trying to grow a vegetable garden.

But I haven't given up on trying to make sense of creation. And thankfully, God hasn't given up on us either. Forward Movement has assembled a group of gifted and inspired writers to provide daily devotions as companions for the year, and I look forward to sharing the journey with all of you. With each illustration, I offer a few brief words about how God inspired my process of creating—and how God continues to inspire me with the amazing gifts of all of creation.

May God bless you as you live and participate in the miraculous unfolding of creation.

Kathrin Burleson
Artist, Trinidad, California

FOR THE Beauty OF THE Earth

January

Formless and Void

In the beginning when God created the heavens and the earth, the earth was a formless void and darkness covered the face of the deep, while a wind from God swept over the face of the waters.

Genesis 1:1-2

Artist's Note: Trying to express a formless void in watercolor presents a bit of a challenge. After exploring several directions with no success, I decided to let the paint do the work. All of the paintings in this series are done on clay panel. One of the selling points of the clay platform is that the artist has better control over the paint, can lift pigment, and make changes. I like it for the opposite reason—it allows me to let go of control. If I put enough water and pigment on it and just watch, it takes on a life of its own and does things I would never think of doing—or be able to do deliberately. It's kind of a metaphor for life. The trick is to know when to let things happen and when to try to control the situation or force a solution.

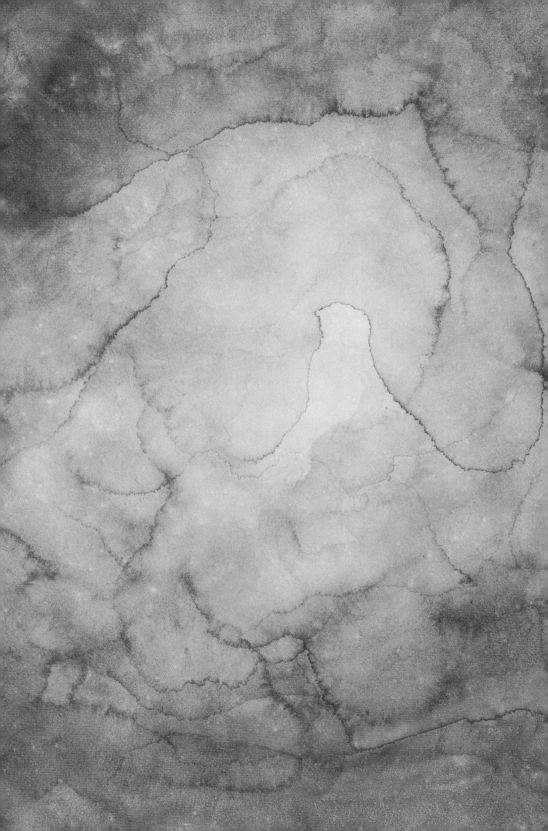

Let There Be Light

Then God said, "Let there be light"; and there was light. And God saw that the light was good; and God separated the light from the darkness. God called the light Day, and the darkness he called Night. And there was evening and there was morning, the first day.

Genesis 1:3-5

Artist's Note: Visual art is all about contrasts. If you want a line to look bold and really stand out, you surround it with faint, delicate work. Want green to look really green? Place it by the color red. Light? Surround it with dark colors. Like just about everything else, this can be a metaphor for life. We can't help but compare ourselves and our lives to others, sometimes believing that we're on the lower end of the spectrum, and it can be depressing. It's also a dead end. We may find it helpful to remember that just about everything is relative. Maybe the only thing that isn't relative is God's enduring love. Next to that, everything pales in comparison.

In the beginning when God created the heavens and the earth, the earth was a formless void and darkness covered the face of the deep, while a wind from God swept over the face of the waters.
                                                        - Genesis 1:12

We are here together, you and me. We're beginning this year together, pondering the beginning of all beginnings. It is kind of a big moment, this doorway space before there was such a thing as a doorway or space or moments.

I grow cross-eyed at the concept of infinitude—of utter emptiness, but not really empty because to be empty means there was something that could have filled it. There may not even be a container for emptiness to reside. See why I go cross-eyed and wobbly? This is the time for me to remember: God calls me to be still and let God be God. The concept of infinitude is real as roses but actually understanding it is beyond me.

There have been moments of creation in my life that have left my face in pain from smiling so broadly, my throat raw from laughter, my eyes running with happy tears. I marvel at how much bigger and broader God's smile must have been at the moment of creation, how God must have laughed with deep joy and profound contentment at calling the chaos into order and watching light form, watching stars wink awake, watching as something to watch takes shape. In this time before time, you and I might feel despair over the emptiness; skepticism about how things will gather, form, and fly; reluctance to keep adding things like planets or plants or animals or people. And still, God knows better, and keeps on making all things—all of the things—with love and intention and hope. This is literally more than we can ask or imagine.

Stay and sit here, in this beginning stillness, just for a minute, here in the midst of this first day. God is doing something new, something amazing—and in this very present moment, that thing is not the whole of existence or the universe or physics or string theory—it is you.

January 2

We thank you, Almighty God, for the gift of water. Over it the Holy Spirit moved in the beginning of creation.
The Book of Common Prayer

There is something mystical and fascinating to me in realizing that nowhere in our account of creation do we see God creating water. Water seems to be already part and parcel of God. When scientists look into the universe to find places that look like Earth, that could cradle life the way this place does, they search for water. Water could mean life.

One summer almost half a lifetime ago, I swam in the waters off of Key West, Florida. The water in that part of the world is especially saline, and floating is a breeze for most folks. There in my snorkel mask, staring wide-eyed into the array of plants and animals that make their home in those waters, I felt overcome. There was so much to look at, so much to marvel over, and suddenly my mask was filled with my own special blend of saltwater—tears. I closed my eyes and allowed the gentle motion of the sea to hold and comfort me. There must have been some kind of cellular recognition of a similar moment in my being—of being in the warm waters of my mother's womb, of feeling so at peace, so embraced, so safe, and so precious.

Water—whether it is the womb-water of our individual births or the present and potent waters of creation—is inseparable from the Creator. Mountains, molehills, mendicants, millionaires, and a Messiah are all— every last one of them—born of water and buffeted (sometimes gently and sometimes not) by the wind of God.

January 3

Wind—like water—has seemingly always been part of our story. Wind sweeps over the face of the water, pointing us toward the fact that something major is about to happen. I think about the way my mother's perfume wafts into a room before she does.

Young's Literal Translation of the Bible renders the first and second verses of Genesis this way: *In the beginning of God's preparing the heavens and the earth—the earth hath existed waste and void, and darkness [is] on the face of the deep, and the Spirit of God fluttering on the face of the waters.* One of the things I particularly love about this translation is that almost all the verbs are rendered in present tense—everything from creation to revelation happens in present time, right now, right this minute. And that is amazing to me. It's also true, which leaves my heart fluttering with awe and wonder.

Time, in this moment of creation, is not a concept. There is no sun or moon, and the earth is merely a waiting pool for what has yet to be called into being. Our best estimate of the age of the universe as we currently understand it is around 13.8 billion years.

I have a hard time remembering major details of my life from the mid-1990s and am only moderately sure I turned off the coffeepot this morning, so 13.8 billion years is a lot to wrap my head around. But I know that 13.8 billion years puts my piddly life into some serious perspective. I love thinking that I am so close as to be cuddled up next to this holy moment of God's breath hovering over the water, just before the command to let all things be.

January 4

When I was 26, I quit my job and moved home to live in my mother's guest room. My new job was taking care of my cousin who was born with a catastrophic injury. This was the most important year of my life. During the year, I learned more about grace and mercy than I ever thought possible, and this injured little boy without sight or speech taught me more about the power of compassion and love than anyone besides Jesus.

The depth of Austin's injury is difficult to plumb, because he can't really tell you about it or respond to external stimuli. Even his doctors have a hard time sussing out what might be going on inside of his body and how to fix or mitigate it. I assumed a lot of chaos abounded inside of Austin's mind. This was a very unfair assumption to make—and one that Austin corrected for me in short order.

One morning when it was still dark, I came into the house from the garage and made my way down the hall to Austin's room. As I was about to enter his room, I stopped dead in my tracks.

Austin was laughing...belly laughing. He was laughing so hard that he had tears streaming down his face. He made that little sigh we all make at the end of a gale of laughter and then started right back up. It was the most joyful, unprompted, unexplainable, and beautiful thing I have ever heard in my life. All this time, I had imagined chaos and confusion inside of his broken self, and he showed me—giggled it right into my heart and mind—that God is always doing more than we can ask or imagine, making a world for each of us to understand and marvel over in our own ways, even when no one else can see it.

January 5

One of my favorite authors asserts that, "Time is a face on the water." I love this image of time being a living and breathing creature. It is easy for me to imagine time as either a taker or a giver, but rarely do I imagine it with a face. Personalizing time makes me less irritated by it—the way time seems to jump or drag or fly by.

I can far too easily imagine my own face reflected in water, not unlike the myth of Narcissus, so I have to be careful not to fall in love or in thrall with myself. Of all the things I know, I am most certain that God is God and I am not, and this is a very good thing indeed. There are too many days when I struggle with just being myself—I would be terrible at being God.

Think of your favorite face—the face you love best—and imagine it gazing over the deep, looking at all the possibilities and probabilities and prognostications with joy and gladness. Imagine the desire to reach out and hold, to squeeze and murmur over, to place a hand of blessing and comfort on your own face—no brooding or pouting or quivering lips, only the satisfaction and contentment of sharing space.

This is how I imagine God looking out across the waters—God's face like time on the water—like my beloved's face or my grandmothers' faces, or my parents' faces, or the face of my best friend. These faces are constantly changing, but I know their lines and wrinkles and texture and brightness so well that all I have to do is close my eyes to see them.

January 6

We are almost a week deep into this new year. I'll be honest with you—
I've already said some things I shouldn't have. There are dishes in the sink
that I have not washed, laundry in the basket that I have not folded. I am
struggling to keep the integrity of my resolutions, and I am half-tempted
to just bag them and wait until Lent to start over. Maybe you're in this
same boat, or maybe you're making it just fine and haven't put any door-
dings in this new-model year.

I was 26, almost 27, the year I bought a powder blue VW Bug with a
gray ragtop—the car I had wanted since I was 17. I had it for less than
24 hours before I put a ding in the door. For the rest of the time I owned
that car, this door ding drove me crazy. I had a hard time looking at the
driver's side door without seeing this tiny, itty-bitty, drive-in restaurant-
tray scratch. I had marked up this thing I wanted and finally got, and I
was frustrated and ashamed that my depth perception wasn't better, that
I hadn't been paying enough attention to what I was doing, that maybe I
didn't deserve nice things, after all. Mind you, this is simply a door-ding.
But I got a little wound up.

We're going to put some dings in the doors of this year—we might even
crack or shatter a window or two, and let's be honest—the wheels could
come off entirely. But God is still making this place, making us, making
all things new. All things shall be well. Thanks be to God.

January 7

Even though we are just at the beginning of the beginning, today is a day for rest. I'm not sure I believe that God rests on the seventh day because God is tired (I mean really, God needs a nap?), but I have no trouble believing that God stops to rest and enjoy creation.

For today, let us linger here, hovering with God over the face of the deep, feeling God's Spirit churning and making a way, readying to light the sky, form the ground, divide the waters, fill the seas, furrow the land, paint the flowers, breathe breath into all that lives.

Something amazing is happening, and we will bear witness to it together, you and me. But for today, we get to be quiet and wonder over the power that is being summoned up in the mind of God, about to burst forth into all that is yet to be, making space and filling it at the same time. And this will be a wonder to behold.

January 8

This week's author
Nancy Hopkins-Greene

> *In the beginning when God created the heavens and the earth,*
> *the earth was a formless void and darkness covered the face*
> *of the deep, while a wind from God swept over the face of the*
> *waters.*

Genesis 1:1-2

Most biblical scholars agree that the oral history of the Children of Israel—Genesis, along with the rest of the Pentateuch (the first five books of the Hebrew Bible)—is finally written down during the Babylonian captivity during the sixth century BCE. The Jerusalem temple has been destroyed, the Israelites have lost their holy city and their promised land, and they have been carried off to Babylon.

These are trying years for God's people. As we hear in the laments of prophets and throughout the psalms, they struggle to make sense of it all. "How shall we sing the LORD's song upon an alien soil?" they ask (Psalm 137:4). Having lost their grounding, they are in the midst of chaos; their very existence as a people is threatened. One of the only ways that they can hold onto their identity and their faith is to tell and re-tell their stories. These include stories of how God has chosen, delivered, and redeemed them as a people.

And they include stories about how this same God creates all of life. The story of creation reminds them of the One who brings all things into being and who remains faithful to them. Some say this first chapter of Genesis is a liturgy the exiles recited as a way to comfort themselves, providing a sense of order and meaning in the midst of disorder and displacement.

Many of us, at one time or another, have experienced the loss of our center, moments when we feel disoriented, displaced, or shaken up. Often the world around us can seem equally unmoored. Like the Israelites, we can find comfort in knowing, even if we cannot sense it yet, that the Spirit of God is hovering, even now, bringing order out of the chaos— bringing new life and possibility.

January 9

As a child, I remember wondering, "What if there was nothing?" I guess that question was my way of wrestling with existence itself and of how I came to be—how *anything* came to be. It was mind-boggling, and if I think too much, it still is.

"The earth was a formless void, and darkness covered the face of the deep." Our minds can grow muddled with the thought of it: Before form or substance. Before light. Before there was anything. Yet this is where it all begins. How can we imagine it, this formless void? This nothing before anything?

In his work *Pensees*, seventeenth-century philosopher and mathematician Blaise Pascal wrote of an empty place, a craving inside every person. We try unsuccessfully to fill it with all sorts of things, but this infinite abyss can only be filled with God. Some have called this empty place the "God-shaped hole," and it is present in each of us.

Each of us has a place of yearning, a void we try to fill with material things, money, or alcohol. We try to fill it with busyness, self-importance, or control. Yet none of these satisfy, because what we need—the only thing that can fill this space within us—is God.

Standing before this formless void that existed before anything, we can be present to that God-shaped hole—that void inside us that only God can fill. And then, with all of creation, we can watch and wait for the wind—the Spirit—to breathe through it and fill it with God's presence and God's love.

January 10

It is still a few months before Lent, but I am reminded of the Easter Vigil. The liturgy begins in darkness as the Paschal Candle is lit from a newly kindled fire. The congregation processes into a dark worship space; a cantor sings the *Exsultet*. Sitting in darkness, worshipers listen and pray as the "record of God's saving deeds in history" is read (*The Book of Common Prayer*, pages 288-291). The first of these readings is this account of creation. This part of the service is liminal. There is a great sense of anticipation. We are on a threshold, about to cross over from death into life, from darkness into light.

It reminds me of other liminal times in our lives—in-between times. They can be as simple as the interval before dawn when the sound of the crickets dies down but the first birds have yet to begin their song. Something has ended, but the new has yet to take form. These times can be long, hard, and often chaotic, and we can lose a sense of belonging or rootedness. But liminal times can also foster spiritual growth. A classic example is the Hebrews' years of wandering in the wilderness. The new year can be such a time, as we leave behind one year and move into the new.

In these first verses of Genesis, we are on a threshold, in a liminal moment. We are in darkness and waiting for light to come. Similar to our celebration at the Vigil when the first Alleluia is proclaimed, we believe God will bring light. We wait, knowing that God will act. "I am about to do a new thing; now it springs forth, do you not perceive it?" (Isaiah 43:19a).

January 11

We are only two verses into the Bible, and there is already an apparent contradiction. Verse one would suggest that God created out of nothing—that "formless void." Verse two seems to say that there was something already there: the wind from God and the water. Which one is it? What *actually* happened?

Living in southern Ohio, I am not far from two tourist attractions that seek to answer this second question: the Creation Museum and the Ark Experience. I confess: I have not visited either, but as I understand it, they both promote a literal interpretation of Genesis. The Creation Museum portrays a "young earth creationist" perspective, in which the earth is only 6,000 years old and dinosaurs and humans walked the earth at the same time. The Ark Experience is a theme park that includes a life-sized ark like the one that Noah built, with measurements and specifications taken from Genesis.

I am not a scientist or a paleontologist, but I do wonder if in asking, "What really happened?" we are simply asking the wrong question. The writers of this creation account are not trying to give us a scientific explanation for the origin of things. They are making a statement of faith about God the creator and the relationship between this Creator and creation.

Debating whether God created out of something or out of nothing misses the point. What we know throughout the Bible is that God keeps taking lost causes and impossibilities: a childless couple, a group of slaves, a people in exile, a crucified man—and bringing new life. In the words of Paul, God "gives life to the dead and calls into existence the things that do not exist" (Romans 4:17b).

January 12

I love the color green. People who know me will confirm that I like to wear green. I also like to walk through green fields and forests, to grow and eat green things. I even joke about the fact that I like the color so much that I married someone with the last name Green(e)!

About ten years ago, I was delighted to hear about a new edition of the New Revised Standard Version of the Bible called *The Green Bible*. Like red-letter editions of the New Testament in which Jesus' words are printed in red, all verses and words about creation are set in green. Of course, this whole chapter of Genesis is a sea of green.

The first words of the preface to this edition asks, "Is God green?" Before you conjure up an image of a green monster-like deity, note that they were asking if God cares about creation, if Jesus was an environmentalist. The book's editors—and my—answer to that question is a resounding "Yes!" I believe that God cares passionately about the earth.

But where we are in the story *now* is before the first sunrise. It is before the dry land is created—there's no soil yet in which green things can grow. It is before the color green. I wonder if God was already thinking up the rainbow, blending yellow and blue? Had God already imagined photosynthesis?

And what else was God imagining? Lions lying down with lambs? A man rising from the dead? As for me, at this point in the story, I'm anxious for God to get going and to create the color green. And if God can create green, imagine all that God can do!

January 13

I am a gardener. I get excited when the first shoots of green emerge from seeds I plant in early spring. I take delight in eating the first ripe raspberries along the fence. I love looking out the window to see my flower beds in bloom in the summer. I love growing things. But I am equally a cultivator of the soil itself. I not only compost our yard and kitchen waste, but I also have a worm bin in my basement for vermicomposting during the winter months. And as much as I love a lush and fruitful garden, I sometimes enjoy most the space in between: the dirt itself.

As opposed to dust or dirt, soil is full of decaying matter, minerals, and microorganisms. Rich and balanced soil anchors roots and stores water, air, and other nutrients needed by plants. It might look like dirt, but there is a lot going on below the surface.

The wind of God sweeps over the face of the waters in these moments before creation. God hasn't created the soil yet, but this wind invites us to pause and reflect on all that goes on out of our sight, below the surface of things. Somewhere in God's plan are all of those growing things above and below the surface. But for now, creation is fallow and waiting. Perhaps we could ask this of our own lives too. What rich and abundant things could be stirring below the surface? What seeds might sprout in the year ahead?

January 14

For a number of years, my colleague, Charlie, and I had offices across from one another. His office was beautiful. Not only did he keep it orderly, but it was full of antiques and artwork. Just next door was my office. In contrast to his, mine was austere: walls mostly bare, surfaces clear. Folks gave up asking me when I was going to move in.

At that stage in my life, my children were young, and our house always seemed cluttered. Coming to my office in all its emptiness was a breath of fresh air. When people commented on the contrast of our two offices, I finally told them that Charlie and I were simply demonstrating two dimensions of the spiritual life: His was the aesthetic "yes," and mine was the ascetic "no." We need both, I told them.

Also known as the *via positiva* and the *via negativa*, these are two ways of knowing the Holy: by what can be seen, felt, and understood and by what cannot. The *via positiva* sees God in the beauty of creation, in the arts, and in the very fullness of life. The *via negativa*, often associated with the mystics, suggests that God is known in the unknown, in the emptying of all. In the words of Wayne Muller in his book *Sabbath: Finding Rest, Renewal, and Delight in Our Busy Lives*, "All life has emptiness at its core; it is the quiet hollow reed through which the wind of God blows and makes the music that is our life."

In a way, this point in the prehistory of creation epitomizes the *via negativa*. All surfaces are clear. There is nothing. And it is in this empty space that we wait for God to act. God is about to say a resounding yes to sunlight, to lush green growing things, to incredible diversity, to unfathomable beauty.

January 15

This week's author
Nicholas Knisely

Then God said, "Let there be light"; and there was light. And God saw that the light was good; and God separated the light from the darkness. God called the light Day, and the darkness he called Night. And there was evening and there was morning, the first day.

Genesis 1:3-5

There is a wall that separates us from the actual moment of the birth of the universe.

When we look out into the darkness of the nighttime sky, the farther we see in distance, the more ancient the light we observe. Astronomers call this "lookback time." The farther a light source is from us, the longer the light takes to reach us. What we see is not the actual astronomical object, but how it appeared when the light we see left its surface and began to travel toward us.

You might think that, given a sophisticated enough instrument, we would be able to see all the way back to the beginning of the universe. We can't: There's a literal wall of light blocking our view. That wall represents the universe as it was hundreds of thousands of years after it began and demarcates the moment the universe cooled down sufficiently after the fire and heat of its birth so that atoms could begin to exist and electrons and protons begin their dance. Before this instant, there is only the chaos of the act of creation.

Because of this wall of dazzling light, we cannot directly observe what happened in the beginning. But by observing the light—and the universe we now inhabit—we can make some pretty good guesses. But, when we do that, we speculate. We do not know—or at least, not fully.

We do not know God fully either: God's light blinds our vision. We know only in part. But we do know Jesus—and in Jesus, God's will for us is made known in a way we can comprehend. We can see the light of the fires of creation. But that light shrouds a mystery—a mystery unveiled in the incarnation. But first, there is light.

January 16

The first verses of Genesis make a surprising claim: The light God creates exists apart from the sun or the moon. In the period of history during which this story was written down for the first time, this was a startling idea—that light could exist without a source.

People imagined that the light that God created was the light that illumined all of creation—often described as a sign of the presence of God in the community. Think of the description of the experience of the shepherds in the fields on the night Jesus is born: The glory of the Lord shines all around them, and the angelic host sings and gives thanks.

When we meet God fully in the person of Jesus, we hear that Jesus is the light of the world, that in him there is no darkness at all. It is not the light of the sun or the moon or the stars that Jesus refers to when he says this; it is the cosmic light created in the first moments of God's creative action.

This light, the light of the beginning of creation, makes it possible for us to comprehend the world God has created around us, the world God has created for us. The light that God creates is good, and without it we are left groping in the darkness. It is that same primordial light that makes us wise and is the foundation of holy wisdom.

Today, give thanks for the light of the dawn that drives away the darkness of the night. That light is only a shadow of the light of God, but it points us toward the truth.

January 17

If you put a thin piece of paper between you and a light source, much of the light vanishes. It seems an odd thing for us to believe that light will always overcome the darkness when it is a simple thing to block the light and make a shadow.

The problem seems to be rooted in the way that we experience light. For humans, light is that which we can perceive with our eyes, and darkness is the lack of that perception. But our experience of visible light is not the whole reality of light. We perceive only a small portion of the vast expanses of the phenomenon of electromagnetic radiation that is light.

Light contains x-rays and gamma rays, ultraviolet and infrared, microwaves and radio waves—both short and long. And while a piece of paper might block a tiny portion of visible light, the paper is transparent to pretty much the rest of the entire spectrum. The light of a simple candle, which contains all the wavelengths of light (though in teeny, tiny amounts) has portions that pass through a piece of paper and create a partial shadow.

While it might seem a simple thing to block the light, it is almost impossible to create a place that even the smallest candle cannot illuminate.

We have been given the Light of God as part of our birthright as humans—redeemed by Jesus and given the light of Christ in our baptism. There is nothing that can fully resist that light that is within us. It might appear that shadow remains, but that is only because we do not yet fully see the full spectrum of God's goodness in those difficult and dim moments.

January 18

As I look out my window this morning, I see the leaves of a holly tree bouncing in the wind. I see the flash of a cardinal's wings as he flies across my yard. I see brilliant white clouds framed against a blue sky. And I see all this indirectly by the reflection of sunlight.

If there were no sun shining brilliantly in the sky this morning, I would see only darkness when peering out my window. The tree and its leaves would still be there as would the cardinal and the clouds, but I wouldn't be able to perceive them. It is the light created in the belly of the sun, which escapes the surface and hurtles through interplanetary space that makes it possible for me to marvel at the picture presented to me by my window. That light is reflected from the objects it encounters and makes it possible for us to see and know what God has created in the world.

The light that God creates in the first day allows us to know the world around us. It is a sign that points us to the greater truth that it is love.

January 19

When I was ordained a bishop, I was given a mitre—a tall, pointy hat that is a symbol of the episcopate. Because I serve in Maryland, the Ocean State, I asked that my vestments reflect our experience of being people who live our lives on and beside the water. The symbolism we chose to emphasize was the water of baptism. The design of the mitre incorporates this in the form of stylized waves with foam. When the light strikes my mitre just right, people say the foam on it glows as if there's a light inside it. Who knew foam could do that?

When there is foam on the water, it is a sign that the water beneath is living and in constant motion. The foam is created by the mixing of the wind and water as the waves move across the surface of the deep. The faster the waves and the more active the motion, the greater the chaos, and the more foam is created. When I look far out to sea and see the waves, it's not the waves I really see but the foam that creates flashing in the light.

Created by chaos at the boundary of sea and sky, the foam is lit up by the light—it dances and sparkles and plays. The chaos is the source of the beauty that the light illumines—marking the motion and transformation of the wave as it travels.

It seems to me that the light created by God often does such things— lighting up the chaotic regions of our lives in such a way that they become places of beauty and creativity. What seems to be useless can find purpose when it is brought fully into the light.

January 20

When God acts to create light on the first day of creation, there is a consequence. God's creation of light also creates possibility for there to be an absence of light, named darkness in Genesis. In a sense this yin and yang is echoed in other parts of holy scripture: God's creation of light makes God the creator of darkness, too.

It seems odd to think about darkness having its genesis in God's creative act. But imagine for a moment if the cosmos were filled only with light: We wouldn't be able to see. The totality of illumination would dazzle us. Without shadow and boundaries created by an absence of light, we would miss out on the beauty of the differences that God has embossed on creation.

The darkness is not a thing in and of itself, as it has a derivative existence. But darkness is fundamental to God's plan.

At times, light seems absent. And if you're anything like I am, you probably imagine that you could manage quite well without having to experience dark moments. But as I read the story of God's creative acts, I see these difficult times are the unavoidable consequence of the gifts that God gives us—the dark and the light.

January 21

The Agony & the Ecstasy, Irving Stone's biographical novel of the life of Michelangelo, maintains that the artist would rise before dawn so he could see the marble he intended to carve in the first light of day. The light of dawn, with the sun's rays pouring over the distant horizon, made it easy to see the imperfections in the marble.

The light of dawn lets us see truth in a special way.

To me, the light before dawn is beautiful. There is something magical in watching the deep blue of the night sky lighten in the east as dawn approaches. The lighter blue of early morning twilight—the way the horizon begins to emerge as the stars disappear—is a sign that day is gathering its strength, just before the sun leaps above the horizon and day begins in earnest. Somehow, watching the darkness disappear makes the light and the gift of the day all the more precious to me.

I am inclined to believe that we find the greatest truths at the boundaries, frontiers, the liminal places where we move from one state of being or understanding to another. Twilight is the archetypal boundary, and it is the boundary that can only exist because of God's creative action and the effects it has on the cosmos.

Jesus is most often found at the boundaries, at the margins. Perhaps this is why disciples first encounter him after the resurrection at early dawn, in the twilight as the night recedes and the light waxes stronger—flooding the shadow-filled places with light and life.

January 22

This week's author
Jonathan Melton

Then God said, "Let there be light"; and there was light. And God saw that the light was good; and God separated the light from the darkness. God called the light Day, and the darkness he called Night. And there was evening and there was morning, the first day.

Genesis 1:3-5

Every day turns into night. Brilliant, I know. But the process of every day turning into night is not as obvious as it used to be, what with our fancy smart homes and smart phones filling our lives with light. Some days, I fool myself into believing that both the light around me and the light inside me have switches I control, that I can flip on and off at will.

The refinery outside the town where I used to live had lights that were literally never turned off except when they were being replaced. I found the sight of the blazing refinery at night depressing, but the picture of endless "daylight" also resonated with me. There is so much in each day to accomplish! Who has time for it all? I recently read that the average person today reads more information in a day than an average person in the 1800s read in an entire lifetime. No wonder we are all so tired. No wonder we stay up late trying to sneak in one more productive thing under the blanket of a night that would like to give us rest.

Like my kids, who tap me on the shoulder nearly every time I'm about to find a groove with my chores or complete a sentence with my wife, the sleep that comes with the night interrupts the work and productivity from which I am tempted to derive my worth.

Night breaks life into pieces, tiny steps, daily surrender. It's as if, on Day One and before anything else, God built into the order of things this reminder: Walking with God, one unfinished step at a time, trusting, enjoying, and trusting some more, really is the thing this life—indeed all of creation—is about.

January 23

When I camp, and only when I camp, I become a morning person. The birdcalls at 5 a.m. sound like they are made through megaphones or by birds inside my tent, some standing on my pillow. The sunlight at seven feels like noonday. Throw in the fact that the previous day at the campsite likely ended with the sun's setting or shortly after, and I find myself happily emerging from my dew-drenched tent at ungodly hours, as if summoned by the beauty of the new day and the vitality of all the life already busily embracing it. It feels good and right to welcome the new day together.

Sure, part of my eagerness to get out of the tent no doubt stems from the discomfort of the ground and the way the rainfly traps body heat. But I also feel an accountability to creation. The birds are singing! Who am I to lie sleeping? All of the mysterious, nocturnal creatures who took their waking turn during the night have retired and given me the space to live and move again. We are all cooperating, making room for each other. We are all connected. We are all the good work of our Creator. I am grateful.

I am still grateful when I wake up inside my climate-controlled home to an alarm clock whose heralding of the new day I will fight with reluctance and generous use of the snooze button. But my gratitude on those days is more likely to be for *distance from* creation rather than *connection to* it, and some days, I wonder what kind of gratitude that is, really.

January 24

The liturgy of Compline is practice for death. The beautiful night prayers of the Episcopal tradition are not less a practice for death for their beauty. The antiphon bracketing the *Nunc Dimittis* calls out, "Guide us waking, O Lord, and guard us sleeping, that awake we make watch with Christ, and asleep we may rest in peace." Lord, help us *rest in peace*, we pray.

As a kid, my granny taught my brothers and me a familiar childhood bedtime prayer that shared the prayer book's sentiment: *Now I lay me down to sleep. I pray the Lord my soul to keep. If I should die before I wake, I pray the Lord my soul to take.* I only found out later that my granny's choice of this particular ending, as opposed to a happier, death-free version, was controversial in the bedtime prayer circles of other eight-year-olds and their families. The effect of Granny's bedtime prayer was to make me aware that each day is a gift. Fancy plans and worry do not entitle me to another one. Rhythms of days and night become occasions of surrender.

"Give us this day our daily bread," Jesus teaches his disciples. Because tomorrow, should it come, will also be for asking for bread, for walking with and relying on God. To walk by myself—to have enough on my own— is never the goal. But each and every day is for walking with God.

So guide us waking, O Lord, and guard us sleeping...

January 25

In high school, I dabbled in art. I still do sometimes. My favorite medium is charcoal, which is an immersion exercise in light and dark. I like to notice where the two are separated and where they connect. Also, I find smudgy hands delightfully satisfying.

Sometimes the transition from dark to light is tender and gradual. Other times, as when a light source is directed at the side of one's head, the separation seems total and abrupt, slicing along the bridge of the nose. One side is drenched in light, the other in darkness. Even in that instance, though, there's a line, a place of connection, like the line marking the far side of the moon.

The interplay between light and dark acknowledges that our lives too are a mix of sunshine and shadows, joys and trials. Certainty and honest doubts. Whether seasonally, by daily rhythms, or simultaneously, we will know the truth of both the light and the dark. We will learn our need of both, and we will learn by these rhythms the nature and substance of our needs.

I grew up thinking of darkness as the place where scary things hid, but of course there are gifts in the darkness. Nicodemus, for example, discovers permission in the dark to seek Jesus and name his doubts about the certainties he has carried all his life. For him, darkness means a thrilling possibility: Openness to the learning that requires unlearning and new relationship with God. Darkness gives birth to light. Nicodemus is my reminder that the social pressure to appear "all sunshine" is good to resist. Who knows? Even in the shadows, maybe God is about to do a new thing I do not yet see.

January 26

The communion of saints names our connection to all the saints before us, after us, and around us. Truthfully, the *before us* understanding of the communion of saints comes most naturally to me. When I was little, my daddy would tell me that he didn't go to the cemetery to remember his father, but that he remembered his dad at Holy Eucharist, where Grandpa Jack is even now present with "angels, archangels, and all the company of heaven." As a kid, this made sense. It still makes sense.

After us makes sense too, even if it can be uncomfortable imagining an earthly future in which the uniquely human desire to make a difference has been surrendered.

Around us may feel obvious, but my experience is that seeing the communion of saints *around us* takes the most work. I am daily surrounded by amazing, holy, hilarious, and incredibly gifted people of God. The communion of saints means these incredible people of God across the world are beginning their morning prayers just as my evening prayers are ending, that we are entrusting the work of ceaseless prayer to each other and to the rhythm of the earth's turning around the sun.

Around us takes work because it requires me to surrender my competitive tendencies. To entrust the ceaseless work of prayer to someone who "works while others sleep" is to acknowledge the interdependence of people in countries at war with each other. The communion of saints names the primacy of baptism over every other allegiance or accomplishment any of us could claim. In place of these things, we trust the love of God that is the truest thing about us. Trusting this love, we see one another anew, as gifts and holy friends, as collaborators enjoying the privilege of communicating this love in the world.

January 27

Author C.S. Lewis wrote, "I believe in Christianity as I believe that the sun has risen: not only because I see it, but because by it I see everything else." I love that line, which takes as its starting place the assumption that the Gospel of Jesus is meant for touching everything about our lives and the world around us. The Christian faith is the discovery that gives our lives back to us as strange gifts to be received and reimagined in light of the love and presence of Christ.

Of course, C.S. Lewis was writing for the daytime. At night, it is true that we are less able to see some things, but also that there are other things we can only see by darkness, like the stars. My mom and dad live out in South Texas, and my dad has this nightly ritual of walking to the edge of the property and staring up at the sky to name his late-night appreciation for the grandeur of creation. When I visit, I like to make the walk with him, and I'll pull out my phone with an app that acts like a cheat sheet for the cosmos, identifying the various constellations. Dad doesn't disapprove per se, but he doesn't need another screen to tell him that life is mysterious and beautiful, magnificent and strange, a stunning and overwhelming gift.

When God appears to Abraham and Sarah and promises a stunning, overwhelming gift, God points to the stars to convey the extent of the promise. C.S. Lewis' sun by which we see the rest of life doesn't erase the other stars: It's simply the one whose nearness gives us life. Christ is the fullness of the love the stars have signaled all along. Christ *is the love* that sets the stars *and us* in motion.

January 28

So I've been thinking about light and dark a lot this week. Noticing both of them and paying them a kind of reverent attention. The week has reminded me that I used to notice the dark a lot more when I was a kid— and that I was usually afraid of the dark.

The other day, my daughter said from the back seat of the car that she doesn't see me cry much. She's probably right. I tear up a lot and unexpectedly, but I can count on one hand the number of good sobs I've shared this year. But as I've been thinking about light and dark and fear this week, what bothers me more than the frequency of my tears is my reluctance to name my fears to my children.

Of course, there's developmental wisdom in my reluctance. My five-year-old son doesn't need my fears. He's got plenty of his own. But as he grows older, I hope I will possess the courage to be afraid in front of him, because I know the blessing it has been to have my wife hear me say, "Babe, I'm scared," and have her put an arm around me, look me in the eye, and say, "I'm scared, too. I'm here, and I'm with you, and I'm scared, and let's do this."

When my daughter was four, she came home from school one day and said, "Daddy, work was hard today. Really hard." I stared at her in amazement. "But you know what," she said, straightening up and putting her hands on her hips. "Daddy, *I can do hard things!*"

More than anything, I know that admitting my fears is essential to staying honest with God.

God, forgive my attempts to do this life on my own. Amen.

January 29

Uncertainty is the thing that makes darkness scary. It's the not knowing what's in the cave that makes us feel like running and screaming. Light holds our imaginations accountable and reins in our fears, because we can see for ourselves that the danger we were sure was there is not, in fact, there. But in the darkness, we anticipate all of the things...or at least, all the worst things.

In an interview about his book, *The Sin of Certainty*, Peter Enns observes that people sometimes talk about faith like a wall. When we become less certain, we describe the wall as crumbling, and our job, we think, is to repair the wall. But faith is "not a wall, but a journey or pilgrimage." In other words, we have to move, even though it is dark...even though we may be scared. "You're not allowed to stay where you're in control."

In the beginning: Day and Night. Light and Dark. Certainty and uncertainty. Times to stay. Times to move. God gives the cloud by day and the fire by night to lead the people through the wilderness. God uses both light and dark as vehicles to lead us. Because sometimes the leading is not just to the deep well but to deeper trust.

Most of the hymns we sing in my church are songs of certainty. I open the hymnal to a page and the words I sing are all held captive, like flies on flypaper. Numbers show me where the song will start and end. All is clear.

But not all songs are like this: Some require me to listen and echo or respond without a script. Some songs don't promise to tell me how they will start and when they will end. These songs may expose my desire for control. But only these songs can be sung in the dark.

January 30

"What time is it?" An honest question from my loving kid. But already I can feel the unkind answer lurching out of me, as if by instinct. "Time for you to get a watch!" I say, triumphantly. I always say it, succumbing to the instinct, because my kids are always asking me what time it is. I know parents are supposed to be patient, thoughtful, and kind...but this question, more than all others, triggers a third-grade level response in me.

When I grow up, I'll tell my kids that watches are, of course, only one of the possible tools to keep track of time and the rhythms of light and dark we call our days. For centuries, Christians have kept present to time by their prayers. Benedict had his communities praying every three hours! It is hard to overstate how far removed our Fitbits and Apple watches keep us from appreciating Benedict's world.

Most of us are trying our best to pray once or twice a day, but saints still exist who measure their days by their prayers. It's pure speculation on my part, but I imagine these saints have an easier time remembering their right place in the order of creation than the rest of us. Gratitude may come more easily to them, too. After all, the dominant chorus throughout the prayers of every time of day is ceaseless and unchanging: "Glory to the Father, and to the Son, and to the Holy Spirit: as it was in the beginning, is now, and will be forever. Amen."

January 31

Where I live in Wisconsin, the days are starting to grow noticeably longer. Truthfully, we've been tracking the later sunsets since just before Christmas. The musical artist *Iron & Wine* calls these our "endless, numbered days," and they are. But so much change exists in the handoff of one day to the next. Longer, shorter, sunny, and overcast...days repeat, but are not the same.

Jesus, with all his emphasis on *today*, wants me to keep from comparing my days. But it's hard. A friend once said, "Comparisons are demonic," and I thought, "Demonic is a strong word, but I think it's the right word." Whether on Facebook comparing lives or sitting in this day comparing it to one that hasn't come yet, comparisons block us from the gift of this present moment into which God has come to meet you and me. Comparison erodes daily trust. It's asking for manna...for daily bread...for minute-by-minute grace...again.

There's a fantastic bakery in my neighborhood called Manna. Manna serves day-old bread, and I'm the only one who gets worked up over this. It's funny, of course, because the only rule about manna is that it couldn't be saved. The people in the wilderness have to get up and gather their portion each new day. God's people have to get up and meet God each new day in an attitude of dependency, vulnerability, and trust.

Lives that have been met every day by the goodness of God—and know this truth—surely give glory to God. But I know how difficult it is to resist the temptation to take the smallest good thing in my life and twist it into a sign that I'm somebody. Who cares if I am somebody? I am *somebody's*. Thanks be to God.

February

The LORD God Made the Earth and the Heavens

In the day that the LORD God made the earth and the heavens, when no plant of the field was yet in the earth and no herb of the field had yet sprung up—for the LORD God had not caused it to rain upon the earth, and there was no one to till the ground.

Genesis 2:4b-5

Artist's Note: This scripture describes God's blank canvas, primed and ready to go, waiting for the first stroke or splash. The first step is completed—now for the details and the fun stuff. But the visual task of representing this moment was to keep it simple: the heavens and the earth, above and below, waiting.

In the Midst of the Waters

And God said, "Let there be a dome in the midst of the waters, and let it separate the waters from the waters." So God made the dome and separated the waters that were under the dome from the waters that were above the dome. And it was so.

Genesis 1:6-7

Artist's Note: I took a fairly primitive approach to this piece, simply placing a cross-section of a dome over the waters. It seemed to work. Afterward, I felt moved to do a little online research and found some interesting explanations about moisture, aqueous vapor, and condensation, but after a few paragraphs I realized I would rather think of a dome in the sky and live with the mystery.

February 1

> *In the day that the LORD God made the earth and the heavens, when no plant of the field was yet in the earth and no herb of the field had yet sprung up—for the LORD God had not caused it to rain upon the earth, and there was no one to till the ground.*
>
> **Genesis 2:4b-5**

I often attend events that begin with an acclamation fairly close to this: This is the day the Lord has made. Let us rejoice and be glad in it.

Indeed, I believe that the Lord did, and does, make every day. And indeed, the Lord makes all that is around us—the earth, sky, sea, and the air we breathe.

We usually read scripture in one of two ways, either using it as a window or a mirror. Often, we read it as if looking through a window, peering through the story to see something or someone from the past, to look at what happened back then. But when we read these holy stories as if we were looking into a mirror, our connections to the stories change, and what we read becomes about us in this present moment. I gently invite us to use the mirror method of reading scripture more often.

For when we look into the mirror of the stories of God's love for creation and creatures and contemplate, "In the day that the LORD God made the earth," we may find that this is not just a story about that first day, long ago but rather about every day since, and most especially for you and me, *this day*, this one, the one we inhabit now, this moment.

God's great work of creation did not end that first day or on any day. *This day*, the Lord makes the earth, sky, sea, and the air we breathe...this day.

February 2

What I love about art is the way it can take an abstract idea and give it dimension. Art can take a linear idea and give it depth, perspective, and color. Art can, in the best of ways, take a seemingly simple idea and make it more complex.

When I think of the heavens and the earth, it is easy to make these two separate things butted up against one another. However, I only have to study and reflect on the life and preaching of Jesus to note that he never sees heaven and earth in this divided way.

I have learned to see—and prefer to look at—the heavens and the earth as one unified reality. I started thinking about what goes on between these two massive and miraculous parts of creation. In my estimation, this holy space where they meet is where life is.

As I step even further into this vision, I see heaven and earth are entirely infused by and running through one another. I learn over and over that these are not two separate and independent pieces of majestic creation but rather one holy, whole expression of God's delight and imagination. This is what the Lord has made.

February 3

As I flew thousands of feet in the air over a huge swath of desert in the Southwest, all I saw was barren and dry land. I looked down and opined to my friend and seatmate, "What a God-forsaken land." Without missing a beat, my friend gently asked, "So *that* is the God you believe in?"

I can't recall how many times I have used the phrase God-forsaken, even though—as my friend (and spiritual guide in that moment) made clear—this profession stands in direct opposition to my life, my beliefs, even my ministry. Without saying it, he was asking me, "Is anything truly God-forsaken?" Of course, the resounding answer is "No."

The earth, even with no plants yet in the field, is not a God-forsaken place at all. In fact, in the desert, life abounds, even when we can't see it or understand it. Even if the desert were devoid of life, and even if we did not know what science and our own experiences have taught us, our belief is this: God is in the desert and is every bit as present, alive, real, and potent as anywhere else in the entirety of creation. There is no place—no land, no field, and no heart—forsaken by God.

February 4

I am quite lucky to have Mount Saint Helens (*Lawetlat'la* or *Loowit* in two of the local indigenous languages) practically in my backyard. I did not live here, on the edge of the Pacific "Ring of Fire," when the volcano erupted on May 18, 1980. Those who did beheld a mind-boggling and awe-inspiring event that most humans never see. The way this cataclysmic eruption changed the landscape was unprecedented and unbelievable.

I once had the chance to tour the eruption site with a man who was head of the lumberjack crew in 1980. Most of his colleagues did not survive. He was not present on the mountain that day, but he knows the terrain well—and he knew it well before the eruption. My lumberjack friend told us about a post-eruption experiment on the mountain: The authorities agreed to let the timber companies cultivate and grow one section of the desolated site and let nature take her course on the other.

When I visited a few years ago, the lush green mountainside cultivated by the timber companies was about to offer up its first harvest of trees. The natural side was also abundant but in a totally different, more unstructured way. As I stood on the line between the cultivated side and the wild side, I thought about how often we seem to be forced to make a choice between two things, to decide which is better. And here I was, standing and looking at two equally wonderful and beautiful results. In all of these scenarios, God is present and active—and cannot be stopped.

February 5

I live in the Pacific Northwest: We don't tan; we rust. In other parts of the country and the world, our home is known as "that place where it rains all the time." The truth is that we often have droughts in the summer—and long ones too.

Washington rain is not like the precipitation I experienced when I lived in the South. There, the rain of the year came in short, often-violent outbursts. Here, it gently falls in curtains of mist and permeates the earth over the course of hours.

The honest truth is that this region is gray–which is to say slightly gloomy—but perpetual rain is more in the realm of legend. After having lived here for years and endured some of these droughts, I can relate to this line: for the LORD God had not caused it to rain upon the earth.

There is something truly special after the long, hot days of summer when rain has become a memory and then finally comes. This is the part of weather where I make a connection to faith. When the rain seems to never end, I know the sun will come out...sometime. I believe it will. And when the sun is beating down and it seems no relief is in sight, I know the rain will come.

The rain will come. I believe that too.

February 6

We have work to do. The work of creating is not just God's. Or maybe I should say that it is all God's to do, but God does much of this work through us. Yes, I like that better.

God—who is in us—works through us to create and change this world. God has set this beautiful (and also sometimes terrible and devastating) creation in motion. And God knows the earth needs tending. I believe God has created something—this earth, this universe—very wisely, in such a way that it requires all the things within it. The universe has not been created as a static and strange object, carefully made and then left to simply churn on, with no stewardship required.

No, this earth—our island home—needs to be cared for, nurtured, utilized, and replenished through the work of our hands and by God's creative majesty. Dominion over this world does not equate to mastery over it nor does it give us license to deplete, destroy, or use as if there are no tomorrows.

In short, God needs us to till the ground, but it is not *our* ground. This ground, this earth, is God's—always has been, always will be. Our job is to care for creation—to leave it better for the next generation of workers, and finally to offer it back to God.

We have work to do.

February 7

Most of my meditations have been about nature and the earth, but we often forget that we humans are part of the natural world. I most often forget this when I am cut off in traffic, or I see a person step ahead of me in line, or...well, you fill in the blank. When faced with such moments, I have actually found some real comfort in these words: *God created them all*. This simple phrase can actually bring a smile to my face.

A man swerves and nearly runs me off the road and then gives me the thumbs up sign (or maybe that was another sign he was giving me?) I think, "God created them all." Perhaps this is akin to the way many of us from the South would think or say, "Bless their hearts," a polite pejorative.

Of course, I can't use, "God created them all," as a flippant statement. I have to believe it. Try using this phrase today. Try acting as if you truly believe it.

In the end the truth remains: God created them all.

February 8

This week's author
Linda Gelbrich

> *In the day that the LORD God made the earth and the heavens, when no plant of the field was yet in the earth and no herb of the field had yet sprung up—for the LORD God had not caused it to rain upon the earth, and there was no one to till the ground.*
>
> **Genesis 2:4b-5**

In preparing to write about the creation of our amazing planet, I discovered books on a shelf I had only thumbed through in past years. One of these books, written by Robert M. Hamma, is called *earth's echo: Sacred Encounters With Nature.* I feel a kinship with the author based on our mutual love of the natural world, a sense of camaraderie with all that has been created, and a deep gratefulness to the Creator who has opened our eyes and our hearts to the wonders of creation.

Hamma writes about ways of experiencing nature—and all of those ways involve paying attention. He writes about those who want to know the names of things, those who notice shapes, forms, and colors as an artist might, and a third way, which is simply to be present—to fully be where you are. When I am outside, I do all these things.

While in Tucson, Arizona, last February, I took a walk by myself. My first inclination was to name the birds I saw: cactus wren, phainopepla, raven, verdin, hummingbird. I even began counting them. I found myself wishing I had brought my bird book along so I could name others. Later in the afternoon, the sun's rays fell on the landscape at a lower angle, highlighting the green, oval ears of prickly pear and the tall stretch of saguaro with their many arms reaching in all directions. I noticed the jagged uplift of massive rock outcroppings on the mountain and the wavy line of hills. But most satisfying was to just be there, to stand with all that was growing, flying by, or just resting.

Rather than listening to my own thoughts, I began listening to the voices of the desert.

February 9

In the part of the world I inhabit, February is an in-between time. Winter is still sputtering, and spring—which is around a long corner—is doing most of her work in secret, underground and inside tight buds. Crocuses, snowdrops, and daffodils are shyly poking up above the winter-sodden soil. Sun breaks through heavy clouds and then disappears; rain slaps the earth again. Snow may fall tonight.

In spite of these day-to-day and minute-to minute weather variations, this time in-between, I love February. I love having more daylight minutes every day and the fresh smell after the night's rain. I love the sense of expectancy, knowing something is happening that I can't see, then finding something new beginning to grow. And look how bright the green grass is!

February is my birth month and that means a new beginning for me. I love new beginnings, whether they are my birthday, New Year's Day, Epiphany, or Easter. As a matter of fact, I count on them.

As a child, the first day of school each year was a new beginning—as is taking a new job, getting married, or the day one becomes a parent or grandparent. But I recently started thinking that every morning we wake from the mysterious land of sleep, we have a new beginning. We enter a new day—a shoreline without footprints—a clean slate, a space waiting for us. In a way, even each breath we take offers a new beginning, an opportunity to pause and be grateful before moving further into the blessing of our life.

February 10

I have a friend who gathers with a group to knit hats, scarves, and lap blankets from skeins of yarn. My sister-in-law quilts, producing unique and beautiful items from fabric pieces. Another friend creates with shards of glass and bits of stone to form stunning mosaics. Another works with copper wire, fabric, feathers, wood, and other found items to fashion sculpted stories. Maybe you are someone who likes to create things—recipes, a bookshelf, a garden, or a poem.

Each day we wake to the bare material of our lives. Each of us has a creative spirit that is expressed in our own unique way—through music, problem solving, managing a difficult conversation, or with our hands. Whatever our creative endeavor, it has a beginning. And sometimes beginnings are scary.

There are moments when a blank sheet of paper on the table feels like a vast prairie I can't cross; at other times, it feels like pure opportunity waiting to be explored. I learned some time ago to begin my writing time with the portion of Psalm 51. It starts out, "Open my lips, O Lord, and my mouth shall proclaim your praise. Create in me a clean heart, O God, and renew a right spirit within me."

When I offer this prayer, I'm asking God for help: to move through me and wash away fear, judgment, and a muddled mind; to help me be open and receptive; to create something new in me. The words from the psalm, even if only held in my awareness for a few seconds, allow space for God's grace to enter. I let go and have been blessed from time to time with the wonderful experience that author Madeleine L'Engle calls being a co-creator with God.

February 11

Last February my husband and I went on a road trip through the American Southwest. We left behind the record-breaking rain, saturated ground, and heavy gray sky of the Pacific Northwest and headed south through forests, mountains, farmland, cities, and then into the desert— dry land with cacti.

One of the first people we spoke with in Tucson told us about a local wildlife preserve that is being developed by a man who loves the outdoors. We made arrangements to visit. This kind and caretaking man gave us a tour, telling us that when he bought the land, it had been scraped clear in preparation for building slabs. The native plants had been stripped away.

Our new friend had a dream when he saw that land, picturing a place where native plants and creatures could find a haven and be in harmony. He dug, planted, and found ways to irrigate—forming little pools, running hoses, and using sprinklers and mist systems. Native plants began to grow and thrive.

This man has also placed numerous bird feeders around the property and tends them daily. We saw twenty-five species of birds that day— plus butterflies, bees, and a couple of squirrels. We heard about the populations of bobcats, skunks, packrats, and snakes who also make the preserve their home. It was like a little Eden.

Everything was at home in this place. Hummingbirds darted over our heads on their way to feeders. We watched the sun's rays dance along their feathers, changing from green or gray to vibrant crimson. It was hard to head back to the car after our visit. Like the hummingbirds, we too had been fed with an indescribable sweetness.

February 12

While on our southwestern road trip, we attended two Episcopal churches. Both had clear glass windows behind the altar. The hills and saguaro cacti were visible when we sat, stood, or came forward for Holy Eucharist. In the little parish in the town of Sisters, Oregon, three iconic mountains—usually snow-covered—were visible through tall, clear glass windows behind the cross.

In our home church all the sanctuary windows are made of stained glass so brilliant and beautiful that people sometimes come in just to see them. The glass is deeply colored and thick, forming figures and scenes in the tall, slender windowsills. When sunlight streams in through each piece of thick glass, bands of color fall gently on parishioners. In the churches we visited on our trip, the outdoors had been invited into the worship space through the glass. In our home church, we can't see outside from the sanctuary, but the outside comes in anyway through the stained glass.

What an important reminder it is for me that, no matter what walls we build or roofs we construct, the natural world is present and all around us—in the materials used for construction, in the air that flows in and out, and in the views we glimpse or gaze upon through the windows. This is just like God. We can't shut God out because God is there—and here—fully present to us, as in the first day before buildings, before the mountains and cacti.

God, who created the vast expanse of earth and sky, loved and continues to love it all into being. We are more than people who sometimes venture out into nature—nature is *in* us.

February 13

The soil in many parts of the Southwest has a cryptobiotic crust: alive, composed of algae, moss, and tiny filaments that form a protective layer over the soil. This crust helps hold water and nutrients in the soil, rather than allowing them to simply evaporate into the arid desert atmosphere. I first read about cryptobiotic crust on a sign I encountered at a national park that directed hikers to stay on the trail; the crust breaks down with each errant footstep. Once broken, this crust takes years to rebuild.

When I've gone barefoot at the beach, I love the crusty feeling as my feet break through to softer sand. I look back at my footprints and then gaze out over footprints others have made. We all leave our marks, but the ocean will always come back in and smooth the surface again. Our footprints will be erased.

Imagine soil with no footprints, no holes dug, no concrete poured—nothing but soil under a high blue sky. Each and every day is like this, like the very first morning. We wake to a fresh start, nothing has yet been trampled—not us, the ground, or our tender hopes. We are clear, smooth, and available.

What will we do with the soil of our lives today? What will begin to grow? What will be worn away or buried? Can we trust that something will happen, that something dwells within us and will take root and grow? What is happening today in the soil of your life?

We did not bring this into being, but we are all continuously being created.

February 14

I decided to plant a garden in our shady yard of fir trees and white oaks. There was only one sunny area, and it was in the side yard by the street. This was before people in our neighborhood had lawns or flowerbeds near the street, much less vegetable gardens.

Creating this garden was not an easy project—the soil in our yard was dense with clay and thickly marbled with pebbles and broken bits of rock. To make things more challenging, tree roots ran just under the surface of the soil and a heavy crop of wild onions seemed to shoot up everywhere. Undeterred, I used railroad ties to form borders for the bed, had a load of soil delivered, and then smoothed the new dirt with the back of a garden rake. By this time, it was February—a good time to plant peas in my part of the world.

When I went outside the next day, my garden plot was no longer smooth. It had been scuffed up, and endless hoof prints pressed into the soil. A well-worn path had formed overnight: I didn't know I had set up the garden on a deer trail.

I laugh about this bit of folly now. There I was, ardently smoothing the soil and trying to create something new in a plot of ground, and the rest of creation was just going on about its business. Maybe that's part of God's dream for creation—that all of us creatures live side by side and learn how to get along with one another.

February 15

*And God said, "Let there be a dome in the midst of the waters,
and let it separate the waters from the waters." So God made
the dome and separated the waters that were under the dome
from the waters that were above the dome. And it was so.*

Genesis 1:6-7

I live in California, and I have a Californian's relationship to water. My
family and I, along with our neighbors and friends, are used to going for
long periods with limits on the amount of fresh water we can use. We
also know seasons when endless days of rain wash hillsides away.

I live very near the world's largest body of water, the Pacific Ocean.
Sometimes I look out over the water and realize how foolish it is to
attempt to see the other side. I try anyway. If it's a clear day and I climb
a hill, I can see the Farallon Islands, some thirty miles away. When
I look out over the ocean from the top of Mount Tamalpais, I can
almost discern the curvature of the earth along the horizon. I imagine
the billions of life forms living in that water—some thriving, some
encountering human-made challenges to their very existence.

We have little control over the waters of creation. The only way to restore
the health of the oceans—or to live within the cycles of droughts, *el niños*,
and *la niñas*—is to realize that creation is an ongoing process and to join it.

In our relationship to creation, we are called to be Christ's "living water"
(John 4:10). This is God's work of reconciliation. God, the acting agent in
our lives, seeks to be reconciled to all of God's creation. For the waters of
creation to live, we must be part of the living water too.

*Jesus said to her, "Everyone who drinks of this water will be
thirsty again, but those who drink of the water that I will
give them will never be thirsty. The water that I will give will
become in them a spring of water gushing up to eternal life."*

John 4:13-14

February 16

The first time I entered a mosque was in Esfahan, Iran, in 2007. The lapis blue mosaic domes pointed to the heavens. Outside the mosque were long pools with benches next to them and spigots of constantly running water. I followed the example set by my guide: Wash my head and face, hands and lower arms up to the elbows, then wash my feet up to the ankles, all the while offering prayers.

There are ritual baths, immersions, and ablutions in each of the Abrahamic faiths. The washing that Muslims do before prayers is called *wudu*. The more complete ritual washing is called *Ghusl*. Many Jews make a *mikvah*, the fulfillment of the *mitzva of tevilah* or commandment of immersion at specific times and for specific reasons.

Many Muslims and Jews describe their ritual washings as nothing less than spiritual metamorphoses. Prior to these experiences, the grit of the world is worn on the body like dust on the skin. These cleansing rituals provide a portal into the presence of the Divine.

As followers of Jesus, we celebrate the sacrament of baptism, and I welcome a well-placed font filled with holy water as the gateway into worship. If a church's font isn't by the front door, I seek it out. If it is not filled with water, I touch the font anyway. Any encounter with God makes the object of the encounter holy, set apart, consecrated. If you are like me (or our sisters and brothers of other faiths), a portal into God's space is helpful preparation to live a life of love.

If you have been baptized, I invite you to repeat the welcome you received from the assembly as you came through the waters of your baptism:

> *We receive you into the household of God. Confess the faith of Christ crucified, proclaim his resurrection, and share with us in his eternal priesthood.*
>
> **The Book of Common Prayer**

February 17

I love listening to Mavis Staples, either as a solo act or with The Staples Singers. There is a song that she regularly performs and has recorded called "Wade in the Water."

> *Wade in the water,*
> *Wade in the water, children,*
> *Wade in the water,*
> *God's gonna trouble the water.*

The Staples Singers were not the first to record this song. The lyrics were first published in 1901. The first known recording is from 1923, but it is said to be much older. Harriet Tubman reportedly used this song and others as instructions to slaves seeking freedom along the Underground Railroad. One source says the song reminded runaways to find water to wade through, making their scent harder for dogs to track. Other sources say the song provided direction for slaves to cross the Ohio River, the border between slave and free states.

To wade in the water is not unlike partaking in the ritual baths of *wudu*, *mikvah*, and baptism: The condition of the person entering the water is not the same when he or she steps out. What piques my interest the most is God "troubling" the water. God troubling the water reminds us of the healing waters of the pool of Bethzatha in the fifth chapter of John's Gospel. When the water is troubled, only then do the blind see and the lame walk. Likewise, when God troubles us, we are stirred to act. If we are truly to be the hands and feet of God in this world, we are also to be God's holy troublemakers. God does not trouble us in order to maintain the status quo. God is troubling us so that we can be agents of healing and hope to a world sorely in need of both.

> *...Wade in the water,*
> *God's gonna trouble the water.*

February 18

I have known a certain politician throughout my life. He is a Christian, but his theology and mine don't exactly match.

My acquaintance's God seems vengeful to me, punishing people harshly for their sins. The God I know is loving and forgiving. The divide between our theologies is such that whenever I hear this politician mention God and God's wrath, I can't help but think that the God he knows and the God I know are not the same God.

There was a time, though, when I recognized his God as my God. Early in his career as a governor, one of his first acts was to remove the language in state laws that called floods, tornadoes, and other natural disasters "acts of God." He explained that disasters befall the good and the bad, so they could not be categorized as acts of God.

When events are beyond our control, when it seems that the world—or nature—is out to get us, God's goodness and compassion are found in those who show they have the capacity to care for others and respond in love. God is not made known to us in the destructive force of storms or earthquakes but in the sure hands of those who respond when the wheels come off, when the roof flies away, when the floor drops out from under us.

When destructive events occur, the beloved community that tends the injured, feeds the hungry, shelters the homeless, and visits the displaced and disheartened are the tangible, visible, and felt presence of the Divine.

February 19

Baseball season is a time of rituals for me. These rituals keep me grounded and sane. I tend to lose a bit of my centeredness in January as I long for the return of baseball and the rituals that sustain me.

My home baseball park has a cove next to it. People float on rafts or kayaks, waiting for a ball to be hit out of the park and into the water. Like me, they have their own rituals for observing the season and the game. Almost every time I go to the ballpark, I walk out to the wall over right field so I can look into the cove and acknowledge the keepers of the water ritual. This walk is a part of my ritual.

Rituals ground us and keep us sane. They focus our attention and assure us that even though some things are out of our control, we can always return to the center.

Many of our personal and religious rituals include water. Much about how we bathe is ritualistic—when we bathe, what we wash first, and what we wash last. For gardeners, watering can become a ritual. Even the washing of dishes can have ritualistic elements.

Wherever and whenever water is present in our lives, whether in leisure or as part of a task, water invites a certain reverence. Water is the primal element of creation. John baptizes people in it. Jesus uses it as an agent of healing. And, for me, it adds a sacred element to baseball.

February 20

I started carrying a water bottle fairly recently. I got a new fangled bottle that keeps water chilled for a long time. I like the bottle because it is neither big nor bulky. Because I carry the bottle around with me, I have started to drink more water. I understand this is a healthier choice for me, and I feel pretty good as a more hydrated human.

I also put an app on my phone that reminds me to pray. I haven't always had a regular, daily habit of prayer, but this app is a good reminder. It's simple—it sounds a lovely tone at different times during my day and shares a name from my prayer list. At the prompting of the tone, I stop and pray intentionally. These prayer times focus me on one thing for a set amount of time on three occasions during the day. In the time between my prayers, I feel more focused. As with my water intake, I was doing okay in my spiritual life before I started praying more regularly, but with this new practice, I feel better.

I don't plan to give up my new water drinking habit: I'm reaping the positive physical effects of drinking more water each day. I also don't intend to stop my new, more regular prayer habit. I'm feeling multiple positive effects from it too—spiritual, mental, and even physical improvements. Taking the time to pause and pray slows my heart, my breathing, and makes me feel more deeply connected to the family member or friend who has asked for prayer.

Our bodies are more than 60 percent water. To replenish our water is a life-giving habit. Christians make up the Body of Christ. To replenish the connective tissue, the spiritual bonds we have, one to another, waters our souls.

February 21

The baptismal font in San Francisco's Grace Cathedral stands at a kind of architectural and spiritual apex. It is the first thing a person encounters after coming through the front doors. The font is directly on the way to the altar, standing between two windows. One window depicts Moses, and the other portrays John the Baptizer. There is no accident that when a person stands at the font, he or she might be looking either at the Liberator or the Baptizer.

Moses the Liberator leads the children of Israel out of bondage and into freedom through the waters of the Red Sea. When they cross the sea, this barrier of water that marks their transformation into a people who are holy and set apart.

Then there is the wild Baptizer, this misfit cousin of Jesus, standing in the waters of the Jordan River and crying, "Repent!" He invites people into the water to prepare themselves for the inevitable, impending truth: The kingdom of God is near, and those baptized in water and the Holy Spirit will be transformed—made holy and whole and set apart for God's great work of redemption—by the waters of this second birth.

The waters of our own baptisms are something like portals into the presence of God—they knit us to our communities of faith. We know God in Jesus Christ, and we see the face of Christ in community. We enter into that household by passing through water.

February 22

This week's author
Jason Leo

*And God said, "Let there be a dome in the midst of the waters,
and let it separate the waters from the waters." So God made
the dome and separated the waters that were under the dome
from the waters that were above the dome. And it was so.*

Genesis 1:6-7

The way I understand it, Jesus was born in some cave or barn-like
structure full of animals and farm equipment. And then some random
people brought him and his parents some very expensive gifts. I am sure
other people brought them water. There was no avoiding the necessity of
water—the animals had to have it, people had to have it—especially Mary.
I guarantee she was some kind of thirsty after giving birth to Jesus. And
I know she had to work hard to keep herself and the baby Jesus clean in
those first days of his life. Barns are dirty places, so a supply of water had to
keep coming. People were bringing them water, and I thank God for them.

I lived part of my life as a priest in a small farming community, where
I was reminded every day that water is at the very heart of life. In the
baptismal prayer over the water, we hear and say so much truth: *We
thank you, Almighty God, for the gift of water. Over it the Holy Spirit
moved in the beginning of creation.*

This same Holy Spirit still moves over the water, creating and giving life
and health and hope to people in times of both joy and sadness. In times
of hope and in times of grief, water manifests itself as a sign of God's
grace in the most expected—and unexpected—places.

February 23

When my bishop sent me to the small mission church in the little farm town, I was pretty excited. My excitement didn't last long. I looked at the financial report and inspected the church building...and immediately made an appointment to go and see him.

The bishop was surprised to see me back so soon. I told him that the building was falling down, attendance was poor, there was no money to pay the bills, and that he really needed to think about doing something serious in that place. He responded, "I did. I sent you."

When Jesus walks across the water to board the boat, the disciples are amazed. Peter is so inspired that he wants to join Jesus on the water. Jesus does not discourage him, and for a moment, Peter does pretty well. But then he starts feeling scared and begins to sink. Jesus encourages Peter to have a little more faith—he too will one day do amazing things.

As I left the bishop's office, he called to me from the doorway. "Remember," he said, "If you want to walk on water, you have to get out of the boat." *What is that supposed to mean?* I thought about this the whole way home.

The truth is, I still don't know how to walk on water. But I have learned that if I at least have the courage to step out of the boat, miracles can happen. And Jesus comes to meet me.

February 24

God leads the children of Israel out of Egypt through the Red Sea to the Promised Land. I am sure that when some of the Israelites see the Red Sea, they want to turn back. The problem with water is that most of the time, it is hard to see what is happening below the surface. Who can blame them for being reluctant, even scared?

Under the surface of the water, the Israelites find a path to a new home. They step out in faith and continue their journey—apprehensive about the water in front of them but convicted by what they believe in their hearts. I'm glad they—and we—are eventually brave enough to go below the surface of their faith.

In the farming community where I served as priest—indeed in all farming communities—rain is really important. Too much rain is a problem, but too little is even worse. Once we went a long time without rain, and all creation seemed to groan. The ground was bone dry—dry like the story of Ezekiel in the Valley of the Bones. I could see the anxiety on my faces of my parishioners, friends, and neighbors. I could feel their stress. We needed rain—we had to have it. In our little farm town, everyone knew this was non-negotiable.

Our church building was open every day for prayer. One afternoon, I saw a little girl sitting on the front steps. Her family owned a large farm. "Everything okay?" I asked. "Daddy is inside...praying for rain." I noticed that she was holding an umbrella. *Well*, I thought, *that is a sure sign of faith*. She saw me looking at it. "God provides," she said. "My daddy said so."

February 25

When my daughter was five years old, she refused to go to Sunday School. I figured if I told her she had to sit in church, she would become so bored that she would fold like a cheap lawn chair after one week and go skipping back to Sunday School. I was wrong.

Week after week, she sat next to my wife and behaved pretty well most of the time. Once I looked out and saw that my wife was alone in the pew. *Victory*, I thought. Then I noticed my small child sitting by herself on the front row. I was sad she wasn't having fun with the other kids, and I worried that she wasn't learning about our faith on her own level of understanding.

When John calls people into the Jordan River to be baptized, Jesus joins in and fully immerses himself into our humanity and our baptismal waters. Baptism becomes a symbol and one of the primary sacraments of our faith—the means through which all people are raised to a new life of faith in Jesus.

One Sunday, I came home from church, and my daughter had a friend over to play. They were in the front yard as I came up the walk. My daughter was dunking her doll's head in the dog's water bowl while the other girl watched. I was a little curious.

"What are you doing?" I asked. "I'm baptizing her," my little Sunday School dropout responded. This was as close to a Trinitarian baptism as a five-year-old could conjure. I shed a tear of joy, and I knew my fears about what my child was or wasn't learning about Jesus and faith were unfounded. And I understood that all things would be well.

February 26

Jesus asks a Samaritan woman for a drink of water, and everyone gets really excited. She's from the wrong side of the tracks, and in some way, Jesus is honoring her and giving her respect by not only speaking to her but by asking her for a favor. Some people who see him do this are alarmed—and some are inspired. Who knew a drink of water could be such a big deal?

There wasn't much diversity of any sort in our town. We had one grocery store, one restaurant, one movie theater with a single screen, one pharmacy...pretty much one of everything, except for churches. There were a lot of churches. The upshot was that everyone mostly got along, and whenever there was a big event, festival, or fair, everyone went to the community potluck and everyone pretty much looked the same.

A man from the Middle East moved into our community. He was a professor in the agriculture department at a nearby university and had come to our town for a yearlong program. Sure enough, the first big town event that he attended was—unbeknownst to him—a pig roast. We had a lot of pig farms in our county, and pig roasts were pretty common. I spoke with him for a while at this party, and I could sense his discomfort. He eventually shared that he was Muslim and did not eat pork. Uncomfortable with the menu, he was going to head home.

Out of nowhere, a woman came over to us with a piece of pie and a glass of water. She welcomed this stranger into our community by saying, "I thought you looked hungry." He smiled and thanked her and turned back to me. "I think I'll stay."

A glass of water and a slice of pie shed a whole different light on the kingdom of God that was between us.

February 27

The church was small, but this was not surprising for an Episcopal parish in a small farming community. We prayed for growth, both in number and spirit. After several months passed, there were no new members.

A man in our church loved to fish. He spoke to the parish one Sunday about our efforts to grow, likening our efforts to fishing. Our fisherman friend pointed out that if we fished the way we had been inviting people to church, we might as well put an empty bucket of water at the end of a fishing pier and wait for the fish to jump in the bucket. He suggested we try a little harder in our people fishing, and he encouraged us, saying we were a wonderful community that desired to be a blessing to many more people. He reminded us of the day the disciples go fishing and catch nothing. Jesus tells them to try the other side of the boat, and they end up catching a massive amount of fish.

People nodded at the fisherman in agreement, and we kept praying for growth in number and spirit. And the strangest thing happened. People started bringing their friends and family to church with them. Wouldn't you know it...miracle of all miracles...some of them even stayed. We were all shocked and surprised, probably just like the disciples are when their boats are swamped by the catch Jesus brings them.

February 28

One Sunday, a young couple announced their engagement during church. There was much rejoicing and excitement. After worship, I met with them. They were concerned about the wedding. The young husband was just starting a job at the tractor dealership, and the bride was still finishing college. Funds were scarce, but I told them not to worry: God invented church for a reason. I was sure miracles would abound.

Sure enough—and quite miraculously—a tuxedo and wedding dress appeared, as did people who knew how to make alterations to formal wear. The parish hall was decorated by a cheerful committee, and a high school student began his DJ career at their reception. The ceremony was beautiful, and the reception was wonderful—and we have the pictures to prove it.

Jesus' first miracle is at a wedding, turning water into wine. Some people say he does this to prove that he is the Christ, God's chosen one. This rationale may be true. But, I also like to think that Jesus chooses this time and place because he knows that weddings are a special and holy kind of celebration, a sign of the kingdom coming to dwell among us. Jesus wants this wedding—indeed all the special parties we celebrate with people we love—to continue unabated, with no embarrassment to the host for running out of wine or money or time. Jesus uses something so ordinary and holy—water—to make the miraculous abundant and help us remember that miracles abound.

February 29

(A bonus reading for non-Leap Years)

A doctor in my congregation called and asked me to pay a call to the county hospital. A woman in our parish was giving birth, and doctors had determined that the baby would only live a short time. This woman wanted her baby to be baptized. I thought about when the disciples are in the boat on the Sea of Galilee and a storm kicks up. They are scared, really scared—this is a bad storm and they very well may die. And Jesus comes walking out to them, and all is well.

The hospital room was solemn and sad. As I said the blessing over the water, I could see the tears flowing freely down the faces of the family. The baby was beautiful and lived long enough to be named and baptized. In time, there was healing and new hope and new signs of God's grace for the family and friends. Jesus never promises an absence of storms. He promises to guide us through the storms and never abandon us.

I poured the remains of the baby's baptismal water in the memorial garden—holy water for a holy place. I looked at the water as it hit the ground, and for a moment I thought about the water people bring to Jesus and his mother at his birth—to wash him clean, to refresh Mary. In some way, I figured, this water I was pouring out was the very same water...the same water Jesus walks on, that he turns into wine. These baptismal waters were the same water he drinks from a cup offered by a Samaritan woman and the same water on the other side of the disciples' boat. This water flows from Jesus' side when he is crucified and is the same water that he asks for when he finds the disciples in the Upper Room. It is the same water that the Holy Spirit moves over in the beginning of creation and the water that flows from our eyes in times of great sorrow and great joy.

I thought about all of this as the precious drops of baptismal water blessed the ground in the memorial garden of the church, in that small farming community the bishop assigned me to serve, and I was thankful. Water helps everything grow, even me.

Give us all a reverence for the earth as your own creation, that we may use its resources rightly in the service of others and to your honor and glory.

Lord, in your mercy
Hear our prayer.

The Book of Common Prayer

There Was Evening and There Was Morning

God called the dome Sky. And there was evening and there was morning, the second day.

Genesis 1:8

Artist's Note: In spite of the scientific principles of moisture and condensation and other concerns of our atmosphere, here we have it—God called the dome sky. It can be really complicated, or really simple, and we don't have to choose. Layers of meaning and room for interpretation give much richness to life and our understanding. This is a very simple painting—evening slips away as morning appears. Out of the darkness comes the light. Out of our confusion comes understanding.

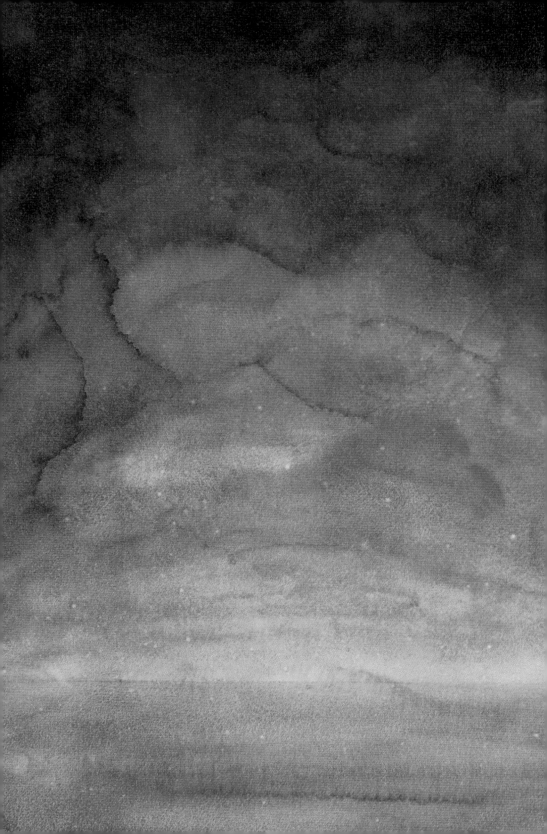

Let the Dry Land Appear

And God said, "Let the waters under the sky be gathered together into one place, and let the dry land appear." And it was so. God called the dry land Earth, and the waters that were gathered together he called Seas. And God saw that it was good.

Genesis 1:9-10

Artist's Note: With this painting, the series begins to be less amorphous. Concrete form begins to take shape in the suggestion of land between the earth and the sky. Most of the painting is painted in transparent pigments that allow the white of the background to shine through, and conversely, give the viewer the sense of looking beyond the skies or into the water. But the land is opaque. The eye stops there; it grounds us and provides the substrate for what has yet to take place. Creation becomes more specific, defined, and differentiated, ready for life. These three environments—sky, seas and land—provide a mere hint of the explosion of variety that lies ahead.

March 1

God called the dome Sky. And there was evening and there was morning, the second day.

Genesis 1:8

One of the concepts about which the late Madeleine L'Engle wrote often and passionately was naming. She believed that one reason for the many problems of the world is that most people don't know who they are—they have lost their sense of being who God created and named them to be. She wrote of the forces of evil that want to un-name, to remove identity, to treat the other as less than God's uniquely beloved.

In the first story of creation, God names everything. "God called the dome Sky." This image of the second day reflects a timeless moment of creation in which the fragile atmosphere that makes our life and breath possible, protects us from radiation and whirls weather around the globe, is brought into being and is named. It is given its purpose. This purpose allows us to take every breath, every day. As the painting illustrates, this dome is complex and simple, beautiful and strong—our protector on this amazing planet.

Thank you, Creator, for calling into being this dome, this firmament, this fragile and faithful expanse. Thank you that, throughout the millennia, it has simply gone on being what you created and named it to be.

March 2

For pre-scientific people, the dome that God calls sky was believed to be quite literally that—an actual dome. This is a logical conclusion: The sky looks like a dome from the perspective of one standing on the land. Rabbinic literature abounds with discussions about the materials used to construct the dome. Some thought the dome was made from beaten metal. One school of thought is that the Holy One combined the primeval elements of fire and water to create the dome. Still others suggested the dome was constructed like a tent so perfectly made that it would never sag or droop.

Today, we have more accurate facts about the elements that make up the sky. We also know more about how our actions impact the complex and protective atmosphere, keeping it from doing the work that God has given it to do by speaking it into being. We know these facts, but in knowing, what have we lost?

What if we were to play with the metaphors that guided the ancient rabbis as they prayed, thought, and wondered about the amazing dome above them? What if we gazed deeply into these adventurous paintings that flowed from the prayer, imagination, and reflections of a modern artist? What might we discover?

O Holy Creator, you have given us the gift of wonder, of imagination, of wild and free vision to glimpse hints of your grace. We thank you!

March 3

So many elements of the painting of the dome of the sky draw the eye at different viewings. In this moment, the line of the horizon pulls me in. Many ancients believed that if they traveled far enough, they would reach the horizon and the edge of the world. Yet we know that our journey into the love of the One who continuously creates, redeems, and sustains us is endless. No matter how far we go (or deep or high or wide or any other distance), we will never come to the end or the edge. The love that spoke us into being draws us eternally—to borrow from author C.S. Lewis— "further up and further in."

Studying the horizon line, I see places where it appears to open into darkness, and other places where it appears a glimmer of light is trying to shine through. This is a reality that certainly reflects my life experiences. As the Holy One continues to create, heal, and challenge me to risk more, I journey through times of fearful darkness, moments of incredible light and insight, and every shade in between. Every time I think that I might be reaching a place of rest and certainty, the horizon recedes further, drawing me onward.

O Eternal Mystery, you are with us and ever ahead of us. In awe and wonder, thank you!

March 4

The dome of the sky is gray this morning. The clouds look as though they are storing more rain to pour on already-saturated land and overflowing rivers. The news tells of drought-fueled wildfires in some places, record depths of snow in others, and unseasonably hot temperatures in yet others. Weather is only sometimes idyllic—death and destruction can come from the sky as easily as life. The first two chapters of Genesis could sing a hymn of praise, telling of the Creator speaking our world into being, naming each new part.

The painting of a sky spoken into existence invites us into these contrasts: darkness and light, hints of shadow, grays and blues and greens, all speaking of a roiling, primeval atmosphere. Our world is uncertain: Our climate, our political and social situations are rapidly changing. Yet we are still privileged to be on this amazing planet, spoken into being by our wildly exuberant Creator. We can choose fearfulness, anger, and aggression in response, or we can choose to respond in praise, living in awareness that God proclaims all of creation to be very good and using that awareness in loving and caring for each other under this unpredictable sky.

Holy God, you have given us this world and these free choices. Thank you.

March 5

O God, the King eternal, whose light divides the day from the night and turns the shadow of death into the morning: Drive far from us all wrong desires, incline our hearts to keep your law, and guide our feet into the way of peace; that, having done your will with cheerfulness during the day, we may, when night comes, rejoice to give you thanks; through Jesus Christ our Lord. Amen.

The Book of Common Prayer

Praying with the painting of the dome brings questions. Is it a painting of evening or morning? Of dusk or dawn? Each is a special gift. In the evening, we are free to reflect on the day that is past, to hand over our worries, failures, successes, joys, and sorrows to the One who gives us the gift of rest and sleep. We can ask for wisdom to be conveyed through our dreams, trusting everything we are and have to the One who created them in the first place.

In the morning, we are free to look prayerfully toward the day ahead—the things we are reasonably sure will happen and the unknown into which we walk. We can ask for wisdom and guidance in each event and encounter and entrust ourselves to the One who gave us life and is with us all the way.

Generous Creator, you have given us evening and morning and are with us along the way. Thank you.

March 6

In the primeval dome of the sky, much is familiar. We see the fertility of the earth. There is horizon, toward which we can go if we choose. There is sky. Then there is the darkness above the dome. Humankind has managed to escape our atmosphere and send people, probes, and inquiry into the mystery of space. It is vast, beyond anything our best thinkers can grasp, and leads us to awe and wonder.

It can also lead us into temptation. *Star Trek* fans know the words "Space, the final frontier." What if we as Christians believed that the vastness of interstellar space really *was* the final frontier? Would we think of it as something to conquer? Something to eventually understand and thus control? What if we forget that it is God who creates and holds it all? The great mystic Julian of Norwich shows us what we must always remember:

> In this vision he showed me a little thing, the size of a hazelnut, and it was round as a ball. I looked at it with the eye of my understanding and thought "What may this be?" And it was generally answered thus: "It is all that is made." I marveled how it might last, for it seemed it might suddenly have sunk into nothing because of its littleness. And I was answered in my understanding, "It lasts and ever shall, because God loves it."

Holy Creator, though we may come to believe that we can understand your creation, you are the infinite mystery we can never control or comprehend. Thank you.

March 7

There is great beauty in the idea of something yet-to-be-finished conveyed in this dome painting. It is a metaphor for our lives—God continues to work on, in, and through us. The painting is a reflection on the wonders of ongoing evolution—all that is unfinished, yet still amazing in its current state of being.

As a woman in advanced middle age and looking at changes to come, I find myself rejoicing in the evolution of self. Some of it has been hard, seemingly impossible to bear. Yet as I look back, I see only grace. As I try to serve others, the hardest parts of my life are those that God uses the most for good. This reality instills a sense of awe and wonder as intense as moments spent in the fecund stillness of an ancient redwood grove, the vastness of the ocean, or when the sky is clear and the night is dark enough to glimpse some of the seemingly infinite stars and galaxies.

Each evening and each morning of another day is a sign of grace, life, and hope for the ongoing work that our unspeakably amazing Creator is doing in us—for the unknown toward which we are being led by the One who knows.

Creator and Redeemer, as you sustain us, we know that you are not finished with us and are lovingly working still. Thank you.

*God called the dome Sky. And there was evening and there
was morning, the second day.*

Genesis 1:8

Each fall, I spend time on my sister's ranch in South Texas. In that arid landscape, the sky goes on forever, and the horizon forms a circle. It is easy to notice the dome shape of the sky hovering above, keeping us safe. One of my favorite features of that full sky—which I attempt to describe and to paint again and again—is that as the sun is still setting in the west, the stars are already visible in the east. I don't doubt this is visible elsewhere, but with an endless horizon in view, it is amazing to see our earth turn toward the night even as the last rays of light shine across the sky.

On one of these evenings, while my brother-in-law started a campfire, I came to understand in a new way the ancient song *Phos Hilaron*. I couldn't help but sing: "Now as we come to the setting of the sun, and our eyes behold the vesper light, we sing your praises, O God, Father, Son, and Holy Spirit." The song came from the depths of my soul, as I witnessed what generations have experienced.

The sun sets, and we make provision of light for the evening, and God is in the midst of it all: the natural darkness and the ingenuity of a campfire. When I sing or hear reference to this evening prayer canticle, I am back at that fire circle and with fire circles of ancient times and of times to come. Daylight gracefully gives way to night stars, tongues of fire lapping up to illumine familiar faces telling and hearing stories ancient and new.

March 9

I spent one Independence Day at an Episcopal camp, and we were told that we were going to see God's fireworks. We walked out, well after dark, to a clearing in the east Texas pines and looked up at the stars. As we lay there, staring up at the sky and beholding the beauty of creation, people pointed out constellations and told Native American stories of the stars' origins.

I still get that feeling of awe at night sometimes. I almost always get that feeling in the early morning when I wake before dawn and see a slightly different perspective on the starry sky than I might have seen the night before. I wonder at the purity of the morning sky illumined by specks of light collected from across our universe and how generations have interpreted their alignment to tell their stories.

I wonder at God's work in me and in the universe as it expands and my life unfolds in the same cosmic story. Before the rush of morning takes hold, I ponder: How can one gigantic star and one tiny person become constellated?

March 10

There are few places I have experienced the natural progression of evenings and mornings more intimately than along the San Marcos River in Texas. The San Marcos flows from springs that are a constant 72 degrees and provides a pristine habitat for five species that exist only in and around those headwaters. I'm told that this area is one of the longest continually inhabited sites in North America. It possesses an Edenic quality and is one of the places I call holy.

I had the good fortune of going to college near the headwaters of that river. In those years, and ever since, I have swum, fished, waded, canoed, and camped on the banks. I have watched the changes in light, activity, and animal presence from dusk and sunset into the night, then at dawn and sunrise, again and again in a variety of situations.

I have even been caught on a canoe trip as the world around me darkened. It was a challenge to complete that trip but not impossible. It reminded me why we sleep at night and canoe in the day and why God created the natural rhythms of light and dark.

March 11

At one point in my life, my great hope was to find a vocation through which I could teach people how to pray while riding a bike. At the time, I didn't realize there were many ways to do that: It was a new experience for me, and the desire to share came from my first experience of riding my bike in the middle of the night.

I was working at a summer camp, and I would ride along the empty roads during a new moon. I learned to soften my gaze so I could use my peripheral vision to spot the guides: the tree line above revealing the night stars, the road's edge below, the pitch dark of pine forest on either side. I could just barely make out the road as I glided through the cooling air of the summer night. It was bliss, and it felt like something everyone should do to know God's presence just the way I did.

Years later, I understand that the combination of nature, trust, exercise, and discovery can come from many things we humans encounter in life. The experience of praying while riding a bike is not limited to riding a bike. It can happen any time when we are caught up in the joy of the present moment.

March 12

"Go back to bed, it's just the natural stirring of your soul...don't go back to bed, it's just the natural current of your soul." Those words from musician Justin Stewart come to me in the wee hours of the morning when something unexplained wakes me at 2:30 a.m. or 3:40 a.m. What has stirred me in these early hours? Is it worth the risk of just turning over and going back to sleep? Has my soul roused me to remember a dream or to write about a waking life issue that has come to a new light?

Every time I have actually climbed out of bed and sat with my restless soul, the sitting has proved fruitful. The time between evening and morning is certainly meant for rest, but when I am stirred by a creative impulse, I worry about what might be lost for the sake of sleep. Sometimes I wake and sit. Sometimes I write a dream down and reflect on it. Sometimes I argue out a problem with myself until clarity emerges.

I remember Abram walking beneath the stars and pondering with God, and I know that the darkest hours of the night are just as sacred as the brightest, when most of my fellow creatures stir and work.

March 13

There is an even tie, in my life, for what makes for the most sacred morning experience. On the one hand is presiding at the altar of Christ for Sunday Holy Eucharist. That is, without a doubt, one of the most sacred things I am privileged to do.

The other sacred morning event comes when I go down to our local Gulf Coast pier with my surfboard for a pre-dawn paddle out. Those are mystic mornings when I ride on the energy of the vast ocean coming into contact with land. The natural pattern of the wave is pushed up by sand bars to form rideable waves. That interaction with nature and then witnessing the first rays of light touching clouds in pinks and oranges is another sacred experience.

The Book of Common Prayer describes sacraments as "outward and visible signs of inward and spiritual grace." In the eucharist, and while surfing in the early hours, it is difficult to distinguish between outward and inward. In each, the visible sign melds with the spiritual grace to become a whole experience that is happening in the present moment.

March 14

In 2005, I was given the opportunity to study in South Africa for five weeks at the College of the Transfiguration. In the final week of my visit, I stayed at Mariya uMama weThemba, a wonderful monastery near Grahamstown in the Eastern Cape. This was a time of reflection and an opportunity to begin the transition back to the United States after four weeks immersed in the culture, church, and spirit of South Africa.

Each morning, I played my mandolin. Actually, that's not totally true: I played my mandolin in the late morning. In the early morning, I prayed psalms with the monks. I can't even remember how early we rose in those winter months to pray the sun up. We gathered and prayed the psalms as the horizon eventually lightened, and I thought we might be crazy, especially the monks, who do this sort of thing on a regular basis. I only did it for a few days during my visit; those brothers are still at it, though.

Now on Sundays, one of the few days I intentionally rise well before dawn, I remember the monks who are up before me, praying for the world, praying through the psalms, praying the sun up. As I pray and review my sermon for the gathering that will take place hours later, I remember the monks in South Africa, gathered hours before me, sitting with God, and praying the world back to life. I trust their prayers are with us all.

This week's author
Barry Beisner

And God said, "Let the waters under the sky be gathered together into one place, and let the dry land appear." And it was so. God called the dry land Earth, and the waters that were gathered together he called Seas. And God saw that it was good.

Genesis 1:9-10

On the first part of the third day of creation, God continues the work of separation, connection, and naming. Light and darkness are created and separated on the first day, and named day and night. Then, on the second day, water drawn up into heaven is separated from the waters covering the earth by means of a dome named sky. Then on the third day comes a further separation: The waters that cover the earth are gathered so as to allow the emergence of dry land.

Part of the work of creation is to set apart, to bring together, and to name. With a name comes identity, purpose, relationship—and, in the case of human beings—responsibility and accountability. The earth and the seas have their purpose: Each will become the habitat for rich and varied forms of life.

Earth and sea must continue as intended by God. They must exist together, make a place for each other, always distinct and separate, yet always complementary. Each needs the other in order to be what it is, and all the great complexity of life that follows their creation depends upon their perpetual, mutual integrity. Other parts of creation will never come to be—and can never be sustained—unless earth and sea continue together, distinct and united.

We too are part of the creation. The story of earth and seas is a story about how we are to live in this world and with each other—distinct and united.

March 16

On this day in 597 BCE, Jerusalem fell to the Babylonian conquerors. Forced deportation followed, and the people faced a long exile far from their land and homes. Dreams died, hope was lost.

God's prophets had their work cut out for them. In the midst of so much profound tragedy, would the people of God look to their Creator and be saved? Could they ever return to their homeland? Could they recover their distinct identity, rediscover their purpose, and live as a light to the nations? Would the Creator, the true and living God of all, be discernable in their life as a nation?

Would they renew their foundational commitment to live as God intends and so reveal to the world what human society might look like in right relationship with the Creator and creation?

If all that sounds like an impossible ideal for any nation, we should recall that it is, in fact, an absolute mandate for all nations. Human society and culture—and our organization into nation–states—are part of creation, God's creation. Each of us, and all of us together, who walk the earth and sail the seas, are made by God for God's purposes. Each of us, and all of us together, are gifted by God to do that work. Each of us, and all of us together, are accountable to the Creator and creation—and to each other—for living lives consonant with God's vision for us.

March 17

I will be wearing green today—not only in a display of solidarity with my Irish friends or to give expression to the tiny bit of Irish genetic material I carry, but also because I want to rejoice in God's beautiful green earth this day.

There is a time and a place in our world for deserts. Those places can certainly be a venue for encounters with the Holy—sometimes the Spirit even drives us there. Deserts are places that will never be green or once were green but cannot be now. They too are part of God's good creation, beloved by God.

But today I give thanks for the lush and verdant, spreading and climbing, blooming and reaching-skyward part of creation that springs from the land that the Creator brought forth. The earth emerged at God's command, according to God's blessed vision for the universe, and now life thrives on it—just as it does in the seas from which it all emerges.

Saint Patrick, whose feast is celebrated today, is of course associated with a particularly green place, set amidst the waves of the sea. He was once a slave, and later, he embraced the power of Christ's reconciliation unfolding in the world. In that power, Patrick brought the good news of the Creator's forgiveness and love to those who had enslaved him.

Where Patrick and others like him did the Creator's work, slavery was abolished. A way of living together in harmony with the will of the Creator, empowered by Christ's work of reconciliation, took hold, and peace and justice followed.

Green today says to me: Be right with your Creator, be right with creation, be at peace with all—and flourish!

March 18

On this day in 1965, Cosmonaut Alexei Leonov became the first human to perform a spacewalk. An astronaut I know spoke of her first spacewalk as the most "awesome, amazing, and terrifying" experience of her life. Many who have made spacewalks as part of their missions have expressed similar feelings, just as many who have been in space commonly describe the first time they saw the earth and seas from space as a profoundly life-changing moment.

These moments reflect a shift in how the planet—and its inhabitants—are seen. Suddenly, Earth is not a huge extension of familiar surroundings, predictably stable and enduring, but something more vulnerable and alone in "the vast expanse of interstellar space." It is seen as our fragile and beautiful "island home." The earth is understood as something that should never be taken for granted, requiring our respect, protection, and devotion.

Today is the Feast of Cyril of Jerusalem, a fourth-century saint and bishop. He is especially remembered for developing liturgies for Palm Sunday and Holy Week that connected to holy places, helping shape the devotional experiences of numerous pilgrims.

It strikes me that a spacewalk is a kind of liturgy—and space exploration a kind of pilgrimage—by which we are brought into the presence of the Divine, helped to see ourselves and our world from a new perspective, and invited to live differently. We are called to live more like what we are: parts of creation—and stewards of it.

This revelation, this invitation to transformation, is given to all of us on our earthly pilgrimage (non-astronauts included). We only need to learn to look through the lens of creation.

March 19

Deep, powerful currents run through the oceans of the world. They circulate the nourishment that is the basis of marine life. They create climate and embrace and impact our lives in many unseen but interconnected ways. These currents impact all of earth.

We sometimes speak of currents running through human history. Interpreters of events and leaders of nations, pundits and presidents alike, seek to identify such currents and to articulate their understanding of them to the rest of us. Every human organization requires some working sense of what the currents are in order to have a vision for the future.

Today is the feast of Saint Joseph. In deciding to marry a woman who is pregnant with someone else's child, a woman who might properly be punished for adultery, Joseph responds to a deep current within himself. In making the choice to devote himself as protector and provider of mother and her child, he reveals to all that he is a gentle, humble, merciful, profoundly decent, and "just" man. He also shows himself to be a partner with the creator in the great plan of salvation. He moves in a deep, divine current.

What do the wise and powerful have to say about the currents of history in Joseph's day? How do they make sense of King Herod's scandals or the politics of a republic transitioning to empire?

Joseph perceives the truly deep currents—the creator at work—in the world, in history, and in his life. And, with Mary, he responds, "Yes."

March 20

At this point in the creation story, earth and sea are lifeless. In God's unfolding plan, this will change dramatically. Abundant life will emerge in both places, life that is distinct but forever connected as part of the universal network of purposeful being that is creation.

Archbishop Winston Halapua of Polynesia addressed the gathering of Anglican bishops from around the world at the 2008 Lambeth Conference. He reminded the bishops of a lesson to be learned from his home: As the waves of the seas dance, so God intends there to be a joyous dance of all people in our diversity—a perpetual, holy dance.

For the people of Oceania, earth and sea are interrelated, their existence intertwined and mutually necessary, Halapua explained. Both are places of human habitation. God has established a pattern in creation, and so it is natural that human beings are likewise connected. We depend upon each other. This is how God made us.

Today is the feast of Thomas Ken, an eighteenth-century bishop who made great personal sacrifices for the sake of his conscience. Time and again, he risked his career and life in calling out bad behavior by the kings under which he served. In addition to his example of personal integrity, Ken has also given us a gift of hymns, including the well-known "All praise to thee, my God, this night," which ends with the familiar Doxology: "Praise God from whom all blessings flow; praise him all creatures here below. Praise Him above, ye heavenly host. Praise Father, Son, and Holy Ghost."

Most of us have sung these words as the offerings of the congregation— gifts of ourselves, our lives, and our labors—were brought forward and presented at the altar. These words are an invitation to the dance.

All creation is invited to the dance this day. Are your feet tapping yet?

March 21

Today is the feast of Thomas Cranmer, Archbishop of Canterbury, martyr of the English Reformation, and architect of *The Book of Common Prayer*. In this latter role, Cranmer drew upon many traditional sources to create beautiful and enduring liturgies, vehicles for the worship of the Creator across the planet for generations. He accomplished the profoundly important work of bringing the monastic ideal of a life of prayer into the realm of ordinary life. One important way he did this was through his work to craft the multiple worship services said daily by monks into the two services of morning and evening prayer. Published in English, these two liturgies have become the primary way of worship, public and private, for countless souls.

These souls have been shaped by such words as found in the *Venite*: "Come, let us sing to the Lord….In his hand are the caverns of the earth, and the heights of the hills are his also. The sea is his, for he made it, and his hands have molded the dry land." Having established that God is Creator, the next portion of Psalm 95 then calls us to worship: "For he is our God, and we are the people of his pasture and the sheep of his hand."

The relationship of creature to Creator is intimate, nurturing, caring, and a source of great joy. But the relationship is not static: "Oh, that today you would hearken to his voice!" With this plea comes an invitation into a deeper relationship of knowing and being human, of loving and being loved, of discernment and faithful response.

What is the voice of the Creator saying to us that we need to hearken to today? What gets in the way?

March 22

*And God said, "Let the waters under the sky be gathered to-
gether into one place, and let the dry land appear." And it was
so. God called the dry land Earth, and the waters that were
gathered together he called Seas. And God saw that it was good.*
Genesis 1:9-10

My neighbor Joy worked in her yard every spring and summer. With
her wheelbarrow, shovel, hoe, and hose, she dug, trenched, and carved
out a design that has evolved through the years. When God talks about
cultivating the land, I think of Joy. She not only landscaped her own yards,
she had a landscaping business that she began after her friends begged her
for help in their yards. Joy's parents taught her how to listen to the earth
and let it tell her what to do. She married an engineer, and together they
raised three sons. I spent a lot of time at her house. She always told me:
"No matter what, you create a corner of the world for yourself."

Joy's home and her yard showed that she understood God's call to us to
actively participate in the care and cultivation of our earth. She believed
in making her corner of the world beautiful for everyone to enjoy. She
taught me a valuable lesson that took me forty years to learn. And God
began the promise of what is now ours, our shared heritage. God brought
us all to this moment, right now.

The Book of Common Prayer provides for us the words to offer thanks to
God: "Give us all a reverence for the earth as your own creation, that we
may use its resources rightly in the service of others and to your honor
and glory."

March 23

Procter Center, the diocesan camp and conference center for the Episcopal Diocese of Southern Ohio, is a sixty-acre farm in rural Ohio. This secluded setting offers the perfect atmosphere for reconnecting with the gifts of God's bounty: An old barn and a new chapel provide space for prayer and meditation amid corn fields and green spaces. My favorite feature is a spring-fed lake that sits behind the conference center. I always request a room in the back of the facility. "Are you sure you want to be way back there? It's a pretty far walk." "Yes," I always answer. "I need a view of the lake."

As I sit near the lake today, pondering God's creation process, I try to imagine what it must have been like when God gathered all the waters together. Was it peaceful, like the lake in these moments, or were the seas raging to be released? Were there indications even then of the glorious, yet volatile relationship we would always have between land and water?

March 24

Until two years ago, I never felt like an outdoorsy person. Nature seemed to be for everyone else, but not for me. Between allergies and inclement weather, I thought I was better off indoors. I'd watch people run, play golf, hike, ski—I didn't feel like those activities were for me. Somehow, God's invitation into creation hadn't reached me. Yet.

Then two years ago, a health scare forced me to reevaluate my life choices. Overweight, with borderline high blood pressure and several orthopedic issues, I knew there had to be another way. I started to pray and meditate about my situation. And God said, *You know what to do.*

After several months of walking on the track of my neighborhood high school, I needed another place to walk that would be easier on my joints. Plus, the kids were coming back to school and needed the track for after-school practice. Once again, God said, *You know what to do.* That day, I hiked my first trail in almost forty years. When I was done, I wanted to tell everyone. It was my first experience of feeling completely connected to God outside. I felt completely at home.

Nature, like God, is always there for you. No matter when you hear the message, the message is yours to receive. And God said, "Let the dry land appear." God did this for you. God wants you to have a place in this land. Will you claim your earthly inheritance?

March 25

And God said…and it was so. If we stay on the surface with these words, God's process of creation can seem like a series of magic tricks. But we know better, because we've accepted God's invitation to go below the surface of the words and into the deep well of God's promises for us.

As we wake and begin each day, we have a choice. We can choose to engage and participate in cultivating and caring for the earth, or we can leave that work to someone else. We can tend our gardens. We can recycle plastic bags. We can use stainless steel straws. Or, we can leave that work to others.

What if God had not done the work of creation? What if God had not spoken our world into existence? We wouldn't have this beautiful world entrusted to our care. We wouldn't *be.* And we know God wants us to be here, because we are here. It is so.

Unlike God, we can't speak our care of the land and water into existence —we have to do the work. God has done God's part by putting the earth's care into our hands. What will we do today to make the work happen?

March 26

Just as God separates the water from the land, we sometimes separate land into smaller, more manageable pieces. As I started my labyrinth walk at camp, a gentleman was standing across the labyrinth on the bricks, looking confused. "I've been trying to figure this out, but I can't make sense of it," he said. "If you walk between the bricks, on the path, it will make more sense," I explained. "The path lies between the bricks."

In a labyrinth, a small space contains a great distance. The outer edge does not indicate the terminus, nor does the center. The path keeps moving, doubling back on itself. You don't have to worry about how far you've gone, because you're safely guided to the end—which is also the beginning. You've been there before, yet it's always new.

God invites us to experience the gift of creation in the same way. We will revisit many paths, double back, find the edge and be pulled back in. God has given us the materials— and the capacity to manage them. How we do so is up to us each day.

What new paths will we create? What will we eliminate? To what will we return again and again? Which paths are meant to be traveled only once?

March 27

We can't live without water. We are made of water. We need water to survive. When God separates the water from the land, God makes it possible for us to live and survive on Earth. In time, we learned to harness water into wells and reservoirs.

One April day, I found myself standing on the shore of the Pacific Ocean in Oregon. I had been to the beach in California, Jamaica, New York, and Virginia, so I thought I knew what the ocean was. Nothing could prepare me for the majesty of the swells, the rock formations rising out of the water, and the cold sea air whipping my face.

My two friends and I walked along the beach as the sun began to set. I had been nervous, because we missed a worship service to visit the ocean. I shouldn't have worried. God found me out there, and God said, *It is good that you are here. It is good that you found me here. I was waiting for you.*

We can't live on water from the ocean. But without the ocean, we can't live. God finds new ways each day to bring us deeper into creation.

Whether you like rivers, oceans, streams, or beaches, what can you do to get close to God through water?

March 28

One thing all people have in common is the weather. Just met a person for the first time? Chat about the weather. In line to pay for your groceries? Talk about the weather. Waiting for the bus? Talk about the weather. I wonder what God would say in these conversations.

When God separates the water from the earth, God sees that it is good. God does not equivocate. God does not say, *Well, this is good, until people plan a picnic. Then, the water falling from the sky isn't good anymore.* What would happen if we changed our thinking to be more like God's? What if we looked on each day as inherently good?

During a recent health crisis, I decided that I had to change my thinking about the weather. I decided that all weather is good weather, and I could only control my response to it. Now, I travel with a poncho, two hiking sticks, and gloves. I always have the gear I need to walk outside, no matter how hot, cold, wet, or dry the earth might be.

God intends for us to care for and cultivate the earth, which includes caring for and cultivating ourselves. The daily invitation into creation includes the sunny days, the cold days, and the rainy days.

Dear God, thank you for the gift of another day in your creation. No matter the weather, help me to view this day as your greatest gift. Amen.

March 29

I just read about a new island off the coast of the Outer Banks in North Carolina. Talk about "let the dry land appear!" When I searched for more information, I found this response from Stanley Riggs, a retired geology professor and author of books about North Carolina's coast. "Nothing here becomes a fixture. Nothing is the same from one hour to the next. There's no such thing as 'normal.' Everything here can change overnight. That's what makes it so amazing."

New land appears; someday it will be submerged. Water and land have a tenuous relationship; water gives and destroys life equally and indifferently. As much as we try to control water, it controls us.

Land is no different. Walk on a nature trail and you're sure to find exposed roots. Both flowers and weeds break through concrete in search of life and light. We've spent the last fifty years spraying chemicals on our lawns to get rid of clover, dandelions, and other weeds, only to find that we're contributing to the extinction of bees and creating environmental and health issues for all forms of life.

The emergence of this island became news because we are enamored of the sea's ability to transform the land. Perhaps a new island will be formed. Perhaps a beach will be destroyed. It's beyond our control.

God separates the land from the sea, but they remain inextricably linked. When I compare my euphoric and catastrophic experiences with water and land, I think about how they represent the ultimate struggle in our lives: Although we try to command our life to form around our ideas of what it should be, God can throw a storm, a flood, or a drought our way to remind us that God is always the captain of the ship.

March 30

Now he is God not of the dead, but of the living; for to him all of them are alive.

Luke 20:38

I've discovered the most beautiful arboretum in which to walk and relax: Spring Grove Cemetery. It's the second largest cemetery in the country, with expertly maintained gardens spanning 733 acres. I grew up in Cincinnati, but I had never spent much time there. Who hangs out at a cemetery?

One of my friends posted on Facebook some photos of monuments from the cemetery. Intrigued, I decided to drive through it. I came back every day for three weeks—I couldn't help it. It was as if God had called me there and forced me to discover my peace.

This cemetery is always filled with life—from workers pruning and cutting the grass to folks using the cemetery as a shortcut to avoid traffic. There are walkers and runners, mourners and peace-seekers; wild turkeys, turtles, hawks, cardinals, swans, and other animals inhabit the lakes and woods.

Then there are the trees—more than 1,000 different trees—and the cemetery offers numerous benches and trails from which to enjoy them. My favorite trees, weeping willows, have their own trail section. If you've longed to walk under a canopy of your favorite tree, your wish may come true at Spring Grove.

I'm sitting in one of my favorite spots as I write this meditation. The peace I find is indescribable. I thank God each time I'm here that God put it into the minds of some of her children to create a space like this: a physical space that honors death while creating and celebrating life, a place where one's soul may truly rest in peace, whether that soul be on earth or in heaven.

March 31

Ever since the creation of the world his eternal power and divine nature, invisible though they are, have been understood and seen through the things he has made. So they are without excuse.

Romans 1:20

I was an inside person for most of my life. It's not that I didn't appreciate the outdoors. I went to a Montessori school, which valued experiential learning. We learned about leaves by walking the grounds of our school and about animals by walking the trails down the hill toward the Ohio River, spotting salamanders, newts, rabbits, and snakes. Once I became an adult, I just didn't think the outdoors was for me.

Pain brought me back to nature. That's how God showed me that the seas and the earth were separated for me, too. I sought comfort for aching joints, and God provided the shade of the trees, the damp of the ground, and the soft rushing of the water in the creek beds. God brought me joy in discovering that I belonged to creation. I felt part of something bigger than me. I stopped searching for my purpose and my reason for being. When I am in the woods, I understand that my reason for being is to experience what God has created for me, my ancestors, and generations to come.

Since I've rediscovered myself outside on trails and tracks, I want everyone to join me out here. I've become an evangelist for the healing benefits of trails—that's how I know it is spirit-led. Being in the woods or on a trail is the closest thing to being in church that I've ever experienced—people smile, nod, say hello, or even stop and chat. Maybe they feel the same way I feel—happy, peaceful, and thankful. I pray that you let God lead you into your peace in creation. Maybe we'll see each other there.

April

A River Flows

A river flows out of Eden to water the garden, and from there it divides and becomes four branches. The name of the first is Pishon; it is the one that flows around the whole land of Havilah, where there is gold.

Genesis 2:10-11

Artist's Note: Once Genesis starts describing places and geography, the paintings needed to make the transition from conceptual paintings of creation to something more concrete. Formless void and the cosmos are amorphous and indeterminate; a flowing river is something more concrete and literal, so this necessitated yet another shift in approach, from abstract to more realistic. I wanted to invite the viewer in, so I settled on a very simple, stylized painting of a river flowing out of the Garden of Eden, the beginning.

That Land is Good

And the gold of that land is good; bdellium and onyx stone are there. The name of the second river is Gihon; it is the one that flows around the whole land of Cush. The name of the third river is Tigris, which flows east of Assyria. And the fourth river is the Euphrates.

Genesis 2:12-14

Artist's Note: Paintings rarely develop in a straight line. More often than not, the process involves a few twists and turns, kind of like rivers. When meditating on this scripture, I was drawn to two very different approaches. The first line, "And the gold of that land is good: bdellium and onyx stone," introduces some compelling elements. I fooled around with related imagery, but it just felt too static. Once I finally started painting a landscape, I found that I really enjoyed it even though I've avoided them for years. Now that spring is here and the rains have pretty much stopped, I'm looking forward to getting outside and painting. Who knows where that will lead? Oh, the gold we find when we accept a challenge and face our fears!

> *A river flows out of Eden to water the garden, and from there
> it divides and becomes four branches. The name of the first
> is Pishon; it is the one that flows around the whole land of
> Havilah, where there is gold.*

Genesis 2:10-11

The images found in the first two chapters of Genesis are rich and meaty with multiple meanings. It's hard to imagine this is an accident. Reading these words and contemplating on the responses they evoke in us can bring us closer to the author, closer to our community, and closer to God.

This verse opens with an image of division that separates the primordial river flowing out of Eden into four branches, which flow out into the furthest reaches of creation. Why does the account specify that there are four branches? Is it related to some deeper mystical meaning? Is it a memory of some historical geography? Saint Ambrose imagined that the number four corresponded to the four cardinal virtues: prudence, temperance, justice, and fortitude. Saint Cyprian of Carthage thought they represented the four gospels.

To me, the four rivers evoke the four cardinal directions: north, east, south, and west. From this perspective, we are invited to open our thinking outward from Eden, which is at the center, toward the rest of God's work and design. The four rivers also make me think of the three dimensions of classical space and that of time, so that they represent the entirety of the universe as we have known it from the beginning—and mark out every moment of history, every event and instant.

This last idea is the most evocative for me in our twenty-first century context. It reminds me that the origin of all experience and the unfolding of God's plan for creation is the Garden that God created for us to inhabit. We have departed from the Garden, but we remember and long to return.

April 2

In my experience, great rivers are created when small rivers and tributaries add their currents and water to that of another river. Think about how the Mississippi River is made greater as the Missouri and the Ohio rivers are added to the Mississippi as it flows south to the Gulf. Or consider the Amazon, as the Purus and the Madeira and the hundreds of other streams combine to make one great, majestic current.

But in the Garden, the situation is reversed. Here, the great river flowing outward from the navel of creation divides into four. I'm reminded of how rivers like the Nile or the Mississippi break out into thousands of smaller streams as they make their final push through a delta into the sea. But I don't think that's the image this part of the creation account is meant to evoke in us. This is different—this is a great river dividing into four great rivers, each with their own story.

This reversal seems more about connection and unity than it is about division. We are asked to recognize that all the great rivers of the earth are expressions, children of the water that God creates to water the Garden. If we could, we would travel up the waters of the rivers of creation, to find the places where they rejoined one another, and following on, we would find the center.

Looking at these verses in this light invites us to see the underlying unity of the world that God has made: a world where all waters spring from the same source and are available to everyone. The waters of the rivers in the account are one, just as we all come from the same source and are all one family.

April 3

Scholars are divided on the location of the river Pishon. Other rivers mentioned in this passage are commonly understood to represent the Tigris and the Euphrates rivers, so it's reasonable to imagine that the Pishon isn't a metaphor. Likely we have forgotten that a river was once named as such. We have either lost track of the name, or the river itself has vanished. Either way, the Pishon has become lost to us today.

Technically a lost river is one that loses water as it flows toward its mouth. Such rivers are not uncommon in the deserts of the Southwest. These lost rivers dwindle as their waters are diverted into reservoirs or spread out into irrigated fields. Sometimes, all that is left is a dry bank that only runs with water once a decade or so when mighty rains restore it to its former glory and intention.

The Pishon is lost to us in time—it flowed and watered a great land once upon a time but does so no longer. A river such as this invites me to wonder what other gifts God blesses us with that we have lost over time. What gifts have become the lost rivers in our lives?

When you encounter a lost river in the Southwest, you can find living, flowing water if you journey (make a pilgrimage) back toward the source. The pilgrimage restores us to that which has been lost. How is God inviting you to seek the wellspring of waters today?

April 4

Though certainty about the original river named Pishon is lost to us today, we are more confident in locating the land of Havilah. The construction used with the name in this verse is uncommon and translates as "the land of sand." This verse describes that as the "place where there is gold." Mostly likely, this is the Arabian Peninsula.

The sands of the Arabian Peninsula can be overwhelming in their immensity, and they are often described as being like a great sea. It's a striking contrast to compare a sea of sand to a river of water in the same verse, and it is even more striking to point out that in this land full of common sand, we find the rare and valuable. This gold that causes war and strife is worshiped as an idol and offered to gods in other parts of the Bible.

I am drawn to the paradox that the thing we greatly desire as human creatures and describe as rare and precious is found in the place where there is an overwhelming abundance of a common substance. How often do we imagine that the things we seek the most are hidden away in a distant place—an uncommon, fantastical place unlike the everyday locales of our regular lives? But here is a hint that creation doesn't work that way. The things we desire most can be found in the great, everyday sea of common things. The paradise we search for is not found over the next mountain but right here under our very feet.

It is in the land of sand that there is gold.

April 5

I lived for six years in the Sonoran Desert in Arizona.

It took me time to see the beauty in the desert, to see the ways that the brown and gray stood in rocky contrast to the deep blue of the midday sky that was nearly always devoid of clouds. When I looked out across that vista, anything green, anything with trees, was immediately noticeable.

North of where we lived, a river of water rambled across the desert floor. It's called the Verde River, the "green river," because its banks feature trees and grass. It is a meandering river oasis.

Before I lived near the Verde, I had never seen a river that so clearly gave and supported life in such a hostile place. The lush plant life was only possible because of the water moving between the river banks. Those banks were alive not just with the trees and the plants but with the birds and small animals who found a place to make a home. When I looked closely, I could see the ruins of the buildings, towns, and communities that the Indigenous people had built there too. The water of the river created an entire ecosystem and told an old, old story.

I imagine the rivers that flow out of Eden did the same in the beginning—and they do the same for us today. The water from the Garden calls to mind the water of our baptism, which makes life possible. The teeming river banks of the Verde River remind me of God's creative action in our lives and our need to stay close to the life-giving waters that flow forth from the wellspring of the Divine.

April 6

I'm quite taken with the image accompanying the verse we are praying with this week. I love how the artist echoes the blue of the stars and the sky at the top of the frame with the deep blue of the water at the bottom. The water reflects what exists beyond, outside of it, and what glows above it.

When the sky is a deep azure blue, the water below takes on that quality. When the sky is green before a storm, the water is too. When the heavy rains come and flood the ground, the rivers rise and rush with brown foamy water filled with topsoil that the rain has stripped from the surface of the earth.

The character of the river's surface comes from the winds that blow across it. On a calm day, the surface is smooth and glassy. When the wind comes in puffs, you can see the small ripples on water. And when the storm winds blow, the water rises in chaotic fury, with whitecaps and crashing waves that foreshadow the life the water will have once it reaches the great sea.

Bodies of water like mighty rivers have their appearance because of the external reality in which they are placed. They are protean, without permanent form or structure. Perhaps that is why we love to live beside them but rarely on them. The creative energy that their changing form gives us is able to be expressed only when we combine it with the stability of the earth and ground. Perhaps that is why it is the Spirit that gives us life, but we can only truly live if we dwell in Christ.

April 7

Most cities exist in a particular location because of the environments that surround them. They straddle a safe harbor, sit at the bottom of a mountain pass, or hug the banks of a river. In the days when cities were being founded, rivers were the highways civilizations used to flourish.

Imagine London without the Thames, Paris without the Seine, Rome without the Tiber, or Cairo without the Nile. They wouldn't have thrived, and they wouldn't have endured their numerous cycles of destruction and rebirth.

It's quite striking that the Bible's account of the story of the world beyond the Garden begins by describing the rivers that flow outward, dividing and organizing the lands that God sings into life. It's quite striking too that water, which is essential to the nature of a river, so often plays a central role in the great stories that we tell across generations: stories of seas divided, lakes calmed, rivers crossed, waters that drown and give life. This river of Pishon that flows from the Garden begins the story of our experience of God outside of Eden. The river places us in the beginning of the story of salvation and gives us our sense of location in the world that God invites us to explore.

There are rivers in our lives today—rivers that are part of our stories, that spring from the place where we too have been created by God and in whose waters we travel and discover that God has gone ahead to meet us. Where are the rivers taking you now, and what are they causing to grow inside you?

*A river flows out of Eden to water the garden, and from there
it divides and becomes four branches. The name of the first
is Pishon; it is the one that flows around the whole land of
Havilah, where there is gold.*

Genesis 2:10-11

My grandmother had a love affair with water. She threw herself into
the waves of the Atlantic on our yearly vacations to South Carolina as I
watched from the dunes in admiration and trepidation. I refused to follow
her—the immensity of the water terrified me. This element seemed too
powerful to trust, and I worried that I could lose myself in it. When my
grandmother beckoned me to the water's edge, I firmly refused, banking on
the certainty of land over the ambiguity of the sea.

My grandmother didn't give up on me and spent long afternoons in the
shallow end of the community pool, teaching me how to blow bubbles. She
urged me to trust the water and to lean into it. One day, we were having
so much fun at the pool that I lost myself in the action, and rather than
drowning or disappearing, I found myself swimming alongside the other
kids, delighting in the buoyancy of my new state. When we returned to
South Carolina the following summer, I didn't think twice before following
my grandmother into the waves.

The element of water is enigmatic, powerful, and scary—but it is also
transformative. Water reminds us of our interconnectedness and urges us
to have faith. The very practice of faith is akin to stepping into the great
unknown of the ocean, shedding layers of ego, fear, and separation, and
learning that we are part of a greatness upon which all life depends. I
can still see my grandmother standing at the water's edge, beckoning me
toward her. When the Spirit calls, will you follow?

April 9

I just returned from a trip to Haiti, the poorest country in the Western Hemisphere and the largest diocese of the Episcopal Church. Haiti's natural landscape is breathtaking, with majestic mountain peaks overlooking rolling valleys, yet this natural environment also shows the scars of degradation. Haiti continues to wrestle with sustainability challenges as deforestation and prolonged drought exacerbate food insecurity for the Haitian people. Beyond issues of land conservation, Haitians also face the enormous challenge of access to clean water.

Speeding through the lush countryside of Haiti's Central Plateau, I caught my first glimpse of the Artibonite River, a major source of drinking water for Haitians and a gathering place where locals bathe and wash their clothes. In 2010, this essential community resource was poisoned when United Nations peacekeeping troops dumped infected waste into the Artibonite, introducing a deadly cholera epidemic that ultimately killed more than 8,500 souls. While the United Nations has since accepted responsibility for the tragedy, international partners have yet to mobilize sufficient resources to end the cholera epidemic in Haiti.

The mighty Artibonite River, once a source of life, was transformed into an instrument of destruction by one irresponsible act. As ripples emanate from a raindrop crashing into the surface of a pond, our small works have large consequences. How often do we pause to consider the effects of our actions?

Life is fluid, yet as we go with the flow, we can also increase our awareness. Today, let's look up from our stresses and our screens to see the landscape before us through new eyes. May we conscientiously alter our words, our habits, and our goals to promote healing and wholeness in the world. Let us move with intention, and wherever we can, bring life to those whom we touch.

April 10

The image of Eden's river rolling forward, bringing life and growth to God's abundant garden, is a rejuvenating vision. The river is a powerful, providing source, and even as I long for its refreshment, I am simultaneously inspired to emulate Eden's river by serving as a life-giving force in my daily interactions.

From 9 a.m. to 5 p.m., I work in a policy advocacy office in Washington, D.C., on behalf of the Episcopal Church. Each day, I spend my hours drafting action alerts, responding to emails, planning advocacy trainings and events, and meeting with congressional offices and advocacy partners. If I don't work with intentionality, I lose awareness of how my actions impact my colleagues and my organization's wider advocacy network. Rather than going through the motions, I must remember that everything I do has tangible effects on those I touch.

Our Indigenous partner advocates remind me to "do things in a good way." After watching these advocates' good example, I am beginning to understand what they mean by this phrase. *Doing things in a good way* entails being a compassionate, aware, and conscientious person. The good way calls me to make eye contact with people living in the shadows, to focus on seeing more than being seen. The good way bids me to be patient and kind to the colleagues who rub me the wrong way, even when I'm under stress and time is short. The good way challenges me to take a deep breath, conscientiously considering how an action or strategy will affect those living today as well as generations to come. When I fully live into this good way, I too can be a source of life.

April 11

More than a decade ago, a harsh drought struck the Shenandoah Valley of Virginia where I grew up. I remember feeling the dry, crackling grass beneath my feet and inhaling the unmistakable scent of wildfire smoke when I walked outside. My family watched as our pond diminished to a meager puddle before evaporating entirely. Our neighbors whispered nervously, wondering if this year's pitiful crop would sustain them through the winter. That summer, we all longed for a River Pishon to materialize and rejuvenate our withering land and economy.

As greenhouse gases precipitate climate change, my community's experience is hardly unique. Our world is witnessing more frequent and more severe droughts in many corners of the globe, and even as we strive to address climate change, we struggle to understand the link between environmental damage and spiritual drought. Mainstream culture often fails to emphasize our role as subjects within God's creation, a magnificent ecological web that we are called to steward even as it sustains us. Given the massive challenges confronting our society, how can we begin to repair this disconnection?

Maybe we can start by addressing the spiritual drought within ourselves. When I have gone too long without grounding myself in faith, I feel dried up and overwhelmed by the problems facing our world. Often, I ignore my inner drought and push forward, mechanically completing tasks as my mind races ahead, stressed and distracted. At times like these, if I can just remind myself to take a ten-minute break, go somewhere quiet and meditate or pray, I am rejuvenated. I emerge from my time away feeling reconnected and ready to serve. Perhaps the River Pishon is closer than we ever imagined, and as people of faith, we need only seek its waters to drink deeply and be renewed.

April 12

Healthy rivers support healthy communities. When I was a kid, a local chicken corporation offered my neighbors free sludge fertilizer for their crops. The sludge would save these farmers a lot of money, yet it also contained hazardous chemicals and pathogens that could leak into our ground water and rivers. Eventually, the proposal pitted neighbor against neighbor and ultimately led me to believe that issues of environmental sustainability and human need are intrinsically linked.

I saw this linkage again many years later on the banks of Lake Oahe, a reservoir of the Missouri River. I traveled to Lake Oahe with other faith leaders to stand in solidarity with the Standing Rock Sioux tribe and to oppose construction of the Dakota Access Pipeline. The Missouri River is the Sioux's main water source and constructing the pipeline under Lake Oahe would jeopardize the Sioux's access to clean water. When I arrived, I saw the lake and surrounding prairie landscape transformed by the presence of police vehicles, road blocks, law enforcement wearing riot gear, and hundreds of water protectors. Like my farming community, the Sioux face a Goliath corporation intent on exploiting local need for financial profit. This critical issue of environmental justice offers us the opportunity to live our faith through advocacy and action.

We do not have to travel to Standing Rock to join the ranks of water protectors. God invites us to be water protectors wherever we are, for where there is human life, there is water to be savored and safeguarded. "*Mni wiconi*," say the Sioux. "Water is life." This day and every day, may we have the courage to face down our giants and stand up for clean water everywhere.

April 13

In the age of free and easy information, social media feeds bursting with calls to action added to a constant stream of print, radio, and digital news, we can easily feel overwhelmed by the problems of the world. Refugee crises, national debt, environmental degradation, crumbling infrastructure, famines, our rapidly changing climate, gun violence, the prison-industrial complex…the list goes on.

With these challenges confronting us, how can we systematically address the injustices of the world? Are we even equipped to take up these causes and be effective agents of change? The information deluge often makes me want to shut down my computer and clear my head with a good novel rather than heed a moral call to action.

This week's scripture passage details a mighty river that "flows out of Eden to water the garden" and then divides into multiple branches. I like this image of a potent river dividing and conquering. Powered by one source, this river waters generously, expanding its original impact to reach thirsty foreign lands.

While we do not have to tackle every problem in the world, we can certainly address some of them. Is there an issue that directly impacts you or people you know or your local community? Is there a movement that especially ignites your sense of injustice and calls you to act? The Spirit—that mighty source of life and action empowering every agent of its works—will speak to you and tell you where to go. Like the branches of Eden's river, no one of us can be everywhere at once, but together, we can cover significant ground.

April 14

One river takes many forms: a tiny trickle emanating from a mountain rock, a singing brook, a tumbling waterfall, a wide and steady tributary feeding into the sea. The shallower the river, the more frenzied it appears, gushing over impediments en route to its destination. Deeper waters often seem calm, even leisurely, but their surface is deceptive. Beneath their tranquility lies a powerful force that flows with certainty. A shallow river frenetically fights forward, but deeper waters peacefully advance.

In your everyday tasks and interpersonal interactions, do you feel more like the babbling brook or the mighty river? This morning, I found myself sprinting across the U.S. Capitol complex to make a morning meeting, only to realize that I had gone to the wrong building and my colleagues were waiting in a different office two blocks away. I was frazzled and angry at myself for not paying better attention to details, and at that moment, I felt like a shallow, frenetic river.

The Latin proverb *aqua profunda est quieta* reminds us that still waters run deep. To move with the peaceful surety of a mighty river, we can ground ourselves in the depth—and strength—of our faith. I am still working to grow into the full potential of this awesome depth. Some days are easier than others, and I try to approach the process with patience and humor (the lighthearted brook is a good teacher, too). We are on an adventure, a course that bows and bends even as we move forward to the sea.

Journeying in our faith, may we reach the faithful depth of a mighty tributary, surely progressing toward fullness of life in Jesus Christ. Amen.

April 15

And the gold of that land is good; bdellium and onyx stone are there. The name of the second river is Gihon; it is the one that flows around the whole land of Cush. The name of the third river is Tigris, which flows east of Assyria. And the fourth river is the Euphrates.

Genesis 2:12-14

Water is fickle and impulsive. Life-giving yet treacherous. Strong enough to create electricity but soft enough to bathe a newborn. It can destroy buildings and whole sections of cities, but it is consecrated into holy water and used to bless the rebuilt community.

Our existence begins immersed in the water of our mother's womb. Yet water is a paradox: The water molecule itself is made of hazardous elements, coupled and balanced in a perfect trinity of life-giving H_2O. Water is the most abundant resource on the planet, yet many around the world struggle because of lack of access.

Water effortlessly wanders around barriers on its search for the sea, but with persistence and time, water creates its own path—wearing away obstacles into smooth stone and deep canyons. Water fills the space it is given, and so our lives would follow if we let them. Water shows us the way forward, yet we look upstream. Our life should be one of movement and constant searching, but we often stand still.

We build dams and levees around our lives. We try to contain what should be fluid and free. We bottle emotions for fear of them flowing out of our reach, out of our control. We funnel our rainy days into gutters and sewers instead of letting them soak in to help us grow when spring arrives. Indeed, water is fickle, impulsive. Water is life.

April 16

When I first began fly-fishing, wading through rivers looking for fish to bother, I often slipped or stumbled on submerged rocks. Every step needed to be calculated, but I was in a rush to catch fish. However, when trying to sneak up on notoriously skittish trout, splashing from missteps, even slight ones, leads to a lot of casting—and no catching.

Over time, I adjusted. When I started I took a breath between each step, my fishing trips became less about catching fish and more about catching those breaths, less about trout and more about quieting myself enough to move with grace and ease. One foot firmly planted as the other nudged around and looked for firm footing, even in areas obscured or distorted by the murky water. Step. Breathe. Step. Breathe. Nowadays I slip less, catch more fish, and stay dry slightly more often.

When my daily life gets busy and I start to feel myself rush through tasks at work and home, I remind myself of this lesson. I have set aside daily and weekly time for prayer, exercise, meditation, and other self-care practices, but being human, I sometimes default to approaching these practices as means to an end. I rush, and the entire point is lost.

For most of us, firm footing is hard to find. Slipping and sliding are inevitable as we wade through life. But the more often we pause, breathe, and ensure we have our footing before taking the next step, the less frequently we stumble.

Everyone finds his or her balance differently. What will you do today, that will ensure tomorrow's step is taken with care, ease, and grace?

April 17

There is wisdom and simplicity in using rivers as natural borders. Nations and states, counties and districts, commonwealths and provinces: Look at any map and you're bound to find rivers and streams serving as natural boundaries.

I wonder, though, do we too easily dismiss rivers as simple dividers, barriers to bridge and borders to cross? Do we forget the journey of unity that flows beneath those bridges?

Take the iconic Mississippi River as an example: It serves as part of the border of ten states. The mighty river is wide and memorable, an obvious choice for a natural barrier.

However, the water churning between its banks comes from thirty-one states and even part of Canada. Water comes from Pennsylvania and New Mexico, Saskatchewan and Appalachia. Search for a map of its river basin—seriously, it's impressive. A single river emerges from countless springs, creeks, and even the drainage ditches of shopping mall parking lots. Returning to the ocean, the trickles of runoff rejoin the water cycle and begin their journey anew.

It wouldn't be a stretch to say that, of all the natural features we interact with regularly, rivers unite us more than any other. They are the life-giving arteries of God's creation, for which we are called to care. How might we treat these waterways differently if we spent more time seeing them as such?

April 18

In the mid-nineteenth century, officials planned a large suspension bridge across the Niagara River, a few miles downstream of the famous falls. It was an ambitious project for the era, crossing both the river and an 800-foot gorge.

To get the first line across the ravine, builders considered a number of bold methods: rockets, cannonballs, steam-powered boats, and hoists. However, in the end, a much humbler method was chosen—a kite.

Builders offered $5 to any youth who could fly their kite across the river gorge and attach the string to the other side. A 16-year-old accomplished the feat in a few days. His string was used to pull a rope back across, followed by a heavier rope, and an even heavier rope, and so on. With a sturdy line connected to each bank, construction began. The eventual railway suspension bridge was a landmark achievement for the engineers and the region.

If you're like me, when you run into life's rivers and ravines, you may aim your cannon first and overcomplicate your crossing. It's not our fault—society tends to endorse the bold responses to life's predicaments and celebrates those who overcome their troubles with the force of a cannonball.

But I wonder if we might consider what it would be like to cross barriers with a kite. These daily practices we undertake—prayer, writing, meditation, yoga, running, walking, or your own ritual—begin as a humble string, flown over a river with the simple ease of a kite. Over time, we pull heavier and sturdier ropes across. We build. By creating regular spaces for guidance and wisdom, we are always building—and always preparing to cross the next river.

April 19

The trout was a healthy size and whipped its head back and forth as I navigated the river rocks and boulders, trying to keep up with the fleeing fish—and maintaining tension on the delicate line that linked us.

I climbed up one larger boulder as the water deepened in front of me, and I attempted to stand my ground. Just as I gained my footing, the line snapped and threw me off balance. I might have caught myself, but humor prevailed.

Luckily the water was deep and slow moving, so I avoided hitting any rocks on the way down. I swam to the nearby shore and climbed out unscathed. I stood there, soaking wet, my waders full of cold river water; I'll let your imagination run with my first words. But I can assure you, I was laughing within a few minutes.

Upon inspecting my gear, I discovered that the thin monofilament had not snapped, but rather the knot attached to the hook had slipped undone. Instead of a jagged end of the line, I had a telltale curly "pig tail" that put the blame on me.

In my haste to get in the river and start fishing, I rushed the knot and likely tied it wrong. Despite everything I did to catch that fish, it was always going to escape, because I hadn't prepared in such a simple, but essential way.

Daily prayer, silence, and meditation are simple enough that we may slip into complacency. However, like the knot tied a thousand times, focus and attention matter every time. Showing up and being present matters. You never know when life may put some unexpected tension on you. And if it does, it helps to know you can rely on your knots.

April 20

Fly fishing is rhythmic, most notably the casting part. Some instructors use metronomes to help newbies find the right cadence. I often find myself singing a song in my mind, syncing each cast to the beat. The technique takes practice and patience. It took me years to feel comfortable, and even still there are times when I probably look like it's my first day out.

The rod whips a heavy line through the air, back and forth, using momentum and the springiness in the bent rod to hurl the line forward and behind. The line is tapered—sometimes to the width of a human hair—and at the slender end is a hook, dressed in feather and furs to imitate a natural bug, waiting to deceive a fish.

For a moment, as the heavy line rolls highest in the air, unfurling forward or back, there is a slight pause in the caster's motion. A sudden stop, as the line completely stretches out. It's slight, but that short moment of waiting is crucial to the timing of a cast. With the amount of line, wind, and casting distance continually changing, you must pay attention to each pause and make slight adjustments. There is never an identical cast.

When the leader of a prayer begins with the words, "Let us pray," there is typically a similar rest, a brief moment of preparation—undefined and unique to each occasion. The pause provides a starting place for the group to enter the same rhythm, the same cadence of prayer. I find peace in that moment, like I find peace in the still moments of casting a fly fishing rod, adjusting to the moment and waiting just long enough. And then, once the time is right, moving forward.

April 21

In the flat lands of Florida, rivers move slowly. Sometimes, very slowly.

Everglades National Park, one of the world's most diverse ecosystems, deceives visitors who see only stillness in its swampy grasslands. The wetland is actually not stagnant; it is a slow-moving river. Carrying fresh water from Lake Okeechobee at only a quarter-mile a day, the water takes over a year to reach the coast just a hundred miles away.

Often called the River of Grass, its 60-mile-wide network of creeping waterways is dotted with sawgrass and small patches of forest. The system is home to an abundance of plant and animal life.

In recent years, agricultural runoff and pollution have caused algae blooms in Lake Okeechobee, suffocating the water, plants, and animals that rely on it. Recent population growth and urban expansion across South Florida is limiting runoff options, and the lake's polluted water is regularly dumped into the Everglades and nearby river systems for flood control purposes.

The slow, tainted water crawls 1,320 feet each day, causing lasting harm to the entire ecosystem. Perhaps if the waters moved faster, the problem would be less visible and easier to ignore. But the problems linger here and soak in. Even cutting off the pollution today would mean over a year of damaging water continuing to meander along the coast.

When our own lives are flooded with poisons, the slow, seeping march of life doesn't always wash away the damage as quickly as we would like. Patience in the seemingly still waters of waiting doesn't come easy. Even if recognized and remedied at the source, it can take time for our own troubled-life waters to reach the coast, and no healing comes without scars and lasting signs of struggle.

And the gold of that land is good; bdellium and onyx stone are there. The name of the second river is Gihon; it is the one that flows around the whole land of Cush. The name of the third river is Tigris, which flows east of Assyria. And the fourth river is the Euphrates.

Genesis 2:12-14

I have spent the majority of my Sunday mornings inside dark churches, where the only sunlight is filtered through stained glass and beneath my feet there is red carpet or tile. As much as I love Sunday mornings in church, some of the Sundays I remember best are in a chapel with no walls at a summer camp in Texas and a few Sundays at campsites in Colorado, where my father, a priest, set up a card table and we stood on a carpet of pine needles.

It's a bit of a cliché—going out into nature to find God. Nonetheless, out in creation is where many people feel closest to the Creator. There is a benefit from worshiping out where our experiences of the natural world are not mediated through glass and stone and artificial structures.

In fact, there is some evidence that simply walking barefoot on grass has health benefits. I can't vouch for how good the evidence is, but it makes sense to me that connecting to the earth, unencumbered by anything invented by human beings, is good for us. Here, we can quiet ourselves and listen, away from the noise and clatter of our everyday lives. Being in creation, outside of our manmade walls, is a way to remind ourselves that we are part of this creation, and that whether we're worshiping or merely walking, God is there.

April 23

Genesis tell us that the land of Eden has valuable natural resources—gold and bdellium and onyx, minerals that could power an economy. If we were to write these verses today, we might list oil and natural gas, the fuels that run the world. Yet these are also the things that can destroy us. Love of gold and wealth at the expense of human life has caused much conflict, and excessive burning of fossil fuels is already costing lives as global temperatures rise.

The land is good, but it can also be exploited in ways that harm others. I think about climate change often and worry that we are in danger of destroying the gift that sustains us, and in so doing, destroying ourselves. We easily forget that we are stewards, and we are not called to consume the earth but to live on it.

Soon, I hope, the most valuable lands will be those with sunlight and strong winds that we can use freely without harming our land and ourselves. Soon, I hope, we'll remember that the treasures we extract from the earth are only borrowed.

April 24

In 2017, the Whanganui River in New Zealand became the first river to be recognized as a legal person. The law, pushed by the Indigenous Maori tribe, acknowledges that the river is a "living whole." I am not certain exactly what this means legally (though apparently the river has lawyers of its own now), but it does mean, in part, that no one can own it.

The four rivers in these verses from Genesis—the Pishon, Gihon, Tigris, and Euphrates—are a central part of what makes Eden good. They water the land and provide sustenance for the people living there. Yet if you divide a river, block it, pollute it, damage even a part of it, you affect the entire river—you can easily destroy a community or permanently change a landscape.

Today, one billion people do not have access to clean water. That is one-seventh of the global population. There is enough water to go around, but we've spent centuries dividing up the land and its waters rather than sharing them. At times, ownership may be the only practical way for a society to function. But what would it be like if we thought of the earth as a living whole, another being in God's creation, rather than something that can be divvied up among us?

April 25

When I was a child, my family took a vacation every summer. We would drive from Texas to Arizona and then up into Colorado to visit family and camp in the national parks. The back of our van was always a little heavier on the way back with various souvenirs we picked up—smooth stones, fossilized sea shells, gnarled pieces of driftwood. I don't think we ever found onyx, and I wouldn't know bdellium even if it was in my hand, but nonetheless the world was full of treasures.

I no longer grab things I see from the side of the trail when I'm away from home (at least, not often). We don't have enough space in our little apartment to keep driftwood. But the world is still full of treasures.

Now those gifts come to me in the form of a beautiful day after a long, wet winter, a brilliant sunset, or the view from my car window as I leave the city. These experiences, like the shiny stones we collected on our shelves as children, are touchstones that help me recall beauty.

April 26

When I lived in Houston, I loved taking road trips across Texas: driving from Houston to San Antonio where my parents lived, or down to Padre Island with friends, or up to Dallas for a wedding. These trips could take anywhere from three hours to seven—everything *is* bigger in Texas. I like the openness of those hours on the highway, the large, blue sky, the simplicity of driving. You can't do anything but watch the road, maybe listen to music or the radio, or talk to whoever might be in the passenger seat. On these trips I would often think about relationships or the future or wrestle with my faith.

Living in a city as I did then and do now, it's easy to feel disconnected from the land, like we are on separate planet from the rest of the animals that inhabit the sky and sea and wilderness. Even on these trips, of course, I was in a moving machine, but I felt more a part of the land, a part of Texas—a state I still love. There's so much diversity there, and after a few hours of driving I could find myself on beaches, in hill country, or driving through flat fields of cotton or corn.

Today, I live in New York City, another city I love—and a city I love to leave, driving north past the high rises, apartment complexes, and parks and out into the woods and small towns along the Hudson River.

Though we never leave Earth, of course, we often have to leave home to feel like we're still on it. In this way, a road trip or a hike or simply an afternoon in the park is like prayer—consciously reconnecting with something that is always there.

April 27

After years of subsisting on peanut butter and jelly sandwiches and cereal, I've grown to enjoy cooking and baking. My wife and I make simple meals for our 10-month-old daughter and oatmeal or fried eggs for ourselves. Most weekends, I bake. I enjoy baking because it takes time and focus and because it's physical. After a day in front of a screen manipulating words in electronic documents, the act of measuring and mixing and kneading makes me feel present and at home in my body.

When we spend so much of our time in the virtual world and our food arrives in neat packages or arranged in supermarket aisles, it is possible to ignore the fact that our food is dependent on the land—and so are we. Our well-being is dependent on the well-being of the earth. We cannot separate them. This seems obvious, but we too rarely live as though this were the truth.

We may not always have time to cook or prepare our foods, but remembering where the food we eat comes from and how it gets there is one way to recall that we are part of a single, interconnected creation.

April 28

The Southwest has a system of water sharing called the *acequia* or "the people's ditch." Small streams and canals carry melt-water from snowfall down into communities that share the water through a communal governance system. These small communities are in arid areas of the country, where water is sometimes scarce. The *acequia* system is more than 400 years old.

In this system, no one owns these watercourses. There are disagreements, of course, but the community deals with them with a local commissioner and *majordomo* who administer the water. It varies a little by region according to the needs of each community.

At a time when water scarcity is growing, I see the *acequia* systems as signs of hope that, like inhabitants of Eden, we can see the rivers that flow through our lands and support our lives as abundant gifts belonging to us all.

April 29

My daughter has just learned to crawl. So I too spend a lot of time on the ground, making sure she doesn't bang her head or eat something that's fallen on the floor. She hasn't quite gotten the hang of crawling around on her knees, so instead, she pulls herself around on her hands while doing a kind of sideways push with one leg. We try to keep our floor relatively clean, but because she likes to stick her hands in her mouth, I'm sure she's ingested plenty of dust and dirt.

This is probably fine. Some studies suggest we are too clean. Our body learns to handle bacteria and microbes by being exposed to them. If we never touch anything dirty or become sick, it is harder for our bodies to learn how to handle dirt and germs.

To be very clear, I'm not a doctor, and I'm not encouraging people to go out and feed their children dirt. (Apparently some parents do just that, which I learned after searching the terms "health" and "dirt.") But I try to remind myself as I watch my daughter sit on the ground in the park or at home that we don't have to live in fear of a little dirt. We were created to handle a messy world—and even to thrive in it.

April 30

Land is valuable, and everybody wants a bit of it. Even though few of us are farmers, this desire to have land is ubiquitous. Many of us want to own a home, preferably with a backyard, a bit of earth to call our own. As someone who owns his apartment (and we have a shared backyard), I understand this desire. Sometimes, however, we get too protective of our property.

We've seen this protective tendency surface recently with a growing fear of refugees and immigrants. This fear comes, at least in part, from a belief that there isn't enough: not enough gold and not enough water and not enough land to go around.

The truth is that there is enough. We produce enough food to feed everyone and there is sufficient water to go around. There are many complicated reasons for why people still go hungry and thirsty, from war to poverty to geography. Nothing in this world is simple or ever has been, at least not since Adam and Eve were kicked out of the Garden and became the first immigrants.

But I also believe that if God's creation is good, if it is meant to sustain us and we are meant to use it well, then we have to let go of fear and the need to cling to our little piece of the world while others struggle to survive. There is enough. And it is still very good.

O merciful Creator, your hand is open wide to satisfy the needs of every living creature: Make us always thankful for your loving providence; and grant that we, remembering the account that we must one day give, may be faithful stewards of your good gifts; through Jesus Christ our Lord, who with you and the Holy Spirit lives and reigns, one God, for ever and ever. **Amen.**

The Book of Common Prayer

May

Let the Earth Put Forth Vegetation

Then God said, "Let the earth put forth vegetation: plants yielding seed, and fruit trees of every kind on earth that bear fruit with the seed in it." And it was so.

Genesis 1:11

Artist's Note: As with some other paintings in this book, this work was originally done for another series. Part of the I Am series based in the metaphors in the Gospel of John, this painting is titled *The True Vine*. In the beginning was the Word. Christ goes beyond the story found in the gospels; Christ is grounded in the beginning, the genesis of creation and the source of our faith. Christ is eternal.

I spent a long time in vineyards working on the prototype for this painting. I drew and re-drew vines. But I simply couldn't get away from grapes. The fruit of the vine represents the fruit of our relationship with Christ.

Seed of Every Kind

The earth brought forth vegetation: plants yielding seed of every kind, and trees of every kind bearing fruit with the seed in it. And God saw that it was good. And there was evening and there was morning, the third day.

Genesis 1:12-13

Artist's Note: This was one of the last paintings I finished for this book, and it was a special request from the editors. I admit: It took me a bit of time to get my mind around this assignment. It's inspirational to convey the spirit of a bird or mammal but wheat? This painting took a while to simmer and develop. I needed to look a little deeper and let the intricacies of wheat speak to me. Once I let go of my own preconceptions, I realized the incredible complexity and beauty of a stalk of wheat. This offered new lessons from creation: Don't make assumptions. And make sure to take the time to really look at something. Now I'm inspired to do a whole series of paintings depicting wheat and other grains.

May 1

> *Then God said, "Let the earth put forth vegetation: plants yielding seed, and fruit trees of every kind on earth that bear fruit with the seed in it." And it was so.*
>
> **Genesis 1:11**

Every culture has its own relationship with plants, its own stories about plants.

Did you know that humans share roughly 15 percent of their genetic makeup with plants?

We so easily place ourselves in a different realm, far removed from the lower forms of life such as plants. It might be helpful for us to occasionally remember that we share a common ancestor with Bermuda grass, which I love to rip from my garden beds.

Honor this: We live and breathe this day with each fern and forest. What an island of life we seem to be in the vastness of space, but here, under the same sun, in the same big puddle of water, we have managed to pass on the story, our DNA, for billions of years.

May 2

Good food is good medicine.

We rely on plant life as a food source and as food for animals, which in turn provide us food.

I grow cabbage. It takes around ninety days to grow and mature. Summer campers pick the worms off and feed them to the chickens. We cut the outer leaves off and also feed those to the chickens. Then we cook our cabbage with a couple of eggs. The chicken manure and eggshells are put into the compost pile where microbes feast.

Within these ecological cycles we may find all that we need. And if we are lucky enough to find enough to make it to tomorrow, then this moment is worth all song and highest praise.

May 3

If you have never really hugged a tree, I encourage you to do so.

Some humans tell stories of the deer people, plant people, tree people, and the human people. These ancient stories inspire me to treat all forms of life with as much dignity and reverence as I show toward other humans, to other tribes of people.

If you can open yourself up to the tree people, if you can feel the world as a tree feels it, if you can catch the sun with your leaves, if you can watch the years go by in front of you without even thinking of taking a step, then you may hug a tree—and feel the well of compassion within it.

May 4

There is death between plants and humans too.

Socrates was sentenced to death by drinking the poison, hemlock.
Roundup is routinely sprayed along fence lines and sidewalk cracks,
aiming to kill any errant grass or weeds. The blooms of toxic blue-green
algae make for deadly swimming. One hundred years grows a forest that
can be cut and hauled away in a day. Romeo and Juliet visit the apothecary.

In God's creation:

There is food, and there is poison.
We are food, and we are poison.
There is life, and there is death.
There is one sun.
There is one dance.

May 5

Each leaf held just so: stable, yet reaching for the sun. Each leaf is balanced within for what it can be—and what it needs to be.

This is beautiful.

These patterns in nature are spaced so perfectly, shaped just so, so that life may happen, so that this celebration may continue into tomorrow.

May 6

Try to grow anything in the winter: You will work twice as hard to get half as much. Even if the temperature is mild, little will thrive. The daylight hours are too few. There is not enough sunlight to give most plants the food they need to do serious growing. In the winter on a farm, it is better to do the work it will take to be ready for spring.

When the sun crawls back toward the equator, a few extra minutes of daylight brings a surge of energy.

Root systems expand. New leaves appear. Flowers unfold. Eggs hatch. Insects swarm.

And if you can catch that wave of solar energy when it comes, you will find yourself growing too.

May 7

I humbly receive.

In Japan, they say *Itadakimasu* before a meal. It can be translated into English as, "I humbly receive."

The farming institute I worked for in Japan taught a deeper meaning to this phrase. They talked about it as if it were to mean, "I humbly receive this life."

This interpretation points to the ecological fact that we must consume life to continue living. So we honor all the life that has been sacrificed to allow us to continue into tomorrow. Today as you chew each bite of your food, try to remember: *Itadakimasu*. Remember to be humble. Give thanks and celebrate the lives that were given to allow you to continue living.

May 8

> *Then God said, "Let the earth put forth vegetation: plants
> yielding seed, and fruit trees of every kind on earth that bear
> fruit with the seed in it." And it was so.*
>
> **Genesis 1:11**

Be very still. Quiet your breath. Don't hold it, but listen: God is speaking creation into being. God's breath is coaxing our Mother Earth as she labors. The seed God planted has been nurtured, and now it is about to break through her womb and be visible.

We try to imagine what it is like when God calls forth creation. But this is almost impossible. We might take a step back and look at seeds—really look at them—and allow ourselves to wonder how plants, shrubs, flowers, and trees come from such tiny seeds. This practice of intention might give us a glimpse into the wonder that is creation. Regardless of how creative our imagination might be, I don't think we can measure up to the creative mind of God and all that God brings forth in creation.

Rogation Days are celebrated in the month of May. The history of Rogation Days takes us back to a time when parishes marked their borders, walking the boundaries of land in a church community. Tradition says that parishioners were to care for the land within the bounds. Psalm 104 was often recited as the boundaries were marked and the earth was celebrated.

> *You make grass grow for flocks and herds, and plants to serve
> mankind; That they may bring forth food from the earth, and
> wine to gladden our hearts, Oil to make a cheerful counte-
> nance, and bread to strengthen the heart. The trees of the
> LORD are full of sap, the cedars of Lebanon which he planted.
> In which the birds build their nests, and in whose tops the
> stork makes his dwelling. (Verses 14-18)*

May 9

From the beginning, fruit trees have had at least two jobs: to feed and to propagate new life—a tree of life.

When we read the biblical account in Genesis, the writers have divided creation up into work days. Words like these have gotten us into trouble. Many people see the earth as a trove of resources created for and intended to meet our every need. This attitude is reflected in one of the eucharistic prayers: "You formed us in your own image, giving the whole world into our care, so that, in obedience to you, our Creator, we might rule and serve all your creatures" (*The Book of Common Prayer,* p. 373).

In more recent times, our understanding of creation seems to lean more to the following prayer: "Give us all a reverence for the earth as your own creation, that we may use its resources rightly in the service of others and to your honor and glory" (*The Book of Common Prayer,* p. 388).

Many Native American creation stories reflect relationships between all the elements of creation and make it clear that there is an intentional interdependence, with no part of creation more important than another. When we see ourselves as intricately interwoven parts of a whole, we are more apt to care for all of creation. One way to mark Rogation Days includes revisiting our promise to use resources rightly so that we might ensure there will be fruit for generations to come.

May 10

Clap your hands, all you peoples;
 shout to God with a cry of joy.
For the LORD Most High is to be feared;
 he is the great King over all the earth.
He subdues the peoples under us,
 and the nations under our feet.
He chooses our inheritance for us,
 the pride of Jacob whom he loves.
God has gone up with a shout,
 the LORD with the sound of the ram's-horn.
Sing praises to God, sing praises;
 sing praises to our King, sing praises.
For God is King of all the earth;
 sing praises with all your skill.
God reigns over the nations;
 God sits upon his holy throne.
The nobles of the peoples have gathered together
 with the people of the God of Abraham.
The rulers of the earth belong to God,
 and he is highly exalted.

Psalm 47:1-10

Just as in ages past, we sing a new song to God each time we pray the psalms. Psalm 47 fits well within the theme of God in creation, reminding us over and over that God is "king over all the earth" and "the rulers of the earth belong to God." Even as Jesus ascends into heaven, God continues to be present in creation just as God is present in the beginning. God is not gone but is very present in and with creation. Were we to think otherwise, it might be easy to see creation—or even ourselves—as abandoned, left behind. God is here, in the land.

May 11

Seeds are as diverse as the plants they hold within them, but you can't tell from looking at the outside of a seed what wondrous creation will be birthed from it. A seed by itself is just a seed.

Add rich soil and nourish seeds with water, and they sprout new life. In this next stage of the life cycle, flowers and fruit are often produced. They in turn continue the cycle of life. My Native American ancestors teach that the life cycle is fragile and could be lost at any moment, if not cared for with love.

Imagine for a moment how our plant relatives teach us about the miracle of life. It begins with soft-spoken words (or at least that is how I imagine it) beckoning life out of fragility—a seed.

A seed all alone is just a seed, but nestled in the rich womb of our Mother Earth, new life bursts forth. First, it is but a sliver cutting through the seed's hull but once the plant pushes itself out, a new life—a miracle—is revealed before our very eyes.

I am a gardener and often start plants from seeds. No matter how many times I do this, I still wait with joyful anticipation for the very first sign that the seed is more than just a seed. I watch as the plant breaks through the soil and when it is strong enough, the plant stands alone and often produces more seeds for future plants. These seeds are like children and require our care.

Plant a seed. Be amazed.

May 12

I love the seasons of the year in the desert. And no matter how many years I have spent marveling at the flora of the desert, I am still surprised and filled with awe as the plants adjust to heat or cold, wet or dry, wind or stillness.

It is particularly wonderful to see the trees move with the wind. In the desert, trees are not very tall but they are strong and many have a full canopy. It won't be long now before our monsoon season begins. The desert comes alive as brilliant greens replace brown and faded green.

I think of Isaiah 55:12 during the monsoons: "The trees of the field shall clap their hands." They really do seem to clap their hands as they sway to the rhythm of the wind. If you listen closely, you can even hear a song that the trees compose with the wind. Once in a while, Brother Thunder grabs our attention, but it soon returns to the trees' song.

It seems almost impossible to believe that these wonderfully diverse trees were once tiny seeds, but they remind us of this fact when they have lived out their life cycle and sprouted another tree. We call the new sprouts volunteers because they voluntarily sprout where the seeds have landed.

Have you ever had the experience of sprouting a volunteer? Has someone ever said that something you said or did impacted them in a way you had not imagined? We are those trees—and sometimes, the volunteers.

May 13

For the last several years, we have been paying more attention to the impact of human endeavor on our Mother Earth. Yet the relentless attacks continue. We hear about global climate change and its devastating effects. I think of my relatives who have relocated their village because of rising ocean levels. I think of my relatives whose water has been diverted from their farmland and re-routed to people living in growing urban centers. I think about my relatives who tell stories of animals who once lived among them and say things now like, "It has been many years since we have seen one."

We teach our children to care for our Mother Earth. She is referred to in this way because we see her the way we see our own human mothers. As God calls forth life from creation, our Mother Earth is bathed in sun and moonlight and with rivers and streams.

O heavenly Father, who has filled the world with beauty: Open our eyes to behold your gracious hand in all your works; that, rejoicing in your whole creation, we may learn to serve you with gladness; for the sake of him through whom all things were made, your Son Jesus Christ our Lord. Amen.

The Book of Common Prayer

May 14

God said...And it was so. I wonder if these words were said in the booming voice of a command? I suppose it is possible to have an image of God in creation as wielding power, ordering creation into being. But I can't quite wrap my head around that kind of tone coming from God. Our ancestors teach us that our perspective of the world becomes our response to the world—it is a reflective relationship. If I were to see the world as a place where power and order rule, then I would treat the world in the same way. On the other hand, I would treat the world differently if I understand that I must listen closely and carefully to hear God whispering in the wind, sound traveling from the most fragile plants, flowers, and trees.

Can you hear a seed sprouting? Do you hear when it makes its first appearance above ground? What about the fruit from the tree? Can we taste it without a sense of wonder? Think of the different types of fruit, their flavors, shapes, and sizes. It is beyond my imagination to understand how God brings all of these and more into creation by gently coaxing our Mother Earth to incubate, nourish, and care for them until they are ready. How else could our Mother Earth respond? As creation is whispered into being, all of creation stands by and rejoices in awe and wonder.

My ancestors' words come back to me again suggesting that if I treat creation with awe and respect, creation will respond with the same—and continue to amaze me and invite my heart to wonder each day.

Listen. God is speaking creation into being. And it is so.

> *The earth brought forth vegetation: plants yielding seed of every kind, and trees of every kind bearing fruit with the seed in it. And God saw that it was good. And there was evening and there was morning, the third day.*
>
> **Genesis 1:12-13**

I was surprised to learn that most organic farmers say they grow soil, not plants. It's impossible to grow healthy plants without healthy soil. The earliest farmers knew this when they wrote, "The earth brought forth vegetation."

We are living creatures with qualities like those of a plant. When we take into account our soil—the unseen spiritual aspects of ourselves—we can learn a great deal. Our ancestors are our soil, the people who came before us and whose DNA we carry. My maternal grandfather, an outgoing and courageous man, was capable of persuading and inspiring people to protect and conserve precious land along the Ohio riverfront in his hometown of Cincinnati. My father, a talented businessman, developed a drinking problem later in life, and so I watch for signs of addiction in myself. These lives and many others shape the characteristics of my soil.

But we're not limited by our bloodlines—we can amend our soil to include the whole communion of saints. I've chosen to add to my soil stories of people like my godmother, one of the most spiritually grounded people I know. A staunch Yankee—and 97 years old—she's teaching me how to live, how to grow old, and how to die. Another amendment I've chosen is William Kent. A prominent conservationist, Kent donated land, giving the world the Muir Woods, among many other treasures. Kent's witness serves as a guide, showing me to think creatively about protecting the land. These are some of the saints who shape the soil where I am planted. Can you describe your soil and what amendments you are choosing?

May 16

Sonora wheat seeds are tiny—like golden grains of rice but plumper. A crease bisects the sides of the seeds. On either side of the crease are the cheeks.

Wheat is not indigenous to North America. Sonora seeds are important to me because they are the oldest variety of wheat in our country, brought over by the Spanish in the sixteenth century in response to the mission friars who wanted to grow wheat for their communion bread.

When I began to plant wheat, I learned how to prepare the land, dig the furrows, sow the seeds with careful spacing (two finger-widths apart), and then cover and compact the soil. I knew those friars did precisely the same thing, along with the countless farmers throughout history. I remember the first time I planted these seeds: I stood over them, feeling an intense tactile connection.

I had joyfully prepared the seed bed and deliberately let each seed run down my fingers. I watched their sand-colored bodies, the rich brown line in the soil like a row of pearls on a necklace. Now I felt an utter lack of agency. I had done what I could do. I could not make the seeds grow, and this fact both humbled me and made me feel helpless. I would now need to endure the waiting before the first bits of green emerged from the soil.

I held those seeds in February. Would I harvest their progeny in August? This is the practice of faith, something farmers have known since time in memorial.

May 17

Seeds can remain dormant for centuries. The oldest seed to successfully germinate—a Judean date palm—was about 2,000 years old. How is it that such power can lie in wait for so long?

Germination takes place when a seed absorbs water and swells, and a radicle bursts through the fruit wall. In botany, the radicle is the first part of a seedling to emerge from the seed. This is the little tail we see in a sprouted seed.

There is a small church in north London called St. Luke's. The rector and I became friends during a research trip I made to his parish a dozen years ago. I traveled to England in hope of finding people who just might share my love of the church and my love of the land. At the time of my visit, a resident artist was installing an enormous painting. If you're standing in their chancel and gaze upward, you will see the beautiful golden branches of a tree spreading across forty panels embedded in the ceiling. A verse from Revelation runs along either side, where the writer has an enraptured vision of a holy city with a river running through and trees alongside: "The leaves of the trees," he writes, "Are for the healing of the nations..." Springing from the branches are hundreds of green-gray leaves, but what you can't see from the ground is that every leaf has a name painted on it—the name of someone who has been part of St Luke's, the name of someone loved and lost, the name of someone venerated because of their life. Several months after our visit, the priest wrote to tell me of a wonderful thing: They had included my name in their tree of life.

The inclusion of my name surprised me. At that time, I was undergoing the process of deep personal discernment and discovery. However, the power of this tiny act—the painting of my name alongside so many other names; permanently written in this holy place—felt as though the seed of my idea had germinated and was now visible. Germinating my hunch, germinating my unformed longing, this small act gave me courage. We never know when the seeds of our longings will be nourished and germinate. But we do know that our yearning retains its fullness, even when it is dormant.

May 18

There's a period most nursery plants go through between departing the comfy conditions of a greenhouse where moisture, temperature, and sunlight are finely calibrated for ideal growing conditions, and being planted in the bare earth with nothing to protect them from wind, frost, and strong sunlight. This period is called hardening off. The tender plants are moved into a cold frame to be gradually exposed to increases in both "bad" and "good" conditions. The plant needs to learn to withstand greater adverse conditions as well as positive conditions of increased sunlight.

During this period, plants stop growing upward and focus their energy on putting down deeper roots. The roots then signal the leaves to prepare for rapid expansion. The seedlings need these deeper roots to withstand harsher conditions and vigorous growth ahead.

When we go through our own periods of hardening off, they don't feel pleasant. We have moved into a more challenging situation, and we're out of our comfort zone. During these periods, we don't see growth—we can't see progress, and our efforts can feel futile. But what we know from the spiritual life is that our roots are being strengthened, and we are being prepared to withstand difficulties as well as to flourish in the future. God desires this for us. If we only grow upward and outward, we might topple over at the first strong wind and ray of light.

May 19

Fallowness—leaving a field unsown for a season—reestablishes subtle soil structure and allows microbes to reset to their natural rhythm. Native life, previously thwarted by overproduction, is allowed to reemerge. Fallowness breaks damaging pest and disease cycles and is an effective means of rebuilding fertility. While a fallow field appears empty and idle, there's actually massive activity happening in the soil, restorative activity that we cannot see.

Most farmers today no longer allow land to go fallow because the practice is deemed uneconomic. This isn't the farmer's fault. The farming system rewards yield. As a result of not resting the fields, the soil is exhausted and loses its vitality over time. The food grown from that land is less nutritious.

The ancient spiritual practice of fasting is based on the natural idea of letting the body go fallow. When we forego food for a period of time, fasting reduces the external demands on the digestive system, allows old waste to discharge, and lets God's vital life-force begin to resurface. The Desert Fathers relied on this practice to clear their minds, mend their bodies, and create space for God. Jesus practices fasting too.

You might consider fasting at some point this year, with your doctor's blessing of course. Perhaps as a birthday gift to yourself, during Lent, or when you have time to retreat into quietness. You'll be surprised how as the physical body quiets, the spiritual mind becomes quite active and has the chance to recognize the elemental nature of life, the need for water and the need for rest. Our bodies have the opportunity to rediscover hunger and what it means to be satisfied.

May 20

Just as every person has a story, so does every harvest. I like to imagine that the seeds remember being blessed and placed in the earth. Do they retain the memory of pushing down their roots during the cold February rain and of rushing up toward the sun, growing five inches, during that first warm week in April? Do they hold the memory of evaporating moisture on long, hot July afternoons, turning greenness into gold? On our harvest day, I want to believe the grain recognizes my daughter as she strides through the field with a sharp sickle, that it hears the sounds of the blade and feels its stalk separate from the earth.

At day's end, she proclaims, "That was fun!" This is my daughter's voice, but do I also hear a duet? Is the earth also rejoicing because of its part in the cosmic dance of life?

Can we taste this story when grain is baked into bread and called the Body of Christ?

May 21

There is an ancient Hebrew blessing prayed over the bread, "Blessed are you, Lord God, King of the Universe, who brings forth bread from the earth." Bread doesn't really rise from the earth, but grains of wheat do. Have you ever contemplated how one gets from a kernel of wheat to a loaf of bread? So many steps are no longer visible. Most people are not familiar with threshing or winnowing. This is why I lead community planting and harvest days every year—to bring people into this dance of life.

The first year, I arranged for a dear friend, a talented musician, to lead plein air music for the event. She researched spirituals and other songs that were historically sung in the fields. On the morning of the event, we made the hour drive north to the farm. As we drove past verdant and tender spring grass, we could sense anticipation in the air—something important was about to happen. Soon we would be carefully planting heirloom seeds into prepared furrows, into the womb of God's earth. We would be farmers, taking our place in bringing forth bread from the earth. All these experiences co-mingled with the words we sang, a tune by David Dodson, called "The Farthest Field:" *Walk with me and we will see the mystery revealed, When one day we wend our way up to the farthest field.* I had a sense of connection and kinship, a shared identity with my great-grandfather, Pa, a wheat farmer from Ohio; with Ruth and Boaz in scripture; and with all those generations who had come before me and had put their trust in the soil.

Every step of the process that day bestowed reverence: beginning with the children removing the rocks from the field, to the stooping and bending of the planters' bodies, to the prayers and the praise that rose up from our mouths.

May 22

*The earth brought forth vegetation: plants yielding seed of every
kind, and trees of every kind bearing fruit with the seed in it.
And God saw that it was good. And there was evening and
there was morning, the third day.*

Genesis 1:12-13

Encompassing approximately 100,000 square miles of the Southwest, the
Sonoran Desert can be a forbidding place. Temperatures routinely exceed
105 degrees in the summer, approaching 120 at times. Buckhorn cholla,
fishhook barrel cactus, ocotillo, saguaro cactus, and prickly pear—even
the vegetation is daunting.

But then it rains.

At any one time, as many as 200,000 seeds per square meter lie dormant
on the desert floor. But following the winter storms, which typically
begin in December, something miraculous occurs. Sonoran toads boil up
from the earth to breed, cactus wrens boldly build their nests of grass and
twigs in the thorniest scrub they can find, and the desert starts to bloom.

Dispersed by wind or birds or animals carrying them on their fur or in
their gut, the seeds of desert plants can lie inert for decades, waiting for
just the right conditions of moisture and sun to explode from the sandy
soil. There are no guarantees, but every few years—when germination
is followed by regular rains and the winter isn't too cold—the Sonoran
Desert becomes a carpet of pinks and yellows and reds.

Lupine and poppy, feather duster and mallow—whether perennial or
annual—they were all at one time a seed. Closed on themselves in the
dark, they labor toward light, drawn by the same deep Mystery that stirs
our souls to life.

May 23

Few sights are as heartbreaking as the image of a mountainside on fire. Watching from the safety of our living rooms, we sense the fear of those who live in the path of the blaze, of those leaving everything behind, of those whose job it is to fight the flames. We think of the creatures too, the ones whose only home is in these woods.

And what of the woods themselves? Ironically, for many of the species that constitute our forests, fire is the source of life.

Lodgepole pines, jack pines, and even the giant redwoods and sequoias all produce what are known as serotinous cones—cones that protect their seeds until exposed to fire. With the jack pine, for instance, cones may remain on the tree for many years. Protected from the fire itself, the seeds are released when the heat melts the resin holding them in place. Finally dropping to the ground, the seeds fall onto soil that has been cleared by fire, prepared by the blaze that may well consume the mother tree.

Adapted to fire, the jack pine and coniferous species like it have evolved not only to survive a blaze but also to depend on it to thrive. Fire frees the seed, primes the soil, cuts through the smothering canopy, and lets the sun shine in.

What has the flame of loss exposed in my own intractable heart? What seed lies waiting in the fresh and fertile soil of the raw places in my soul?

May 24

I am standing in the garden in July, an empty basket in my left hand, a ripe tomato in my right. The compulsion, when it comes, is simply too much to resist. Raising the plump fruit to my mouth, I take a bite. Unconsciously, I close my eyes, blissfully unaware of the juice dribbling down my chin. Such is the lure of a homegrown tomato just picked from the vine.

The long association between fruit and temptation isn't hard to understand. Whether a juicy tomato from the garden or a tree-ripened peach from a roadside stand, fruit connotes a kind of illicit pleasure, something decadent and rich.

And so it is.

In his book *The Botany of Desire*, Michael Pollan explores the ways that plants have evolved to use humans and other creatures to keep their species alive. The process is easy enough to grasp. The plant develops a flower that is fragrant or bright or both, the objective being to entice a pollinator to visit and do its work. Once fertilized, the ovary of the flower begins to develop into a fruit containing seeds: Biology 101.

The beauty of this system is that these seed carriers—these fruits—are often extremely delicious. Try growing dewberries or cherries or figs and you'll find yourself competing with all manner of winged or four-legged thieves. Fruit-bearing plants may lack intelligence as we know it, but they nonetheless possess the wherewithal to ensure their own survival: They trick us and the rest of the sentient world into distributing their seeds.

How easy it would be to think of the plants in my garden as nothing more than scenery, a backdrop for the busyness of my life. But their existence is more complex than I know. To slip into their world, to be drawn to taste the midsummer ripeness of their fruit, is to taste the joy of the created world, to experience the intelligence of the Divine.

May 25

I planted my first garden at the age of six. It wasn't much to look at, a narrow plot of what we called "black gumbo" soil marked off with string on the east side of our crackerbox house. The only seeds I sowed that year were beans, specifically pinto beans appropriated from the kitchen shelf.

Poor soil or not, they grew, but as I soon discovered, these weren't the kind of beans that ended up on my dinner plate. Those beans were green—typically Kentucky Wonders that my parents raised. Unlike my little plants, those were reliable and prolific, things of beauty to a wide-eyed child.

My first venture into gardening may not have yielded much, but it was enough to get me hooked for life. Having seen a seed erupt from that thick clay earth, I couldn't go back to a life that lacked such miracles.

More than half a century later, I am still that six-year-old, wandering through the yard each spring, eager to see what's going on beneath my feet. Did the seeds of last year's larkspur germinate? Will the bluebonnets I planted in the fall come up? There's no predicting either one.

Frustrating as it can be, that unpredictability is something I've come to love about the land. This year, for example, our property is blanketed—quite thickly in places—with seedlings of cedar elms. Why this has occurred is a mystery to me. Granted, these native trees show up with regularity around the yard, but not like this—and never to this extent. Was it the mild winter that allowed this phenomenon to take place? A prolific bloom? The amount of rainfall we received at precisely the right time? Who knows.

What I can say, however, is that these seedlings appeared without any help from me—some dark intelligence, buried deep inside each embryo, determined when they would send out roots, shoots, and leaves. Becoming like a little child again, I stand silent in the presence of this Mystery, the stirring of a kingdom taking shape in the soil of my own soul.

May 26

As ambitious ideas go, this one was basically off the scale: Create a farm on twenty-eight acres of prairie to find a way of growing crops that wouldn't deplete the land. How absurd this must have seemed at the time. Hadn't the Green Revolution of the 1950s and '60s solved all our agricultural woes?

Plant geneticist Wes Jackson didn't believe it had.

Leaving a short but successful career in academia, Jackson returned to his native Kansas in 1976 to create what he called The Land Institute, a nonprofit organization dedicated to the task of developing a sustainable way to farm. The Green Revolution might have helped the Bread Basket produce beyond belief, but it was also taking a big toll on the soil and the microsystems it sustained. What if we looked to the land itself to teach us what it knew?

Before the Dust Bowl—before the widespread use of chemicals, before the practice of planting single crops that would have to be replanted every year, before the plains were transformed by modern farming practices—this land had been fertile for more than 10,000 years, supporting life with a myriad of perennial plants.

What Jackson learned, and what The Land Institute staff continues to demonstrate on roughly 1,000 acres, is that their practice of no till agriculture not only reduces erosion and eliminates the need for chemicals but it also increases the soil's fertility and ability to hold water. The challenge has been to domesticate wild perennial grains and legumes and to develop existing annual crops such as wheat into perennial ones, returning year after year.

Listening to the land, listening to the Kansas prairie, Jackson reminds us of the value of diversity, of roots, of nurturing the givens of our lives. Ultimately, he argues, focusing on what lasts is wiser than making a quick crop and moving on. Jesus would have found a good parable here.

May 27

It's no secret that plants produce the oxygen we breathe. Consequently, when we hear of trees leveled for farming or land scraped bare to build another strip mall, we worry about the quality of our air. What we often fail to recognize, however, is that more than half of the oxygen we depend on is not produced by trees and other terrestrial plants. It comes directly from the sea.

Phytoplankton, one-celled plants whose name in Greek means "wandering or drifting plants," live near the surface of the ocean, where they transform sunlight into chlorophyll and emit an estimated 50 to 85 percent of the oxygen on earth. Making this statistic even more astounding is the fact that the biomass of plants in the sea is .005 percent of the biomass of plants on land. Put another way, phytoplankton and other marine vegetation are 200 times more efficient than grasses and trees and shrubs in producing the air we breathe. And yet—there's always that "and yet"—we too often treat the sea as both an inexhaustible source of consumables and a system that is infinitely capable of repairing itself. Neither, of course, is true.

Author Rachel Carson began her career as a marine biologist working for the Bureau of Fisheries, later known as the U.S. Fish and Wildlife Service. Her main task initially was to communicate information about the ocean in a way that laypeople could understand. This proved to be a labor of love, given Carson's long fascination with the sea. The success of her trilogy *Under the Sea World*, *The Sea Around Us*, and *The Edge of the Sea* was greater than anyone could have imagined. The reason? Carson's poetic language played a crucial role, but another part of the explanation is that at that time, the public knew little about sea life. People were enchanted by her descriptions of the geological and biological processes forming and sustaining this world.

We have learned and seen a great deal in the decades since Carson wrote her first book on the sea, but we still don't grasp the importance of the life—particularly the plant life—that exists beyond our view. Might our hope lie in the power of re-enchantment?

May 28

Many plants go dormant in the hot summer months, but the resurrection fern takes this survival tactic to the limit. Normally lush and green like any other fern, *Polypodium polypodioideshas* has the uncanny ability to "die" and come back to life hours, days, and even decades later.

An epiphyte, or air plant, the resurrection fern lives its life attached to the branches of a large hardwood tree—an oak, cypress, or pecan. Like Spanish moss and bromeliads, this fern draws sustenance not from the host plant but from the air and nutrients that collect on the surface of the tree.

In hot, dry weather, a resurrection fern ceases normal plant behavior—photosynthesis and respiration—and instead puts its energy into keeping microscopic vascular tissues intact; once the rain returns, the leaves must be capable of absorbing water again.

Until then, however, the fern appears to be dead. Its fronds become brown and brittle, shrunken, gnarled. Estimates vary, but it is thought that resurrection fern can tolerate a water loss of roughly 95 percent. Most plants couldn't take more than 10.

Let the rain begin, though, and in less than a day, the fern will be green and plump once again: Resurrection. It's a phenomenon that never gets old.

May 29

This week's author
Alyssa Finke

The earth brought forth vegetation: plants yielding seed of every kind, and trees of every kind bearing fruit with the seed in it. And God saw that it was good. And there was evening and there was morning, the third day.

Genesis 1:12-13

On the third day, God creates an earth that can sustain us all. Spinach rises from the ground, providing us with iron. Bananas grow in bunches on the trees, flush with potassium. An array of other colorful fruits, nutritious vegetables, and hearty grains grow—in trees, in bushes, and in the ground—to provide us with vitamins and minerals.

God creates this sustainable gift for each and every one of us. Yet food deserts exist in most cities. Despite the abundance of food in the United States, many urban neighborhoods have limited access to healthy, affordable food. Nutritious food—which should be a given—becomes a luxury, available to those who live in certain zip codes or who can drive to a grocery store. Food deserts are a result of inequality in our cities. Food inequality *is* inequality.

As God's children, we inherited an earth—and all that comes with it—that is meant to provide for all of us. It is our duty to each other—our brothers and sisters in Christ—to make sure everyone has access to the healthy harvest our earth provides. Set up a "People's Pantry," donate or volunteer at a local food pantry, advocate for grocery stores in the food deserts of your city, and combat the roots of injustice and inequality.

Jesus multiplies the bread and fish for all who are present. He breaks the bread to save us all. Likewise, God creates this wonderful, fruitful earth to provide for each and everyone, no matter the circumstances.

May 30

Every summer when I was a child, my mother took me, my brothers, and a few friends blueberry picking. It was always a big adventure. We had a sleepover the night before because we had to wake up early, before the day grew hot and the berries had all been picked. Our van only had two extra spaces, so you knew you were a Finke family favorite if you snagged an invitation to our blueberry picking excursion.

There were rows upon rows of blueberry bushes—some sweet, some tart. Each of us had our own bucket, but it's hard to say how many blueberries fell victim to our mouths instead of our buckets. We picked until our buckets were nearly full or we sounded too many complaints about being hot or tired. We ended the day with an apple cider popsicle, and we had frozen blueberries available for months to come.

As I reflect on my childhood blueberry picking, I realize how grateful I am for my mother, who was brave enough to take a carload of children on these adventures and who planted the seeds of this favorite summer experience in my heart. I appreciate those who regularly plant and harvest the food I eat, those who toil day in and day out to provide what ends up on my table. I am thankful for fertile land and fresh fruits and vegetables that keep my body fueled and full.

And above all, I'm grateful for God, who provides.

May 31

"Take these marigold seeds," my coworker told me, "They're hard to kill." This sums up everything you need to know about my green thumb, or lack thereof. I'm notorious for killing plants. Sometimes I over-water, sometimes I under-water. But I really, really try.

Plants—from grandiose oak trees to burrowing potato plants to blossoming rose bushes—are an expression of God's love for us. God knows what we need, and God gives it all to us, with the simple requirement that we take care of the earth that sustains us.

Plants are so giving. They provide necessary nourishment for our families. They are a staple as we gather together for family meals, and they make great half-time snacks at soccer games. These leafy wonders make it possible to have watermelon at summer cookouts and warm squash soup in the winter.

Aloe soothes our first burns of the summer, ferns clean our air, cotton is spun into sundresses and bowties. The list goes on. Plants keep the bees buzzing and the earth thriving.

God has given us the Earth, and the Earth will take care of us if we, in turn, take care of the Earth. We must honor the earth and all that it provides.

In the case of my nascent marigolds, I'm nothing if not persistent. Lo and behold, I have eight seedlings about four inches high sitting beside the window, stretching toward the sun and waiting for the day they meet the outdoors, bringing beauty, color, and buzzing bees to my porch.

June

For Signs and Seasons

And God said, "Let there be lights in the dome of the sky to separate the day from the night; and let them be for signs and for seasons and for days and years, and let them be lights in the dome of the sky to give light upon the earth." And it was so.

Genesis 1:14-15

Artist's Note: The sun is one of the most familiar symbols of nature and creation, so painting it was a challenge. This painting is the result of about five attempts on the same board. I would get to a certain point and realize the image was boring, so I'd take the board to the sink and wash most of the paint off. Then I would add a little paint here and there, revisiting the board again in a few days to see it with fresh eyes. I had planned to work on it some more after the last washing, but when I turned it around, it seemed to say, "Okay, I'm done now." And it was so.

To Separate the Light from the Darkness

God made the two great lights—the greater light to rule the day and the lesser light to rule the night—and the stars. God set them in the dome of the sky to give light upon the earth, to rule over the day and over the night, and to separate the light from the darkness. And God saw that it was good. And there was evening and there was morning, the fourth day.
Genesis 1:16-19

Artist's Note: This is a relatively simple composition, but I worked on it a long time. I also used white paint, which I don't often use in a watercolor. The traditional approach is to leave the white of the paper and develop the dark areas. In this case, I took the opposite approach and laid in a lot of dark pigment before adding the light. It felt as if I were adding moonlight, and it was contemplative and satisfying. Someone recently asked me how I came up with the title of this painting: "The Lesser Light to Rule the Night—and the Stars." I was so glad that she asked the question. The answer? It came right from scripture, and it's impossible to improve on that!

And God said, "Let there be lights in the dome of the sky to separate the day from the night; and let them be for signs and for seasons and for days and years, and let them be lights in the dome of the sky to give light upon the earth." And it was so.

Genesis 1:14-15

Depending on the translation, the Bible contains about 250 references to light. Often light is described in contrast to literal or figurative darkness. Sometimes light is a lodestar, a beacon providing guidance and direction. Other times light represents an understanding and awareness that comes to those who were somehow blind. Jesus, of course, is memorably described as the Light of the World.

Light is the very first thing God creates "in the beginning." In the Godly Play story about creation, we describe the light on Day 1 as being different from the light in a candle or a flashlight. It is *all* light—the light that all the other light comes from. This light is created as something separate from darkness, and God uses this light to create order out of a chaotic, formless void.

On Day 4, light becomes more defined. It is given form in the shape of the sun, moon, and stars to order our days and nights. A rhythmic drumbeat enters into creation in the form of seasons and years. We are given a way to count our days and mark the passage of time. And while seemingly linear, the passage of time is actually circular, punctuated by repeating seasons of new life, harvest, death, and rebirth.

Throughout every season of life, God engages creation with marvelous, omniscient intention. In the beginning, the Spirit is already moving over the void, waiting to act upon it. As I think about the places of chaos in my life, it is helpful to consider that the Spirit also hovers over me, waiting to bring light and order into the darkness.

June 2

This little light of mine, I'm gonna let it shine,
Let it shine, let it shine, let it shine.

"In the beginning was the Word, and the Word was with God, and the Word was God." So begins the Gospel of John, reminding us that the creation story isn't just about the world God made. It is also about God: The very nature of God burst forth into the world with so much force that darkness could not overpower it (John 1:5).

I remember a college roommate once talking about the power of light over darkness. Even the tiniest candle in the darkest room can make a huge difference. By contrast, the tiniest amount of darkness does nothing to destroy the light in a bright room. She used to say that the power of God is like that—and because we have the light of God inside us, we have the power to banish darkness too.

When I look at the watercolor at the beginning of this week, the first thing I notice is the burst of light. It is tremendously bright, and it seems to be pushing away all darkness with great force. The lights created on the fourth day of creation are but small representations of the original light God creates in the beginning. They aren't the light, but they are part of it.

Maybe part of me was created on Day 4 too. Because I have the light of God in me, maybe God uses me to "separate the day from the night" and "give light upon the earth." This is very different from the warm, fuzzy security blanket of God's love. This is powerful. It is dramatic and potentially world-changing. I am breathless with the thought of it!

June 3

Take a minute to reflect on the image for this week. Consider the colors, textures, and other details present on the canvas. What captures your attention?

Today, I noticed how far the light spreads and radiates from the center of the sun. It expands all the way to three edges of the painting. As the light travels downward, however, it becomes different. The rays of light encounter the surface below (water, perhaps?) and instead of expanding beyond it, the light seems to interact with it. The surface receives the light, absorbs it and, in some places, reflects it.

Physics tells us that when light encounters an object, it can be absorbed, reflected, or transmitted through it. I believe the light of God does the same thing on the canvas of my life. There are times when the light radiates through me and past me, and nothing I can do will stop it. The light has a power all its own, and I am caught in its path. At other times though, the light is more interactive. It is reflected or refracted through me, causing it to change and become something new because of me.

I wonder where you see yourself in this watercolor. Are you in the center or on the edges? Are you one of the rays of light? Are you somewhere in the deep water below? Maybe you do not see yourself at all, or maybe the image doesn't speak to you. That's okay. Take it for what it is at this moment and ask God to reveal whatever truth is yours—and yours alone. Your relationship with God is a work of art all by itself.

June 4

Sometimes the writers of scripture describe light as a thing to be seen, something bright intended to capture attention. Sometimes, though, light is used to offer us something else. The great lights created on Day 4 are examples of both.

"Let there be lights in the dome of the sky." While this certainly refers to suns, moons, and stars, it also refers to comets, meteors, the Aurora Borealis, and a host of other celestial wonders. Every time I see a full moon, meteor shower, or eclipse, I am reminded of how small I am in comparison to the vast expanse of space. I cannot comprehend a light year, and I have no idea how big the universe is. Like one of the magi following the Star of Bethlehem, I am in awe of the wonder and beauty above me.

And yet for all of their distant power, these lights are personal and close. By reflecting the sun, the moon gives light in the night, and the sun provides light and warmth during the day. Plants and animals need sunlight in order to grow. The cycle of the moon affects the tides and our weather. Stars provide maps in the sky for people to follow—ironically, we cannot see those maps until darkness appears.

How can something so distant be so close? How can something millions and millions of miles away from me have such a direct impact on my daily life? So it is with all of God's gifts, and so it is with God.

June 5

An ecosystem is an interconnected network of organisms that give and take energy as part of an ongoing cycle of life. Producers, consumers, and decomposers all have a role to play, but they must maintain a harmonious balance if the entire ecosystem is to thrive. Nature too has a role to play through changing days and seasons. Old things pass away and give life, giving nourishment to new things.

In the book *Care for Creation: A Franciscan Spirituality of the Earth*, the authors draw a distinction between nature, which has no inherent religious meaning, and creation, which implies the presence of a Creator. From a Franciscan perspective, the distinction is significant because creation invites us to consider the relationship of all created things to the One who created them: "Relationships between the human and non-human created order, the place of the human person within that order, and the response of the person to the created order in its relationship to God."

We all exist within a variety of ecosystems. I understand the importance of paying attention to the individual relationships I have with God, people, and the world around me (even if I sometimes falter in those relationships). But while I sometimes wonder about how my actions (or inactions) impact others in my ecosystem, it is all too easy for me to become caught up in my part of the system and ignore the rest.

What would it mean to become God's partner in the ongoing process of creation? Perhaps I shouldn't just think of my footprint but rather my role in the ecosystem of creation. Where in my life am I a producer? How often am I a consumer? A decomposer? Who would I be if I became a co-creator with God?

June 6

For everything there is a season, and a time for every matter under heaven:

a time to be born, and a time to die;
a time to plant, and a time to pluck up what is planted;
a time to kill, and a time to heal;
a time to break down, and a time to build up;
a time to weep, and a time to laugh;
a time to mourn, and a time to dance;
a time to throw away stones, and a time to gather stones together;
a time to embrace, and a time to refrain from embracing;
a time to seek, and a time to lose;
a time to keep, and a time to throw away;
a time to tear, and a time to sew;
a time to keep silence, and a time to speak;
a time to love, and a time to hate;
a time for war, and a time for peace.

Ecclesiastes 3:1-8

I wonder if the writer of Genesis was thinking of all these moments described in Ecclesiastes. The story of creation, after all, is told before brokenness and sin enter the world. Things were still good. Whole. Surely, though, the writer of Ecclesiastes was familiar with the creation story—and of sin—when writing this passage. This writer elaborates more fully on the notion of seasons, reaffirming the idea that time is cyclical and circular.

Today, of course, we are able to read both of these passages through the lens of the Jesus story. As Christians, we know that all things—even those tainted by sin—are being made new again. The birth-death-rebirth cycle is even more astounding now that we know what Christ's redeeming and restoring love has brought to the world. Amen.

June 7

On Christmas Day 1624, English poet and Anglican priest John Donne preached, "God made sun and moon to distinguish seasons, and day and night, and we cannot have the fruits of the earth but in their seasons; but God hath made no decree to distinguish the seasons of His mercies; in Paradise, the fruits were ripe the first minute, and in Heaven it is always autumn, His mercies are ever in their maturity."

By giving us days and nights, God has given us a way to count our days. Days and nights become seasons, and seasons turn into years. While marking the passage of time is helpful for humans, God is actually timeless. There is no day or night. There are no passing years. As Donne later writes, "all times are his seasons." The rules of time established by God do not apply to God. God is present in all times in all places. In 2 Peter 3:8, the writer says, "But do not ignore this one fact, beloved, that with the Lord one day is like a thousand years, and a thousand years are like one day."

What do we make of this? For me, time and timelessness are reminders that God is omniscient and omnipotent. God knows everything and is in control of all things. Rather than making me feel tiny and insignificant (although this sometimes does), I am reminded to surrender all of who I am into God's care. After all, as Donne says, God "brought light out of darkness, not out of a lesser light." The God who created the universe, who put all the heavenly bodies in their place, also created me. On purpose. What a blessing it is to be counted as one of God's beloved.

This week's author
Douglas Knight

And God said, "Let there be lights in the dome of the sky to separate the day from the night; and let them be for signs and for seasons and for days and years, and let them be lights in the dome of the sky to give light upon the earth." And it was so.

Genesis 1:14-15

We are blessed with the ability to gaze up

From the palms of our hands

Into boundless regions of space

Illuminated by other stars, clusters, and galaxies.

June 9

Deneb is one of the most distant stars that we can see with our naked eyes. It is so distant that the light we see left Deneb and has traveled through space for thousands of years before reaching us. Deneb is still within our own galaxy, and beyond the Milky Way are millions more galaxies.

The exact way the stars and the sun move across our sky can speak to us of so many calendars, so many measurements of time. Time is one thing that comes in many different sizes. The constellations rise and fall as the earth turns, steadily measuring out one more day.

The stars tell us a day has passed. They also tell us that we could fly at the speed of light for thousands of years and never leave our own galactic backyard.

June 10

Some Navajo women still rise early enough every day to greet the sun. What can this mean?

Sometimes the blue-gray light of dawn comes before I am ready, and I hide myself deeper in the sheets.

I curse the sun when it burns my neck as I work in the garden, meaning no disrespect to the same energy that feeds my crops.

Some days by noon, it has become too much for me. I cannot accept the sight of this world (or of myself) in full sun, and I pray for darkness again. I wish the sun away, to shine for someone else who is brave and ready to see.

But some Navajo women still rise early enough everyday to greet the sun. What can this mean?

June 11

I wash the dishes in my household. As I do this, I wish that I instead had time to meditate and be still.

The sun appears to be still. It has always been so, but as the day goes by, so does the sun.

And the earth spins around the sun. And the sun spins and travels around the galaxy.

Being still might be different than I imagine.

June 12

A star will one day guide me to Christ.

It's more than that though. There are many stars, millions in every corner of the sky. There are many moments in this life where Christ can be found.

There are many signs, beckoning us to turn to Christ, even if just for a moment, and to allow ourselves to be open completely and to be filled with light.

June 13

This is the phrase of creation. "Let there be..."

To create is an act of will. To begin, you have say to yourself the mantra of the creator, Let there be.

Let there be a line. Let there be three lines. Let there be another color, another brushstroke, another painting of the bay on a blustery sunny day.

Let there be song. Let there be one more note.

Let there be a story. Let there be one more line of poetry.

Let there be a child. Let there be a star, a light, a love that leads us there.

June 14

Is this all there is?

Imagine everything our sun's light has fallen upon in its lifetime: every day on this dusty planet, every human face, every bird's wing. From the first dawn to the last.

You are a part of it all.
We are stardust.

Energy from the sun.
It is all a part of you.
From the big bang to the quiet applause.

June 15

God made the two great lights—the greater light to rule the day and the lesser light to rule the night—and the stars. God set them in the dome of the sky to give light upon the earth, to rule over the day and over the night, and to separate the light from the darkness. And God saw that it was good. And there was evening and there was morning, the fourth day.

Genesis 1:16-19

One of the gifts of this hymn of creation is that it sings of God bringing forth light long before creating the sun, moon, and stars. Some commentators suggest that this editorial decision was a response to the surrounding cultures whose religions worshiped the sun and stars and sought guidance from them rather than from the Creator. More important than a rejection of astrology, this hymn reflects an awareness of the kind of truth that only poetry can help us sense: All is gift, and all reflects our Creator.

According to Eastern Orthodoxy, the light that overwhelms the disciples on Mount Tabor as Jesus is transfigured is not the light God created on the first day, nor the light of the sun and stars. Rather, it is Holy Light—the eternal uncreated light of God—about which all other light can only whisper. It is a reminder that all we see and think we know points to the One who gives all things being.

Without the sun, there would be no life on this planet. The gravity of the moon and the perfect balance of its orbit influence essential ocean tides. Those who study the stars and the vastness of space are learning more and more that should humble us as we live on this small, exquisite planet. All is gift: The work of God who reveals as much truth as we can bear through the complexities and wonders of the physical realm we have been given to protect and nurture. What can we do but serve with our whole selves, offering praise and thanksgiving and falling into awed silence before such grace?

June 16

What do you see as you gaze deeply into the painting for this week? Do you see a bright moon streaming a path of light across the waters? Do you see the sun beginning to expand into its blinding being? Or perhaps you see stars celebrating the birth of a new sibling. What do you see? More importantly, what is being given to you as you gaze?

This painting—and the entire series of painted reflections on God's acts of creating—can function as traditional icons. In praying with icons, one looks not *at* but *through* the image as through a window to the glory beyond at which they hint. Praying with icons requires setting aside the part of the mind that analyzes the work and instead seeks the wonder and wisdom flowing through it. Some human artists are given the awesome gift and responsibility of creating such windows.

There is no single, right way to see what God conveys through this visual reflection on the birth of our sun, moon, and stars. The painting is, in its own way, like the poetry of the psalms. Both are met where they are. You may have experienced the same psalm in very different ways at different times. That is part of the gift of creativity—both the creativity of God, continually creating, redeeming, and sustaining all that is, and the creativity of the artist. We are invited to be present, watching and listening, open to what God knows we need in this moment. For this, we can give thanks.

June 17

With the creation of the sun and moon, the great hymn tells us that God gives order to the rhythms of the earth and its inhabitants. There are times for doing work: growing, tending, nurturing, learning. There are times for resting, sharing, reflecting, and restoring. There are seasons, each with its own purpose.

The creation of the stars is mentioned here only in passing, but they are not revealed as having any other function besides existing. Perhaps their purpose in this hymn is simply to reflect the beauty and wonder of their Creator. They are given no influence on the lives of humanity. We know the stars are suns in their own right, many of which are far more massive than our own star, the sun. These stars have their own purposes in their own parts of the universe. The poet in Genesis recognizes, however, that they do not control our lives.

The sun and moon, the poet sings, have special purposes for us. They are formed to give light to the earth. Perhaps we appreciate the light less than our ancestors did, since we have the technology to turn lights on and off at our pleasure, even remotely. Yet the sun and moon encourage us to live in reasonable rhythms rather than frenetic activity. They are signs to us of how we are created to live. How we respond to those signs is up to us. For the rhythm we are offered, and our freedom to choose, we offer hearty and humble thanksgiving.

June 18

This painting reveals extraordinary energy. The focus is on the heavenly body that shines brightly, sending out its light on the earth as it was created to do. It practically pulses with divine energy, so eager is it to honor the Creator by pouring its goodness out. This reflects our vocation, too.

At the end of worship where there has been a celebration of Holy Eucharist, Episcopalians offer one of two prayers. Both prayers offer thanks that we are part of the mystical Body of Christ and nourished with the body and blood of Christ. Then we ask God to send us out to do the work that we have been given to do. One prayer says that the work is "to love and serve you with gladness and singleness of heart," and the other proclaims the work as "to love and serve you as faithful witnesses of Christ our Lord" (*The Book of Common Prayer, pages 365, 366*). In both prayers, we—like the sun and the moon—are created and sent into service. Their work is in the heavens; ours here on earth. Both can reflect God's glory. We are to shine with the light we are given, to serve with the strength we are given, and to love and forgive because we are loved and forgiven.

For the grace of God that brings us together, nourishes us with what we need, gives us holy work to do, and guides us in the doing, we are privileged to offer thanksgiving and praise.

June 19

Science is one of the great gifts of God. Those whose vocation is scientific in nature have been given a gift similar to that given to artists—to question, to look closely at what is there, to seek to understand it, and to convey the truths they discover. This is a holy calling. Scientists who study the sun, moon, and stars learn about the functions of gravity, orbits, solar flares, the vastness of immeasurable distances, and the bending of time. Yet, they cannot tell us everything.

I remember a story in which a character describes stars as great atomic balls of fire. Another character replies that fire is what stars are made of, but not what they are. If we limit our exploration to what can be discovered by science, we fall into what author Madeleine L'Engle described as "a vain effort to relegate something full of blazing glory to the limits of technology." Artists and poets can take us closer to the "blazing glory;" They can help us to see past the limits of science. And the best of them encourage us to go even further in our pursuit of knowledge and wonder.

The gifts of science and the art we are given in these pages offer places for reflection and awe. They invite us to stillness and contemplation of the truths they discover. The best of science and art becomes transparent, showing us glimpses of the reality they try to describe. For the vocations of scientists, artists, and poets—for their invitation to go higher up and further in—we offer our thanks to the One they help us encounter.

June 20

One of the joys of entering this painting of the fourth day is watching light emerge from the darkness into the mists that surround it with a sort of aura. The light is not painted in its full power—as though it is not yet fully revealed. This detail tells us about the light God gives us daily, the light by which we live and are guided. Sometimes, the lights can seem so well hidden as to be gone.

A long walk through a misty morning, the air filled with what a friend likes to call "cloud dust," brought this image to mind as I searched for a glimpse of the sun. The light from the sun was faint and diffused, the location of the sun hard to identify. It's a familiar feeling, not just weather-wise but personally and spiritually as well.

We know the painfully familiar questions: "Where is God when evil happens? Where is God when someone I love is suffering, when I have this terrible diagnosis, when so many people endure injustice because of who they are?" Most of us have experienced times when it seems like God is absent. No matter how hard we pray, how faithful we are, we can't seem to locate God. Heavy, cloudy grayness can overwhelm us, leaving us feeling totally isolated.

Yet this painting reminds us that beyond the mist and clouds is God, always waiting, always present. The light will break through, and hope can once again be found. This painting, this icon, reveals what the clouds seem to obscure: Love is eternal, never failing or forsaking us.

June 21

There is such beauty in this painting. There is rhythm, balance, and wonder. It appears gentle, a quiet evening at the beach with moonlight dancing across the water and bright stars dotting the skies. You can become lost in the unimaginable vastness of the sea and the night sky as the rhythm of the surf sends you deeper into peace. It is both an eternal and ephemeral peace.

As with this painting, the peaceful beauty cannot reveal all that is. We know that at any moment, the ocean may send up a dangerous rogue wave, threatening to drag us out into deep water. We cannot predict when someone who has lost their sense of goodness and kindness will act out of what has been warped inside of them. We live in a world of extraordinary beauty, but not one of safety. The peaceful rest of an evening by the shore is a gift and an uncertain ephemera that can slip away in a moment.

But there is another peace, the peace that the world in all its glory cannot give or take away. This peace comes from God. It enables us to cope when the temporary peacefulness is gone. We can sense this peace but not grasp it. This peace upholds us no matter what, even when we cannot feel it.

Thank God for the beauty and wonder of created things and for art that helps us to look with greater care. Thank God for the peace that takes us ever further into the love that calls us into being from the beginning.

God made the two great lights—the greater light to rule the day and the lesser light to rule the night—and the stars. God set them in the dome of the sky to give light upon the earth, to rule over the day and over the night, and to separate the light from the darkness. And God saw that it was good. And there was evening and there was morning, the fourth day.

Genesis 1:16-19

When some people think of the Divine, they imagine light—lots and lots of light. For me, however, precisely the reverse is true: God lives in the dark.

I'm not sure when I came to this conclusion, but it was probably the year I took a course in theology and learned about cataphatic and apophatic—positive and negative—ways of thinking and talking about God. The explanation resonated with something I had known intuitively for a very long time.

But where I found the best language for describing my experience, ironically enough, was in a young adult novel I was reading around the same time, Madeleine L'Engle's *A Ring of Endless Light*. In that book, I first encountered the famous lines from Henry Vaughn's poem "The Night": "There is in God, some say, / A deep but dazzling darkness..."

What could "dazzling darkness" have to do with "a ring of endless light"? What drew me to this juxtaposition was the paradoxical way it spoke of God—a blinding darkness more brilliant than any sun. Rather than posing a threat, this was a darkness in which I could feel undeniably safe and loved. This was a darkness in which I could feel at home.

June 23

I have a confession to make: I grew up unnaturally afraid of the dark. As a result, I slept with a night-light well into my middle school years. I can't really say what scared me—the usual monsters under the bed, I suppose, or maybe the threat of nuclear holocaust that hung like a shroud over the country. Either one could keep me awake.

These days, though, I prefer to sleep in the dark—so much so that when my husband bought a new alarm clock with an LED screen, I objected. Our solution? He kept the clock, and I turned over to face the other direction. As I have since discovered, though, I actually have science on my side in this debate; research has shown that our bodies need the dark not only to get a good night's sleep but to regulate the production of hormones such as melatonin.

Apart from the role darkness plays in sleep, however, we need the dark to remind us of all that occurs beyond our knowledge or control. Granted, some of these things may frighten us, but some may leave us spellbound, awed by their beauty or captivated by their sheer otherness.

Years ago, while on a weeklong spring retreat in South Texas, I made a habit of walking around the unlighted grounds of the center at night. Typically I would go in search of owls, but the barn owls and great horned owls weren't the only creatures active in the dark. The peccaries—or javelinas—were usually out rooting around, as were rodents and possums and coons. My favorites, however, were the frogs singing in the pond down the road and the pauraques, a nightjar found only in the very southern part of the state.

"Purr-WEEE-eer, purr-WEEE-eer," the whippoorwill-like bird sings while other creatures sleep. It is one of the great gifts of the dark. My heart, too, longs for the songs that come unbidden in the night. Hidden, my soul waits for a melody it can recognize and make its own.

June 24

Several years ago, a young friend named Paul Bogard wrote a book about the absence of dark skies at night. Fittingly enough, it was called *The End of Night: Searching for Natural Darkness in an Age of Artificial Light.*

Paul was on a publicity tour shortly after the book came out, so I invited him to the university where I teach to speak on the topic of darkness and mental health. That may sound like an odd combination—darkness and psychological health—but the connection is very real. Ironically, we often speak of "darkness" as synonymous with depression, with despair that is both mental and spiritual. After all, the "dark night of the soul" is not exactly a picnic.

But we are creatures who look toward the heavens for direction, for inspiration, for a sense of connection with The Whole. Take away the night sky, and we lose those things; take away the night sky, and the Milky Way disappears.

"We're all descended from astronomers," astrophysicist Neil deGrasse Tyson has said.

I have no memory of where we were going or where we had been, but I remember very well the night my husband and I stopped on a lonely road in Utah. Pulling off the road—we were the only car on that stretch of road that night—we stood transfixed under the summer sky. It was the first and only time I saw the Milky Way as it was meant to be seen, long and nebulous and bright. I knew at that moment that we were made of the very same stuff.

This is the kind of moment found in darkness and nowhere else. In the glare of a sunny day, I can feel content and full of hope, but I can't feel the sense of connection to a cosmos that exists somewhere in the mind of God.

I'm a creature in need of the dark.

June 25

I was surprised to see him up so early. "Whatcha doin'?" I asked the young man walking toward my tent. It was our second and final morning in the campground, and given how late my students had stayed up the night before, I assumed most would sleep as long as possible.

"I wanted to see the sun come up," he answered. "I wanted to photograph it from the lookout." Had my knees allowed me to make the hike, I would have joined him in the climb. As I knew from experience, there isn't much better than sunrise in the Hill Country of Texas, on a cool day in early spring.

Relegated to the flatland, I headed instead to the river with my camera. Was I fooling myself to think that sunrise on the water was every bit as lovely as the sun ascending from the hills? I don't think I was.

Discovering a trail I hadn't seen before, I strolled along the shady bank, with the only sound the rush of water spilling over a waist-high dam. Empty of the swimmers who would fill it later in the day, the river itself was still, glinting in the sun. With the light just right, the cypress trees made long shadows on the water. I wanted the day to stay like this.

But the sunrise doesn't last.

Some things—the sunrise and sunset, meteors streaming across the sky, a harvest moon hanging heavy above the trees—last a mere second, and then they're gone. That instant when the light appears just right insists we pay attention precisely then. Present to the place where we are, we must keep our eyes trained on the horizon, watching, waiting for those moments when they come.

June 26

For Christmas, my son-in-law gave my daughter a trip to see the Northern Lights. Sometime this winter or fall, they will travel to Alaska, Canada, or Iceland to see one of the most amazing sights on earth. I am more jealous than I can say.

The Aurora Borealis, as this marvel is known in the Northern Hemisphere, has long been the subject of myth. Thought by some to be the spirits of hunters or fishermen or the animals they hunted, the lights have also been explained as the reflection of campfires or torches or as an omen of famine or war.

In reality, these dancing lights are no more than the collision of electrically charged particles from the sun colliding with gaseous particles in earth's atmosphere. The result is an eruption of color, rippling walls of light in shades of green and pink, violet and blue, and every shade in between.

I don't pretend to understand just how this phenomenon works. Yes, I can comprehend the science, but I don't know *why* the science works. What is there in the universe that keeps these solar particles from reaching us? What keeps us safe in the presence of such power? What allows us to look at these lights and live?

I have seen the Northern Lights just once, on a night when they reached the latitude where I live. It's uncommon for the aurora to appear in the southern sky, but I had heard on the news that this was an unusual year, that the lights could be seen just above the horizon. Sure enough, I saw them late one night on the rural road I take to go home. Crossing the railroad tracks and looking toward the trees, I saw a shimmering green hanging low in the northern sky. They danced for a moment and then they disappeared.

Had I really seen the Northern Lights? Against all logic, I knew I had, just as I know when Presence charges through my heart, yet lets me live.

June 27

It's funny how particular lines of poetry stick in your head long after you initially hear them. Among the ones that haunt me are from an Emily Dickinson poem: "There's a certain slant of light, / On winter afternoons."

It's not the meaning of the poem itself that grabbed me so many years ago, but simply the poet's observation that the slant of sunlight changes throughout the year. This isn't rocket science, of course, but it is a phenomenon that intrigues me.

I was a child when I first sensed that the sky in autumn was more intensely blue than at any other time of year. In my memory, I am with three other children from my neighborhood—two boys and another girl—sitting on old wooden lawn furniture beneath mature pecan trees, cracking and eating nuts we found on the ground. Above us, the Texas sky is a brilliant blue in that way it gets in the middle of fall.

Many years would pass before I learned what causes this effect. As the principle known as Rayleigh scattering explains, light coming from the sun is dispersed by molecules of oxygen and nitrogen in our atmosphere—and because blue light has the shortest wave length (not counting that of violet, which our eyes don't pick up very well), this light is scattered the most. This means that blue light, unless it's interfered with in some other way, bombards us from all directions, making the sky appear blue.

For those of us who live between 30 and 60 degrees latitude, the lower angle of the sun in autumn, combined with less humidity, increases the saturation of the blue we see.

"There's a certain slant of light, / On winter afternoons..." How attuned are we to the subtle changes around us—changes in the light, changes in the scent of the seasons, changes in the way the Spirit stirs within us?

June 28

When Halley's Comet last appeared in 1986, my husband and I drove to the scenic overlook at Devil's Backbone, a spot about twenty miles northwest of town, and waited in absolute darkness, hoping to see a ball of fire streaking across the central Texas sky.

It was then or never, we knew, given that the comet shows up just every 75 years or so—we'd likely not be around to see its next pass by the earth, projected to be in 2061, so we had better keep a sharp eye out. Fortunately, we saw it.

But what exactly had we seen? By most accounts, we saw a "dirty snowball," a "rubble pile," a collection of dust and ice and gases, some of it trailing in a tail that stretched for 100 million kilometers or more. I couldn't imagine the actual size of it.

Ironically, the nucleus of the comet itself is small, perhaps only 15 kilometers long by 8 kilometers wide by 8 kilometers thick—roughly the distance I drive roundtrip to work. And yet, it's the only comet of its kind that's bright enough to be seen with the naked eye.

Referred to as a short-period comet for its ability to complete its orbit in 200 years or less, Halley's Comet was first reported 2,500 years ago. Babylonians, Greeks, Medieval Europeans, and Native Americans in Chaco Canyon all recorded their experiences of seeing this fast-moving light.

The Bible, too, is full of references to people who have "seen a great light," making me wonder if this metaphor is based on sightings of this comet, making me wonder if I have seen more than I know.

Walking in darkness, I know a great light moves beyond me. In time its orbit will cause this light to turn toward earth again, and it will shine and shine and shine.

June 29

This week's author
Alyssa Finke

> *God made the two great lights—the greater light to rule the day and the lesser light to rule the night—and the stars. God set them in the dome of the sky to give light upon the earth, to rule over the day and over the night, and to separate the light from the darkness. And God saw that it was good. And there was evening and there was morning, the fourth day.*
>
> **Genesis 1:16-19**

As a child, I dreaded bedtime and begged my parents to let me stay up a little later. One more TV show, one more game, one more book. The sly child that I was, I always chose *The Berenstain Bears,* as it had the longest reading time.

As an adult, I relish bedtime. I love the time between crawling into bed and falling asleep. I love to lie in comfort and listen to the quiet. I cherish the feeling of knowing that whether the day seemed like a sprint or a marathon, it's over and time to rest. My body and mind both know it's time to recharge after a long day, and they are more than ready.

However, I can still have a hard time accepting that the day is over and it's time to rest. I may no longer beg for one more Berenstain Bears book to keep me awake, but there is always one more load of laundry to do or another email to answer. I lie in my bed and wonder what more I could do if the day had another hour. But no matter how long I am awake and wondering, each day still has twenty-four hours—and I can't face the next twenty four without letting myself rest.

God knows the value of rest. After all, God rests on the seventh day. God knows the importance of admiring all that has been done in a day's time—and God knows the importance of recharging in order to have energy to do great things the next day. Perhaps we should take a few quiet moments at the end of each day to step back, reflect on all we have achieved that day, and say to ourselves, "It is good."

June 30

As the sun rises, I thank God for another day. I thank God in the quiet moments of the morning, while the sun peeks softly through the blinds and I pad quietly around my cozy home. I feel God's grace when I sip my coffee, listening to the birds sing their morning praises.

While the sun is high, I thank God for all the blessings the light brings—whether it's during a day's work or a day's play. I am grateful for work I value alongside people I value. And on the weekends, I am grateful to spend time exploring or reading on my porch, with the sun on my skin.

When the sun fades, I am thankful to have a home to return to. I say my thanks to God before I eat dinner (perhaps on my porch, too) and reflect on my day with the one I love. As the light wanes, I cherish the time I have to read and write, to jog the streets of my beautiful neighborhood, or to spend time with friends.

As the sun surrenders to the moon, I thank God for time to rest. I am grateful for the hours of sleep that are sorely needed. I feel thankful for another good day—from sunup to sundown. I ask God to watch over me as I sleep, and I ask God to grace me with another beautiful sunrise in the morning.

July

Swarms of Living Creatures

And God said, "Let the waters bring forth swarms of living creatures, and let birds fly above the earth across the dome of the sky."

Genesis 1:20

Artist's Note: I live next to the Pacific Ocean, a region well-known for its Dungeness crab. Occasionally, I get a text from our friend Zach, a crab fisherman and newly baptized Christian, telling me that he's just off the coast. When I look out at the black sea and sky, I'm able to see the lights of the boat, and I blink the lights to reply. There is something comforting about seeing those signs of human activity out there—something thrilling as well. It's a dangerous way to make a living, and our mission church prays for the safety of our local fishermen. Each year Zach and his wife Susan generously host a crab feed for the church. It's a celebration of the bounty of the sea, the gift of community, and gratitude for God's many blessings.

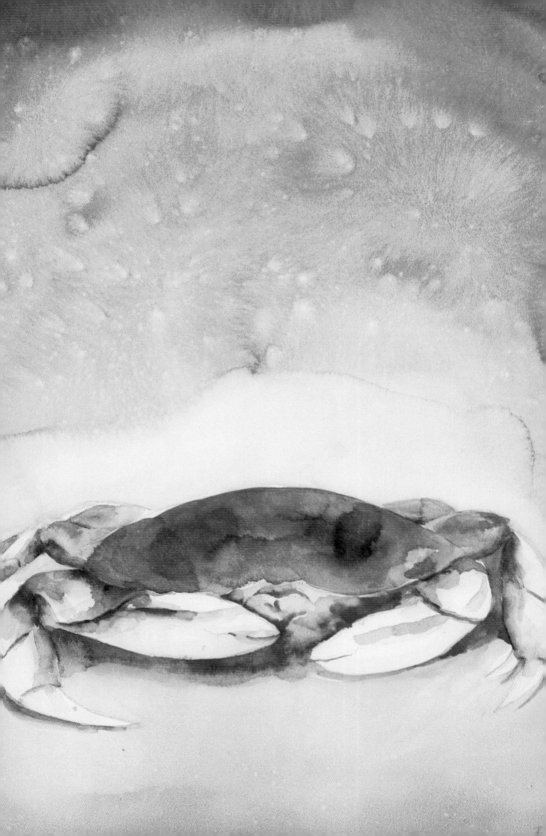

Artist's Note: Egrets are delicate, walking sculptures. We had a lot of rain last winter, and lakes appeared in fields along with some inconvenient flooding. It was such a joy to look out upon these spontaneous bodies of water and see egrets walking along. They are like little exclamation points in the glory of creation. And even though they look so fragile, when they take off in flight, their delicate appearance belies their strength and power.

Swarms of Living Creatures

So God created the great sea monsters and every living crea-
ture that moves, of every kind, with which the waters swarm,
and every winged bird of every kind. And God saw that it was
good. God blessed them, saying, "Be fruitful and multiply and
fill the waters in the seas, and let birds multiply on the earth."
And there was evening and there was morning, the fifth day.

Genesis 1:21-23

Artist's Note: Most of the creatures in this series are familiar neighbors, critters that live in my backyard, but when scripture called for "great sea monsters," I needed to go beyond my usual constraints. I have observed the octopus (pictured on the next page) in the Monterey Aquarium and learned that these magnificent creatures have fairly short life spans of three to five years. The male dies shortly after mating, and the female dies after she tends the young who survive from among 20,000-100,000(!) eggs. The female octopus doesn't leave the brood even to eat and dies of starvation within weeks or months after the babies hatch. This story of sacrifice is even more remarkable than their physiology and a rather grim reminder that life and death are part of existence. How blessed we are to know that through Christ and his sacrifice, death isn't final but is followed by everlasting life.

July 1

This week's author
Richelle Thompson

And God said, "Let the waters bring forth swarms of living creatures, and let birds fly above the earth across the dome of the sky."

Genesis 1:20

We drive a dozen hours for the smell of the ocean, so as soon as we arrive, we fling open the balcony door and breathe it in. The tangy saltiness relaxes the cramps in our necks and the aches in our legs. We exhale the stale air of the car and our offices and pull the wind of the beach into our lungs.

I look past the balcony to the white sand of the Gulf shore. In a moment, I'll strip off my clothes, change into a bathing suit, slather on some sunscreen, and hit the beach. I can't wait to dig my toes under the first layer of hot sand to the cool sediment beneath, and to feel my skin tingle under the rays of the sun, warming and waking me up. Few places make me feel closer to nature than this spot, our family retreat for twenty years.

Between me and the ocean is a patch of scraggy sea oats and a cast of crabs. Despite my desire to rush to the beach, I'm drawn to the machinations of these crabs. They scramble from one patch of sand to another with such fervor. It's hard to tell if they're accomplishing anything other than an occasional skirmish—apparently male crabs tend to fight for the attention of the ladies.

I recently learned that crabs can walk slowly in any direction, but when they're in a hurry, they move sideways.

I'll be honest with you: Except for this vacation time, I'm normally in a hurry too. Manuscripts to edit, projects to finish, rooms to clean, lunches to pack, friends to call, presents to buy. So. Many. Things. To. Do.

In my haste, I move sideways—and sometimes backward. These moments on the beach call me into repose, to recover ways I might walk slowly and, hopefully, move forward.

July 2

Sure, there are thousands of other animals swarming in the waters. I could talk about sharks and snails, coral and fish of all sorts, seahorses and octopi, whales and Leviathans.

But the painting of the crab has entranced me. There's a jauntiness to the crab, a self-confidence in the midst of the swarms: *I am who I am*, the crab seems to say.

My husband would chide me: I am clearly anthropomorphizing the crab, giving it human qualities and characteristics, even though it's just a crab. Still, I feel connected in some way to these creatures. And perhaps that's one of the profound lessons of our creation story: We feel related across space and time, genus and species to the wonders of the world. Somehow the same divine Creator who separates day from night molds man and woman, carves out the hollow of their necks, shapes the curves of arms and waists, crafts fingers that reach and hold.

I don't have to understand this divine mystery of how evolution and creation are woven together into a grand tapestry. I just believe. Not in a naïve, no-questions asked way, but with a deep knowing that God the Creator forms the swarms of the oceans and the birds of the sea. And me.

July 3

I used to have the exoskeleton of a crab—a finely polished and honed tough exterior, designed to keep me safe and protected.

But here's the thing about an exoskeleton: You can't grow. That hard external skeleton prohibits growth. Crabs actually have to molt and go through some crazy process where they remove their legs and eyestalks (yes, that's what they're called), antennae and gills from the old shell and move into a new one.

We humans don't have that capacity.

Twenty years ago, I met the man who helped me shed my tough exterior. He tenderized my heart. My husband gives me the strength and security to be vulnerable and open because his love is unconditional and unyielding. He is strong when I am weak; he carries me when the waves take out my legs.

Letting down my guard means that I feel hurt more often. When I see photos of a party on Facebook and wonder why I wasn't included, I wish for a better defense. When I feel like I've failed as a mother or a wife, a daughter or a sister, I would love to crawl back into my shell and let the world carry on without me for a few days.

But lowering my defense mechanisms has given me opportunities to grow in ways I never could have imagined. I've been changed by the pain of unwise decisions. I've been transformed by the lessons learned from difficult situations and relationships. I don't know if I'm smarter, but I hope I'm a bit wiser and more patient. I know I'm happier.

God knows what God is doing. From sending this amazing man who tears down my walls and builds up my soul to creating swarms of living creatures—some with exoskeletons and some without—God knows what God is doing. Every time. From the beginning of time.

July 4

Wikipedia offers this explanation for the lifecycle of a crab: "Once crabs have become juveniles, they will still have to keep molting many more times to become adults. They are covered with a hard shell, which would otherwise prevent growth. The molt cycle is coordinated by hormones."

Even juvenile crabs have hormones. As the mom of two teenagers, I'd like to wrap my arm around a mother crab's pincers and say, "I feel your pain."

Maybe there's a reason Adam was an adult man instead of a teenager.

Despite the challenges of parenting teens, I also delight in the wonder of new creation unfolding in them. My husband and I witness our daughter stretching and pulling, testing boundaries, molting through the shells of childhood. She is fierce and independent and strong, and I still want to hold her in the crook of my arm and brush my hand across her cheek. There are growth opportunities here for me too.

And there's our son, a creator to his core. Everything is a blank palette: He designs buildings, dresses, and new recipes for slime. He paints river scenes and bakes cakes and sees wonders beyond my imagination.

God is constantly creating, nurturing new life and possibility in all teenagers—and in their mothers.

July 5

Poor crab babies. Their parents actually *do* have eyes in the back of their heads—or at least close enough. Crabs' eyes are set on eyestalks. These eyestalks move in different directions and help crabs see while they're hiding under sand, water, rock, or coral.

Wouldn't it be great to literally see what's coming around the corner or hiding in the shadows?

Early in my career, I took a job as a reporter with a small newspaper in Tennessee. A month after I started, a bigger newspaper from just outside Chicago called me with an offer. A more lucrative job and the lure of the city was hard to resist. I called my dad for advice.

"Did you make the best decision at the time?" he asked. I thought about it, and I had. "Then Chicago is no longer an option. Don't second-guess yourself—and do the best job you can where you are now."

If I'm not careful, I can spend a lot of time looking in the rearview mirror—or sitting in idle while I'm waiting for what might or could happen. Unfortunately, I don't have eyestalks to spy danger (or opportunity) around the bend. But with faith, I can make the best decisions possible with the information I have, and then I settle into the present, offering thanks and praise and letting my heart be glad.

July 6

It's been six years since my parents divorced. The condominium on the beach was theirs, and now it's his. My sisters and I and our families still make our way south from homes in Kentucky, and we know we are blessed to have this special place. But on each trip, I fight a faint feeling of brokenness.

The floor tiles are new. And the bedcovers and appliances. But the wallpaper is the same that my mom labored over to select. There are still notes in her handwriting Scotch taped to the shower doors, explaining how to operate the nozzles.

Around the table, we played dominos and spades; we ate delicious donuts from our favorite shack and peeled the tails off fresh shrimp. We nursed sunburned shoulders on the couch and watched the sunset together from the balcony.

This was our place, and I struggle with the memories of what was and what is.

Then I go back and read the words from Genesis: "And God saw that it was good." And I think about how this scripture isn't just referring to a moment in time, the seconds after swarms of living creatures came forth from the waters and birds flew across the skies. God saw that it was good then—but also good today and good tomorrow. The tides will rise and fall, ice ages and meteor showers will transform the earth. Relationships falter, and people change. But with death comes opportunity for new life, new relationships, new memories. God tells us this through the grand story of creation and shows us this with the new creation in Christ Jesus.

And that is good.

July 7

Crabs are ubiquitous. They live in all of the oceans of the world—the warm surges of the Indian Ocean and crisp swells of the Pacific. Crabs live in fresh water and on land. They show up for dinner and in pop culture. Not only does Mr. Krabs have a starring role as the cantankerous boss of the animated SpongeBob SquarePants, but the King of Pop has a hermit crab named in his honor. Seriously. Paleontologists at Kent State University discovered a new species on the same day Michael Jackson died and named it "Mesoparapylocheles michaeljacksoni." Take that, Elvis.

When something is so omnipresent, it can be taken for granted. It's everywhere, so it's not special. I fall into this trap with my relationship to creation. Sure, I can get lost in a beautiful sunset on the horizon or the first orange and reds of fall. Sometimes, I really appreciate creation—but day in and day out, I don't take notice of its marvels. I don't give thanks for the wind or the ants or the roll of the hills. I'm not aware of the grass unless it's too high or the flowers before they bloom. At the end of each day of creation, God does not rush to the next to-do task, the next set of geological features to shape or creatures to craft. God finishes the work of the day, sits back, and sees that it is good.

May we do so today.

> *And God said, "Let the waters bring forth swarms of living creatures, and let birds fly above the earth across the dome of the sky."*
>
> **Genesis 1:20**

Swarms. That word has some ominous connotations in my mind, most referring to insects: swarms of gnats or mosquitoes or the flies and locusts that plagued Egypt. I prefer the New English Bible's translation of this verse: "Let the waters teem with countless living creatures…" Webster's defines teem as "ready to give birth" or "full"—beginning with abundance. The Spirit of God hovers over the waters, birthing life in countless creatures.

The writers of the creation stories in Genesis couldn't know the worlds of microscopic life that we know are swimming in any drop of water. But they knew fish, crustaceans, mollusks, amphibians, perhaps a few sea mammals (there are those "great sea-monsters" in the next verse), and they recognized that God's creation was overflowing with more life than human senses could comprehend.

In our time, these countless numbers are being drastically reduced by human activity—climate change, pollution, habitat loss, and overharvesting. As oceans warm, coral reefs die, and polluted estuaries can no longer support the tiny lives that feed—or grow up to be— creatures that nourish human populations. We are beginning to realize how much the well-being of the whole creation depends upon the great abundance and diversity in God's teeming waters—and how carelessly we have taken that abundance for granted.

> *For our waste and pollution of your creation, and our lack of concern for those who come after us,*
> *Accept our repentance, Lord.*
>
> **The Book of Common Prayer**

July 9

It is July. I'm nine years old, at Holden Beach, North Carolina, letting my bare toes sink into the sand while waves splash and swirl around my ankles. As the water recedes, I can feel the sand wiggle beneath my feet—tiny, pearly shells in iridescent pastel colors are burrowing between my toes. "Coquinas," my father explains. I scoop up handfuls of dripping sand, letting the little clams burrow between my fingers. I drop them onto the sand, and they disappear. The waves rush back, washing them up again, and again they burrow. So much life, right there between my toes! The beach is alive.

It is July. I'm twenty-nine or forty-nine or sixty-nine, on Sanibel Island, Florida. Wading out of the Gulf, I dig my toes into the sand, feeling for the coquinas. Despite all our pollution of the oceans and alteration of the world's climate, after storms and droughts and erosion of the seashore, there are still coquinas living in the sand at the water's edge.

On the sandbar are starfish and sand dollars and sometimes a conch or a murex, but these are noticeably less numerous than even twenty years ago. It's the coquinas that remain a constant reminder of all the other swarms of living creatures, many too small for the unaided eye to see— the miraculous abundance of the sea, where life began.

I fear for the sea and its creatures, so threatened by our human selfishness. The coquinas seem a sign of forgiveness and possibility. I feel them burrow between my toes, and I whisper, "The beach is alive!"

It's a prayer of thanksgiving—and hope.

July 10

Long before my high school biology classes, someone gave my family a microscope. I remember squinting one eye to peer through it as my father focused the lens over a drop of water, probably from our backyard fishpond. Suddenly I could see a half-dozen tiny shapes darting, colliding, stretching, shrinking, merging—obviously alive, swimming through their own sea.

We are made of water. Our very cells are boxes and sacks of water, contained by impossibly thin walls that somehow hold us together. Our blood flows with every heartbeat, carrying life-giving oxygen; cerebrospinal fluid washes thought into movement and speech; liquids digest food and nurture new life in the womb. And our watery insides, like all the waters of the world, teem with living creatures.

Our intestines, in particular, are host to organisms necessary not only for digestion but also for our overall chemical balance. There have even been studies that show positive effects of healthy gut bacteria on our moods and mental health. This sounds like science fiction—that the right kinds and numbers of tiny creatures living in our intestines could help make us happier!

It's also humbling to realize how wonderfully interdependent God's creation is. We, the species with self-awareness and the power to cherish or to ruin all of creation, are dependent for our health—and perhaps our happiness—on microscopic animals whose seas are our digestive fluids. Poet Walt Whitman was right: "I contain multitudes…"

> We are water—lives
> ride the body's currents, rest
> in our shallows. Kin.

July 11

It's one of my favorite photographs from my years as communications director in the Episcopal Diocese of Southeast Florida: Then-Presiding Bishop Katharine Jefferts Schori leans across the stern of a Coast Guard boat off the Florida Keys, helping to slide a large green sea turtle into the jade waters of the Gulf of Mexico.

Bishop Katharine had visited St. Columba, Marathon, that day, celebrating the congregation's fiftieth anniversary. The parish thought the former oceanographer might want to see—and have a small part in—the restorative work of Marathon's Turtle Hospital.

Covered with a damp towel, Tammy, the rehabilitated turtle, rode in a large plastic tub in the stern of the boat to a site about eight miles offshore, where the turtle hospital's director said she would find ample sea grass for food.

As the boat slowed, Bishop Katharine and retired Bishop Cal Schofield laid their hands on the turtle, blessing her for the journey. Schofield offered prayers for the animal and gave thanks for those who had cared for her. Then the Bishop Katharine and the hospital director tipped Tammy into the water, where she quickly disappeared, then surfaced many yards away, still swimming hard.

> Blessed by bishops' hands,
> she dove deep, swam. We watched till
> sleek head surfaced. Home.

Bishop Katharine beamed. "This says so much about our whole ministry of healing," she said.

July 12

"…and let birds fly above the earth across the dome of the sky."

Looking at the egret that illustrates this chapter, I understand why the writer of Genesis says that the creatures in the water and the birds flying "across the dome of the sky" were created on the same day. Where there is water, there are birds.

When we go to Sanibel Island, we always visit the Ding Darling Wildlife Refuge. There, a glorious variety of wading birds feed among the mangroves, on the sandbars in the bay, or in the estuary's brackish waters. We focus our binoculars on stately herons and egrets and my husband's favorite, the roseate spoonbill, with its spatula of a beak perfectly formed for sifting through the muck for food.

On the beach, we watch pelicans soar over the waves, then suddenly dive, surface with a catch, and take off again. Ibis and snowy egrets with bright yellow feet wade in and out of the surf, gleaning what receding waves leave behind.

In the late nineteenth century, egrets—especially the snowy egret—were hunted nearly to extinction to supply elegant white plumes for women's hats. The birds were rescued only by a successful campaign—led by women—to make egret-plumed hats unpopular.

It seems so hard for us to see beauty in creation without wanting to grab it. I think the snowy egret on the beach who won't let me get too close with my camera may be trying to tell me something: *God made me to fish and to fly. God made you to watch—from a respectful distance—and say thank you.*

July 13

Near our former home in North Miami, Florida, is a park with shaded paths where I used to walk regularly. A pond flows into a canal, and often ibis roost in the trees or graze in the mud and grass at the edge of the water.

Stopping to watch the ibis one day, I noticed a bird that was moving with an awkward, lurching gait. As I drew closer, I saw that the claws of the bird's right foot curled into a kind of fist—a clubfoot. How would an ibis with a clubfoot survive?

It could fly, but it couldn't grab a branch to roost in the trees with the rest of the flock. Except in flight, it would be stuck on the ground, at the mercy of every other animal in the park.

But it *did* survive—I would miss it for a week or so and think that surely it had been killed, but then I'd walk down by the pond and see it hobbling along. "Stumpfoot! You're still alive!" I'd whisper, hoping no one was around to hear.

Sometimes we assume we're so limited by our own defects that we can't possibly be the face and voice of God's love in the world—we're too old or too young or too damaged by our own bad choices and the world's unkindness. But this is simply not true.

God pronounces creation good, not perfect; we are works in progress. Like Stumpfoot, we may struggle on the ground, but we can still soar.

July 14

"Use your peripheral vision," our Tai chi instructor tells us. We need to be aware of each other's movements in order to achieve a smooth and continuous pace through the form. This is what birds do, he explains, when they fly in a flock—each one is aware of the birds on either side so that they move in perfect unison.

You have watched videos of—or perhaps seen in real life—clouds of birds that appear seemingly out of nowhere, wheeling, swooping, soaring, diving—great streamers of birds sweeping across the sky in perfectly choreographed dances.

The entrancing movements of a murmuration of starlings, or flocks of other migrating birds, involve more than simple eye contact. Scientists think that two factors make the birds' coordinated movements possible. The first is each bird's ability to sense quickly the movements of other birds. The second is a constant transfer of leadership—as a lead bird becomes tired, the bird drops back and another takes the place in front.

As the Body of Christ, we are Jesus' flock, and we too need the ability to move in the world as a single organism. We can learn from the birds to be intensely aware of our sisters and brothers, sensing the direction of their movements and taking turns in leadership by not allowing a leader to become so weary that the progress of the whole flock slows.

Who are the people in your life whose movements you see and match? Is it your turn to lead or to drop back and let someone else move forward? This way of being begins with peripheral vision—really seeing each other—and becomes a soaring dance as we move together toward God's dream for all creation.

So God created the great sea monsters and every living creature that moves, of every kind, with which the waters swarm, and every winged bird of every kind. And God saw that it was good. God blessed them, saying, "Be fruitful and multiply and fill the waters in the seas, and let birds multiply on the earth." And there was evening and there was morning, the fifth day.

Genesis 1:21-23

In Genesis, we're told that on the fifth day, God creates all the creatures with which the water teems, including the great sea monsters—and that it is good. Much of what God creates to roam the deeps must be acknowledged to be, to our human eyes, quite monstrous indeed: massive whales, giant squids, jellyfish, stingrays, sharp-toothed sharks. So much of what teems in the world's waters is quite literally outlandish, clearly adapted to survive and thrive in an environment in which human beings do not belong. Yet, God created these monstrous beings to inhabit the deepest waters and sees that it is good. What are we to make of good monsters? God is clearly not judging creation by any set of human criteria or seeing with human eyes.

Most of what God creates on the fifth day, from the sea monsters to the winged birds, live out their lives in environments human beings cannot enter or truly participate in. Only through technological advances made within the last couple of centuries have we gained the ability to even visit these places. We can now tour the ocean depths by means of submarines and scuba gear, travel through the upper levels of the atmosphere through airplanes, and scale the tallest treetops via cranes and dirigibles—but the original writer of Genesis had no such advantages. And much of creation still exists apart from human beings, remaining inaccessible to our observation and judgment. Even with submarines, can we see the great sea monsters as God sees them? Without new eyes and new standards, we will likely fail to see the goodness of much that is and fail to fully participate in God's great act of creation.

July 16

Much of the first chapter of Genesis is full of expansive language: swarm, fruitful, multiply, fill. This is a language of more. Propagation is the order of the day.

From the tiny rotifers and protists that inhabit the meagerest drop of pond water to the fruit flies that descend on every apple and banana left out too long, evidence of God's creative industry covers every square inch of the earth. One really can have sympathy for the ancients who believed that life arose spontaneously from inanimate materials. So ubiquitous are living things that evidence of life can be found in mile-deep caves, geothermal hot springs, ocean vents, and polar ice caps.

What is the meaning of all this abundance? Surely, if God's goal in Genesis is to create life, one creature would be enough? Even a single-celled organism fits the bill. Why doesn't God just create a paramecium on the first day and call it good?

Instead, Genesis tells of extravagant diversity, extravagant productivity, and an emphasis on further growth. "…every…every…every…every… And God saw that it was good." We are shown in Genesis—and in every drop of pond water and with every glance at the sky, if we have the eyes to see—that creation rests on a solid foundation of goodness and that the nature of this goodness is to grow.

"God blessed them, saying, 'Be fruitful and multiply and fill…'" And indeed, they do! That which God creates in the beginning is everywhere we turn. God's fingerprints are scattered over everything. What a vast universe we live in, full of abundance, with more life than we can ever see or imagine.

July 17

Perhaps you learned it in fourth grade, eighth grade or tenth grade, but wherever and whenever you learned it, you likely are aware that one of the characteristics shared by all living things, and one of the surest ways to distinguish living things from non-living things, is growth. The capacity for growth is inherent in all life, from the smallest germs and bacteria to the largest blue whales. Living cells divide; plastic milk jugs do not.

Where does this capacity come from and how did it arise? Scientists still aren't quite sure, but according to Genesis, the ability to grow, to be fruitful and multiply, is an instance of God's blessing. Then, "God blessed them, saying, 'Be fruitful and multiply...'" There seems to be a connection between goodness and growth. God's will, throughout the Genesis creation stories, is for that which is good to not merely remain or hold its own but to increase and multiply.

In this way, virtually all living things push against the walls of their containers. Essentially flightless chickens will hurl themselves into the air when the migratory instinct is particularly strong, seeking to emulate the geese streaming across the sky in the spring and autumn. Octopi are notorious escape artists. Easily bored, they routinely push lids off aquarium tanks, disassemble mechanical components, pull themselves across bare floors, and occasionally disappear down sink drains.

Perhaps the ability of living things to focus and direct their efforts beyond and outside themselves is a natural consequence of their ability to grow—this tendency to slowly (or quickly!) occupy more space and other spaces. In any case, it seems that as we grow—and allow other beings to grow—we fulfill one of God's original benedictions.

July 18

Have you ever been involved in a long-term creative project that required hours of effort spread out over multiple days? Perhaps you've worked on drawings or paintings that demand hours of time. Or perhaps you've worked on home improvement projects that required time in between work sessions for caulk to harden or paint to dry. Maybe you have experienced planting a garden and waiting—hoping!—for those seeds you planted to germinate. Or maybe you have been so ambitious as to build a bike or a lamp or a car and can remember moments when you stopped to test gears, tighten fuses, or try the ignition switch.

If you are one of these types of people, you are probably already acquainted with the urge to periodically take a step back and assess whether the work is going well or not. God operates no differently. After each act of creation comes a moment of evaluation. "God saw that it was good." We're not told whether this seeing is the result of sober and intentional reflection on God's part or a more spontaneous realization. Nor are we told what criteria God is using to judge creation's goodness. Regardless of the specific criteria used, Genesis seems to make quite clear that God is pleased by creation. On some level, each creative act fulfills God's hopes, vision, and intentions.

In human terms, our paintings turn out well, gardens bloom, lamps light up, cars turn on. This is the world we are living in: a world that pleases its creator.

July 19

"And there was evening and there was morning, the fifth day."

This phrase echoes and re-echoes throughout the Genesis creation story: "There was evening and there was morning." It closes out that which came before, and in so doing, points the way to that which comes after. Repeat it a few times to yourself: "There was evening and there was morning…there was evening and there was morning…"

Do you feel a sense of "tick tock?" Like a pendulum swinging left and then swinging right, there is a first part and a second part to the phrase: "There was evening" (tick) "and there was morning" (tock); "there was evening" (left) "and there was morning" (right); "there was evening" (exhale); "and there was morning" (inhale). Like a heartbeat, this phrase provides rhythm and marks the passage of time.

This phrase repeats so many times one might be tempted to grow bored with it. *Yes, I know. There was evening, and there was morning. What else is new?* It's true that in the repetition of this phrase there is an impression of return, recurrence, and circuitousness. But there is also linear progress. Each day (each breath, each heartbeat) is unique and sacred unto itself, inextricably connected to all other days (breaths, heartbeats). In God's creation, today is not yesterday all over again, and tomorrow will be different, as well. Thanks be to God.

July 20

One of the most interesting aspects of the first Genesis creation story is the effortless way in which momentous, unprecedented acts of creation are almost immediately incorporated into and superseded by other momentous, unprecedented acts of creation. The seas and the earth are a really big deal on the third morning; God spends quite a bit of time on them and sees that they are good. Yet now, on the fifth day, the seas and the earth are in the background. They are mentioned only insofar as they provide the substrate for sea creatures and winged birds. If this were a Greek myth, the seas and the earth would no doubt become envious and spiteful and seek to destroy these new beings in an effort to maintain their own importance.

However, the Genesis creation story is pretty far from Greek myth. From start to finish, it presents a world in harmony, in which each aspect, object, and creature has a role to play. What is created on the fifth day interacts with and is an extension of what is created earlier. Without seas and earth and air, fish and birds could never come to be—and they are glorious embellishments! On the third day, God sees that the seas and the earth are good; just as on the fifth day, God sees that fish and birds are good. All receive the exact same evaluation, and later goodness doesn't erase earlier goodness. The focus of God's activity might change from day to day, as each creative act succeeds another, but earlier aspects of creation aren't abandoned. On the contrary, one might even say they increase in importance.

July 21

The fifth day of creation could easily be re-conceived as a play in three acts. In Act I, God creates. In Act II, God sees. And in Act III, God blesses. God's blessing is a new thing in the creation story, and it is echoed in Genesis 1:28 and 2:2. Prior to the fifth day, God blesses no created thing: light, sky, land, seas, plants, trees, the sun, moon, and stars. With the one exception of sky, we are told in each case, "God saw that it was good." But the sea creatures and winged birds are the first works of God to receive God's blessing, the first to be exhorted to multiply.

We aren't told explicitly why this might be. It doesn't seem to be because God is more pleased with how these creatures turn out than with how the plants or sun or stars turned out. More likely, God's blessing points to an essential difference between these latest creations and everything else. To use a later phrase from Genesis, the sea creatures and winged birds God forms on the fifth day are the first creations to partake of "the breath of life." Perhaps by virtue of their animal nature (a word that has its root in *anima*, the Latin word for breath), the fish and birds stand in need of God's particular blessing and benediction in a way that no earlier created thing does.

What is clear about God's blessing is that God's will is for life to increase. God's generative capacities are linked to generosity. We have the sense that when it comes to creation, God withholds no good thing.

So God created the great sea monsters and every living crea-
ture that moves, of every kind, with which the waters swarm,
and every winged bird of every kind. And God saw that it was
good. God blessed them, saying, "Be fruitful and multiply and
fill the waters in the seas, and let birds multiply on the earth."
And there was evening and there was morning, the fifth day.

Genesis 1:21-23

I don't particularly like to swim, especially in the ocean. Something about not being able to see what's around freaks me out. I like splashing in the waves and looking at the sea from the safety of the beach just fine, but I don't have any desire to be way out in the middle of it, with so much dark, mysterious water beneath me. I'm happy here on land where I am dry and comfortable, and I cannot drown or be pulled under by a sea monster.

In Brazil, some practitioners of a local religion called Candomble do not go out into the ocean to fish in the week or so after New Year's. This is because it is the time of Iemenja, the god of the sea. The ocean is hers alone in those days.

While I don't believe in Iemenja, perhaps there is a lesson we can take from this: The ocean does not belong to us. Neither does the rest of the earth, for that matter.

We can only access much of the ocean, like the air above us, with expensive technology. Most of humankind will never see the depths of the Mariana Trench or reach the upper atmosphere, evidence that we are not truly masters of this planet. It belongs to the sea creatures and the birds, too. It belongs to all of us. Our attempts to control this world, rather than live as part of it, lead us to pollute and destroy ecosystems that sustain us. We are only part of creation, part of a whole that belongs to God, not to us.

July 23

My daughter is ten months old. Each week she learns a new trick—a high-pitched squeal she lets out at unexpected times or the ability to hold her bottle by herself. Every day has surprises, good and bad. She might clap for the first time, or she might wake up at 4 a.m. and refuse to go back to sleep (as she is prone to do).

Since she was born, my life has lost much of its former predictability. But even though these changes are more obvious now, my life has always been in a state of flux. I have changed every day of my life and so has the world around me. It's through all those chances and changes that we evolve. Evolution—the process by which we and all life on this planet were created—takes those changes, those genetic mutations, accidents, and surprises that cause species to multiply and change, and populates the earth with an astounding variety of life.

My life will be changing constantly for the next eighteen years (and beyond) while my daughter grows up. But there is a joy in this as God makes a new thing—just as there is joy in discovering a new species or in the change in the seasons. Surprise isn't easy, but it is how we, and all of creation, grow.

July 24

The Great Barrier Reef is the only living organism that can be seen from space. Built by billions of coral polyps, it is home to about 1,500 species of fish. More than 200 species of birds and thirty species of whales and porpoises visit the reef, not to mention the sea turtles, sea snakes, and hundreds of species of invertebrate organisms whose names I cannot pronounce.

The Great Barrier Reef is most likely not one of the sea monsters the writers of Genesis had in mind, but it is without a doubt one of the great living things in the sea.

It is also in danger. As the ocean warms due to climate change, coral bleaching—which is what happens when the algae on the coral dies—is occurring more frequently.

The ocean and the earth are big enough that it seems impossible for us to have a major impact on their health and stability. Yet as we continue to pollute the air and sea and destroy habitats, we put the ocean and the earth in danger.

Solutions to these problems are not easy or always obvious, but they are necessary. We are called to live lives mindful of God's creation and our impact on it. How can we do this every day?

July 25

Toys. Stuffed animals. Candy. As children, many gifts are free and simple. But as we grow older, the blessings in our lives become more complicated. They come with responsibility.

Perhaps the first time many of us realized this was when we got a pet. Even those pets who live in aquariums and cages need constant attention. I received a pet guinea pig for my birthday when I was five or six years old, and though it didn't do much other than squeak, eat lettuce, and leave droppings, I still had to remember to feed it and clean its cage.

One day, you might have a child and realize that while you love your child deeply and are grateful for her every day, you have irreversibly changed your life. You have to change her diapers and be home in time to relieve the baby sitter. You have to make sure there is food in the house and that she does not roll off the bed. Your level of responsibility increases exponentially.

In the same vein, we can longer pretend that the land and the sea and the sky that sustain us do not come without the responsibility to care for them and live sustainably. We have polluted the skies and rivers, destroyed rainforests and caused species to disappear, and now we are in the midst of massive climate change. Everything we are given requires something of us, including the earth we walk upon.

July 26

The American Museum of Natural History features a life-size fiberglass model of a blue whale. It is 94 feet long and weighs 21,000 pounds (a real blue whale can weigh more than 150 tons). I'm amazed by the model whale every time I see it. While I've never seen an actual blue whale, I find great joy knowing that these giant creatures live in the oceans of the earth.

In the museum, the whale is surrounded by displays of various sea creatures and is not far from a room full of colorful stuffed birds. Confronted with the variety of strange and beautiful creatures on this planet, I find these exhibits enthralling.

Of course, it's somewhat strange to experience this variety inside a large building surrounded by skyscrapers and concrete, but perhaps that's just more evidence that this world is larger and stranger and more full of life than we could ever experience.

God blesses the creatures of the sea and sky so they can multiply. We are blessed to live in a world so full of strange and beautiful creatures, so full of life.

July 27

Birds are dinosaurs. This is something I learned not very long ago. My dinosaur-loving childhood self would have thought this was amazing. I always thought dinosaurs lived solely in the past, which made them seem from another world, not the one I live in. We are still constantly learning new things about dinosaurs—finding feathers on fossils, new bones turning up to reveal new species.

The sea monsters mentioned in this passage of Genesis may refer to whales or possibly sea snakes. The writers may have thought there were dragons in the sea. While there are no dragons today (as far as we know), strange creatures like glowing fish and giant squids still exist—animals from the deepest parts of the ocean that we know almost nothing about despite our best efforts.

It sometimes seems as if the world has lost a bit of its mystery. Everything is recorded and photographed. This is a great gift to see and know so much, but it's also important to recognize how much we still don't know. We learn that the animals we once thought extinct still live among us as birds, and sea monsters still swim about in the waters. Our understanding continues to change and grow because creation turns out to be larger and stranger and more full and complex than we ever understood, even when we still thought the waters were full of great monsters.

July 28

I believe it is a blessing to live in this world, but we also all know that the earth God has given us can kill us. Natural disasters and disease cause the deaths of many people. Where is God in that?

In his book Exploring Reality, theologian and physicist John Polkinghorne writes, "I believe that God wills neither the act of a murderer nor the incidence of an earthquake, but both are allowed to happen in a creation given its creaturely freedom." In other words, God gives all aspects of creation the absolute freedom to become themselves. The world is always in a state of change, of becoming something new and holy. This is frightening and also beautiful. It also means, I think, that we are not necessarily the center of God's creation: We are merely part of it.

This line of thinking doesn't totally satisfy me, but it makes some sense in the abstract. We live in a world that God has set free. It's not a clock set into motion nor a Rube Goldberg machine but rather an infinitely complex and changing universe. God blesses creation and also gives creation—all of it—freedom to become itself. That's dangerous and a blessing.

July 29

In the months since my daughter was born, I've often found myself inexplicably on the verge of tears. A song, a movie, a story, or sometimes just the overwhelming feeling of joy I have when she laughs or rests her head against my chest causes my eyes to well up. It's as if my heart is a bit raw—or simply closer to the surface and effortlessly pricked.

I've felt this way at other times in my life—easily filled with joy or compassion. It has something to do with feeling love and feeling full of love (and probably sleep deprivation). In a time when I have often felt besieged by the daily tasks of work and chores, having a daughter has connected me again with the beauty, wonder, and terror of life. Through my daughter, I see this world in a new and less self-centered way, with all its strangeness and danger and beauty.

It has also deepened my love and appreciation for others—especially other babies. My coworkers and I show each other photos of our babies just about every day. I hope that having a daughter never causes me to focus inward and protect my family at the expense of others, but that her presence continues to remind me that she and I are a part of creation, and I am called to do everything I can to love and protect creation, the earth and all its inhabitants, and her.

July 30

The earth and its waters support an estimated 8.7 million species (though some scientists estimate there may actually be a trillion, if we count the micro-life forms we haven't yet discovered). This 8.7 million includes almost 10,000 species of birds and more than 200,000 species of sea life (and possibly another two million species we know nothing about!)

All of these creatures live on about 57 million square miles of dry land surrounded by about 140 million square miles of ocean and 165 major rivers. It amazes me that our island home can support so much life, much of it completely invisible to us. I am amazed that so much life came from a single organism, changing and multiplying and coming to fruition as creatures as diverse as finches and tigers, sharks and bacteria, fruit flies and human beings.

It is worth reflecting on these vast numbers of species from time to time. The scale of it is so big, it's practically unknowable. And perhaps this reflects the largeness and unknowability of God. God—like creation—is near us but always just beyond our comprehension.

July 31

I love springtime in New York City. Growing up in Texas, spring wasn't all that much different from summer. It was hot most of the year, except for a few weeks of cold weather (which were not really *that* cold). In New York, however, I am always pleasantly surprised by spring weather. By the end of March, I am done with snow and cold rain and heavy coats. Since I do not have a car, going out anywhere in the winter involves spending a significant amount of time in the cold, and so I stay indoors most of the time.

Spring comes, and it feels like the city opens up again. Instead of rushing from one building to the next, I walk around outside. I visit the park and might even sit on our small balcony. It is as if the outdoors has been given back to me—a gift. On the sunny days when the weather is perfect, it is easy to see that the earth we've been given is a tremendous blessing.

It's harder to remember this perspective in the winter or when it rains or in times of fear or loss or illness, but I believe it is always true. How do we embrace this sense of gratitude throughout the year? How can we always remember that the water from our tap, the bread on our table, the birdsong coming through our windows—all of this and much, much more—is a blessing and a gift from God?

August

Cattle and Creeping Things

And God said, "Let the earth bring forth living creatures of every kind: cattle and creeping things and wild animals of the earth of every kind." And it was so.

Genesis 1:24

Artist's Note: I was raised in a small rural town in Northern California. Most of my friends were from dairy families, so I spent a lot of time hanging out in dairy barns, riding horses across the countryside, and watching the cows being herded in for milking. To this day, the smell of a ranch (cow manure) brings back fond memories and warm feelings. In scripture, God calls forth cattle, and then the creeping things and wild animals. While I strongly suspect Holstein cows aren't the cattle in question, this is the image I saw in my mind. As we read the story of creation, it is not just a metaphor or story of what happened then. It is inevitably our story as well, and the layers of meaning are limitless.

Most of my encounters with foxes (pictured on next page) have been secondhand. I have photos of them taken by a night camera as they checked out my backyard. I've watched their beautiful tails disappear behind a tree as they fled through the forest. But my experience reached a new and almost surreal level a few years ago when a rabies epidemic hit the fox population especially hard. We would hear of foxes running into the street to bite children on bikes or sneaking into garages and workshops to attack people. Locals were warned to protect themselves and their pets. Fortunately, the epidemic waned, and the fox is once again a welcome, if elusive presence in our community.

Cattle and Creeping Things

God made the wild animals of the earth of every kind, and
the cattle of every kind, and everything that creeps upon the
ground of every kind. And God saw that it was good.

Genesis 1:25

Artist's Note: There is a reason that frogs figure prominently in fairy tales and mythology. These mysterious creatures (pictured on next page) are hard to pin down. As amphibians, they can live both below and above water. For part of the year, they are nowhere to be seen, but when spring arrives, they make their presence known with a finely orchestrated serenade and chorus. If you have ever spent time near a pond, you must wonder like I do how all of the frogs seem to know exactly when to start and stop croaking. It's enough to keep one awake just to listen and wait for the next chorus, and I sometimes imagine a little frog conductor standing on a lily pad marking time and giving prompts.

We lived in West Texas for a few years, a dry, semi-arid landscape. The city designed parks as swales, lower than the streets, so that when the rain finally did come, they would fill up and turn into temporary lakes. It was a brilliant solution to a potential flooding problem, but the best thing about it was the frogs who would come after a deluge. I am sure a biologist could provide a perfectly reasonable answer to where the frogs had been the rest of the time, but I prefer to simply marvel. And that might explain that whenever I paint frogs (and I've painted a lot of frogs), they are witnessing something else, pointing perhaps to the real mystery beyond our knowing.

257

August 1

And God said, "Let the earth bring forth living creatures of
every kind: cattle and creeping things and wild animals of the
earth of every kind." And it was so.

Genesis 1:24

In *The Book of Common Prayer*, one of the eucharistic prayers includes a
reminder that God made humans, "...the rulers of creation. But we turned
against you and betrayed your trust; and we turned against one another."
Having been entrusted with stewardship of creation, particularly our close
relatives—cattle and creeping things—we might look back and honestly
reflect on the varied history of our relationship with the rest of creation.

In those times when we put ourselves in the place of God, forgetting
that we are part of creation, we become like a consuming pagan god—
gobbling up anything we desire without regard for the precious balance
and relatedness of the created family. Considering our collective power
as a species—and the ways we have overwhelmed to extinction other
species—we risk becoming overwhelmed ourselves, frozen with despair.

The antidote to this despair is to invite God's guidance about how we
can make changes in the way we relate to the rest of creation. We might
invite God to be God of all creation, and then look around our front
porch to consider how harmoniously we are living within creation.
What do we contribute to the systems we live in? How do we encourage
and strengthen other species, other creatures of God, to thrive? Are we
taking up a proportional amount of space, or are we lording it over our
neighboring species?

Remembering we are part of the creation and not the god of it might help
lead us into a right relationship as the trusted, temporary stewards of
this creation God has established—to model for future generations ways
to live as good rulers of creation, empowering the totality of creation to
grow, thrive, and continue praising God.

August 2

My wife, son, and I were hiking in Colorado one summer when we heard a moose was spotted along the trail. We tried to remember how to keep ourselves out of trouble with these gigantic creatures. We reviewed the instructions our camp host had given us about coexisting with the moose, bears, mountain lions, and other creatures we might accidentally encounter.

With a mixture of fear and eager anticipation, we hiked onward. It wasn't long until we saw the moose—at a safe distance away—trotting along in a meadow. It was gigantic! We were instantly aware that the moose was wild and that we were most definitely not in a zoo, and not necessarily safe. This understanding heightened our senses, helping us pay close attention not only to the moose but also to the meadow, lakes, and mountains all around us. The giant moose went on its way, and we went on ours. I thanked God for the sighting, and I silently thanked the moose for crossing our path—at a comfortable distance.

Being among the wild animals is a lasting reminder that we are not as in control as we sometimes pretend to be. Hiking in a moose's neighborhood instead of sitting in a climate-controlled environment makes us aware of how precious life is—not just our own lives, but all life. This miracle of understanding leaves us offering thanksgiving to God and to the beautiful creatures with whom we share this life.

August 3

When I reread the story of Jesus' disciples searching for a colt that had never been ridden, I can't help but imagine an episode of "Jesus, the Colt-Breaking Cowboy." We don't know how long Jesus takes to prepare for his entry into Jerusalem, only that the disciples promise to bring the colt back to the owner when Jesus is done riding it.

While I have never broken a saddle animal, I've heard stories and seen movies that illustrate the difficult process. I'm sure the Gospel of Mark shares this story to point toward something beyond Jesus' possession of cowboy elements of humanity. We hear that he makes it through his ride into Jerusalem with no broken bones. And, of course since Jesus is God and can calm the seas and bring healing to humanity, I'm sure taming the unridden colt is less dramatic than I might playfully imagine it—sandals flying, heels down, Jesus' hand thrown up over his head for balance while the colt bucks and starts.

The colt delivers God's incarnated self to the heart of Jerusalem. A creature once wild is brought into relationship—placed in service to God. Here is an example for us to follow. If angels are messengers of God, then this colt carrying the enfleshed Word of God is quite angelic. With invisible wings, I can picture a kind of holy pegasus fulfilling its destiny by carrying Jesus into Jerusalem, starting the fulfillment of his reign—in Jerusalem and Israel—and in each of our wild hearts.

August 4

I had a sacred encounter with a snake one summer evening. I was walking to a worship service at Camp Allen, the camp of the Episcopal Diocese of Texas near Houston. It was my first year on summer staff and my first summer living away from my parents' home. I was one of the staff musicians, so on this particular evening I was walking around the lake with my guitar to prepare for worship.

That summer, I struggled for the first time with deep doubt. Being in leadership and teaching about God, I began to wonder about the God we were praising. I began to wonder what—and if—I actually believed. One night, I sat alone on the steps of the staff lodge and asked God for a sign. In my imagination, I wondered what would happen if a giant angel emerged from the forest canopy and hovered over the tall pine trees. I was afraid. I said, "Never mind," and went to bed.

As I walked around the lake toward the worship service, I almost stepped on what I quickly identified as a coral snake. In all of my previous snake encounters, whether venomous or not, I have jumped and shouted a few non-churchy words. This time, I only felt a deep sense of peace. I slowly backed up a few steps, knelt down, and watched. When the snake moved, its red, yellow, and black bands blurred into a deep maroon color. When it slowed and stopped, they became distinct.

I watched—and I didn't have to wonder anymore, I experienced God's presence in the encounter. I was not afraid but full of awe and peace. I walked on to lead worship, ready to give thanks.

August 5

A friend and colleague is an evolutionary biologist. Known by some as the Frog Lady, her field of study is herpetology. I don't know much about frogs, but I do like to hear them sing at night. Their perfected song is part of their evolution: They sing to one another to find each other and procreate so their song will continue into the next generation.

I find science thrilling. I enjoy learning the "how" of the universe, from the formation of the first stars to how those stars formed the elements of which we are made. I enjoy learning about the emergence of life and when we creatures became conscious enough to be aware of how that happened. It is awesome.

Reading the creation story from Genesis, I turn more toward the imaginative wonderment of "why" all this creation exists. I wonder why we are here. I learn of God's loving creation into being. I learn I am created to pay attention to what God is doing in the world around me. The how and why questions are different—and in harmony.

I give thanks to God for Nicolaus Copernicus, Charles Darwin, and all the scientists who have come after them, people who are learning about the "how" questions of creation. From this place of gratitude, I read Genesis and discover the harmony between science (how) and religion (why). I notice how closely the progression of that first creation poem echoes what scientists now understand: how we got from the Big Bang to being able to write and debate about it. Scientific study is catching up with the ancient, intuitive knowing of religion, and so our songs will continue into the next generation.

August 6

Early Sunday morning, I sit in my studio—a room on the end of a garage—to write sermons. I share my studio with some little critters, including geckos and lizards.

One morning I sat at my desk and saw a lizard. With its forefeet pressed against the closed window, the lizard sought a way out. I slid the window open a bit, expecting the lizard would dart past the opening pane and toward the light. Instead, it ran from the open window. I tried to shoo it toward the opening. I could see its terror at everything that was happening. That little lizard's whole world must have seemed to be ending.

So I left it alone awhile—either to escape or not as its instinct and creativity directed it. Later, I watched the lizard with its face pressed against the window, lungs pumping in exhaustion and terror. I gave it one last scare as I picked it up and tossed it out the open window onto the morning glory growing underneath.

The terrified creature scurried off to a cozy shelter. It lacked the larger perspective I had of its situation. I pondered how often I must look like that lizard to God...my own face pressed up against what seems (to me) an impenetrable barrier, waiting and wanting God to pick me up and set me free—through the open window right in front of me.

August 7

The creatures most deeply present to me are my dogs, Cooper and Porter. They constantly remind me of my own creatureliness. My instinct is mirrored back to me by them, and playfulness is ever-present when I pay attention to my family's companion animals.

These dogs frustrate me, no doubt. They scratch on doors, howl when they feel lonely, and they have no idea what a priest does during Holy Week...and that in itself is a blessing.

We have creation's own needs and rhythms to remind us of the deep commonalities between animals and humanity. Cooper and Porter are with me and always, always ready to play or sit with me or scratch or howl to bring me back to this present moment.

Cooper and Porter bring me back to my createdness. They help me return to the awareness that God is my creator. Our dogs do not care for calendars, not even Sundays. Their routines are, *Feed us morning and night, and let us out...and please, as often as you can, play with us.* When I pay more attention to them than to the calendar, I am healthier and feel closer to God.

August 8

This week's author
Jason Merritt

> *And God said, "Let the earth bring forth living creatures of every kind: cattle and creeping things and wild animals of the earth of every kind." And it was so.*
>
> **Genesis 1:24**

When it comes to creatures of every kind, the scope of "every kind" is hard to imagine. There are the wild beasts we only see on TV documentaries and sugar ants that march along baseboards. Fear-inducing snakes and spiders, spoiled family pets lounging on furniture, lunatic squirrels dodging traffic, and African elephants fleeing poachers. There's the staggering variety of insects. And we haven't even talked about birds and aquatic animals.

Recent scientific assessments predict as many as 6.5 million different species of animals creeping and crawling on land, and over 2 million more swimming in oceans, lakes and rivers. Scientists are quick to point out a margin of error of 1.5 million (or so).

New species are found around the world—an estimated 10,000 are identified each year. Yet we've just scratched the surface of "every kind." We know almost nothing about the life and kinds of creatures in the vast deep oceans that cover 70 percent of our planet. More people have been to space than have ventured to the depths of the ocean frontier. What creatures live in its depths?

The vastness of the animal kingdom—and its seemingly endless frontiers—reminds us we will likely never know the edge of God's creation. The Garden is wide and plentiful, and it is good. Though we may not know its bounds, our faith still asks us to care for it—the known, and unknown, "every creeping thing that creeps upon the earth."

August 9

Imagine the trust that goes into living and surviving as an animal. They do not have the comfort and reliability of well-built houses or cars. Their modes of transportation are feet, fins, and wings, and their homes are where they make them—and can be changed in an instant by a predator or natural disaster. Animals sense that if they do not learn to think swiftly, trust their instincts, and make changes, they will likely become someone else's dinner.

I have always been fascinated by the idea of adaptation. The ability of any creature, including humans, to adapt and change is subtle and amazing. The moment we adapt, we are freed from our ideas about how things must be. We discover flexibility, wisdom, and strength, as well as tenacity and humility. We let go of the ego in our existence.

The adaptation of echolocation is especially amazing. Imagine a species having little-to-no sight and realizing (rather quickly) that to survive, it must develop new ways to endure. The creature begins sending sound into the dark and waiting for its return. Once the sound cue returns, bouncing off barriers on its way, the animal knows which direction to proceed. Out of darkness, a mental picture made by sound waves emerges.

Our prayer life is similar. We find ourselves in unnavigable predicaments, and we send our worries and thanks into the darkness. We sit and wait for an answer, the return of something that sounds familiar. Some signals return quickly, and we know which direction to pursue; some never return, and we move forward blindly. Either way, we continue forward in faith. Imagine the trust that goes into living and surviving as an animal, and remember that you too seek this trust in yourself—and in the Holy.

August 10

Years ago, I helped clean kennels at a dog rescue. Each time I walked through the long row of kennels, I was greeted by dozens of wagging tails and excited yelps. For a dog lover, this kind of interaction was a lot of fun. Predictably, it took a few visits for some dogs to warm up to me, but eventually they all approached, and we gained a rapport.

The shelter was a "no-kill" facility—meaning they would keep animals until they could be placed in a foster home, were adopted, or lived out their natural days. Some dogs had been there a long time. This was the case for one particular pit bull mix. I don't recall his name, but I'll never forget his face, riddled with scars from past mistreatment as a fighting dog. The sign on his kennel read, "Don't allow with other dogs."

Visitors and potential forever families often peeked into his kennel, but no one stepped up to take on the responsibility of a dog who couldn't be trusted. His scars made him look menacing, even though the shelter volunteers knew better. He was gentle and very sweet with humans, but his younger mistreatment had flipped a switch in his brain and he could not be trusted with other dogs.

The situation broke my heart. This poor dog never got to run out in the yard and play with other dogs. He could never run off-leash at a dog park. He spent his days at a shelter, with volunteers who loved him but not with a family of his own.

After moving, I kept an eye on the shelter website to see if he was ever adopted. One day, I saw that his photo was taken down and a blog posted that he had died. A talisman of sorts, the old pit bull had become a symbol of the rescue's commitment to no-kill principles and awareness about animal abuse. Today, I give thanks for the staffs and volunteers at animal shelters around my city, in our country, and across the world, as they care for and protect God's furry creations from abuse and neglect.

August 11

Anyone who has owned chickens likely looks at breakfast differently than people who are not personally acquainted with poultry. Eggs are a staple of our diet, yet fewer and fewer people know what it takes to bring an egg to the table.

I owned three chickens for a few years—Eleanor, Rigby, and Penny Lane. Many people don't name their chickens, but I did because I was raising them for eggs, not the stew pot.

Raising chickens was a learning experience. I grew up in a city and chickens were something we saw on vacation or at the occasional state fair. I had to learn about their health and diet issues, weather concerns, and dangerous predators. Thanks to Google and YouTube, I made it through. My hens provided me with eggs and I kept them safe and well-fed.

Keeping a trio of birds healthy, clean, and safe wasn't easy, but it certainly changed my understanding of the difficulty of raising enough chickens to keep our tables filled with billions of eggs—and chicken nuggets.

As convenience and mass production become more obligatory in our society, we face many ethical concerns and limitations about and around our food production. Not everyone can raise chickens or even start a small garden. And food produced on a small, local scale is often too expensive or difficult to find.

Nevertheless, we can take small steps toward a better understanding of our food sources. And I pray that we will strive to respect and model the natural rhythms found in God's garden. Let it begin with me.

August 12

Yellowstone National Park reintroduced a population of wolves to its land in 1995. This decision and the effects of it became a case study in the interdependency of animals and the environment.

With no wolves keeping them on the move, grazing animals had freedom for many years to linger in valleys, along the edge of streams and rivers, munching the soft, young, and nutritious buds of shrubs and trees. The banks of the rivers became barren. With no foliage to shade the rivers, the temperature of the waters began to rise. The lack of small foliage reduced habitat for many species of animals, including birds and fish. The river banks began to meander and erode.

You may know that trout are a very particular fish. Like Goldilocks, they need water that is *just* right—not too hot, clean, fairly well-aerated, full of food. The fish in Yellowstone suffered from the rising water temperatures, lack of habitat and food, and water muddied from eroding banks.

Then one day, the wolves returned. Their presence kept deer, elk, and other grazing animals on the move, making them reluctant to stop for too long near open water sources. In time, riparian bushes and small trees began to repopulate the banks of rivers and streams. Insects and other food sources reemerged as well—and the trout population recovered.

This experiment shows that small shifts in behavior, outlook, or plans can have big impacts—both good and bad. What have you inadvertently disconnected in your life? It may not be obvious, but what could be reintroduced to recover a lost or languishing aspect of yourself?

August 13

I hear its high-pitched wings on the first pass by my head, but it isn't until the third occasion that I feel bothered. My hand isn't fast enough, but I swing it anyway and for the moment, the mosquito retreats. Then I see the fourth fly-by...and a fifth.

Lighting a citronella candle on the table beside the rocking chair, I hope for a buffer zone. Despite their nuisance, these mosquitos are a food resource for countless other creatures. If I kill every pest that crosses my path, the next critter up the food chain suffers. Even the bothersome creatures have their purpose.

The candlelight and fragrance bathe the patio, but the pest boldly braves the fumes, and continues hassling my ear lobes. It lands on my forearm, and I give myself a solid slap as the mosquito escapes the swat just in time.

Retreating inside, I dig through the junk drawer in the kitchen. No bug repellent spray. Ehh, I hate the smell anyway. Instead, I bring two more candles outside; they allegedly smell like vanilla and ocean breeze—an army of fragrance that I hope is offensive to a mosquito's olfactory system. It doesn't help. The aerial dogfight around my head continues. At least it smells nice as I sit in my rocking chair, read the news, and flail my arms intermittently.

I could go back inside, safely behind the screens and walls, but I'm committed. This patio space belongs to me, but it also belongs to them— all creatures, great and small. After an hour or so, the breeze picks up. I flail my arms less. One candle goes out, then a second, leaving a whispering trail of smoke. I notice that the pests have retreated from the cool evening breeze.

They'll be back tomorrow, and so will I, and my candles too. This space belongs to me, but it also belongs to them. We all have a purpose. Great, and small.

August 14

My dog, Riley, was only a few months old when I adopted her. When I arrived to visit her litter—with little information beyond her breed and gender—my expressed plan was to meet and play with her and then responsibly consider whether to adopt her or not.

The plan failed miserably. Within an hour, she was in the car with me, heading to a pet store to pick up food, a collar, and plenty of chew toys.

When I brought her home, I was excited by visions of playing fetch and going for walks. I couldn't foresee the stressful workdays melting away at my front door, courtesy of a wagging tail. The volunteers at the rescue never told me her presence at the foot of my bed would help me sleep after my divorce.

After a dozen collars, four houses in three states, one hip dysplasia surgery, and more nicknames than I care to admit, Riley has become an integrated part of my life—a steward of my sanity.

Dogs' love is inexplicable—they greet you the same way on good days as on bad. Dogs easily look past flawed characteristics and mistakes. They have a simple view of friendship, love, and companionship. With little effort—and asking for almost nothing in return—they only see the best versions of us.

How would our daily interactions change if we too saw the best versions of the people around us, letting the extraneous details and past transgressions fade to the background? How would your health and happiness change if the next time you looked in the mirror, you saw the best version of yourself?

Give it a try. As you go about your business today, try to see the best version of your family, friends, colleagues, and even yourself.

August 15

This week's author
Lauren Wilkes Stubblefield

God made the wild animals of the earth of every kind, and the cattle of every kind, and everything that creeps upon the ground of every kind. And God saw that it was good.

Genesis 1:25

I grew up on a farm in the lower Mississippi Delta, a lush, verdant place full of living things. From my earliest days, the creatures of the Earth were an important part of that life: the cows Daddy and Grandpa milked, the cats Mother doted on, the snakes and alligators Grandma was vigilant against, the deer and ducks we cousins hunted—all pieces and parts of a brilliant jigsaw puzzle of life, a tapestry of barks and purrs, of downy undercoats and mesmerizing feathers. These were the textures, odors, tastes of a simple life, well lived.

Every sunrise brought unspoiled dew as the deer walked from the pecan grove to the creek; every evening brought the cows back to the barn, dogs to the porch, and cats to their saucers of milk. Thanks be to God for the creatures who teach us to question and explore their sameness and differences—who reciprocate love, loyalty, and affection, who help us learn the responsibility of caring for creatures great and small, and who each help us to live with deeper compassion in the great circle of life.

August 16

Fishing is a holy and sacred meditation on the relationship between person and beast, sun and water, Creator and creatures. There is something deeply sacred in watching the sun break gently over the edge of a lake or river's horizon, in seeing the mists swirl away as the first light of dawn reaches the reedy edge of a backwater.

The only sound you can hear as you prepare to fish is your breathing. Then you cast. With a whiz of the line feeding out of the reel and a plop as it hits the water, you are connected with creation in a manner that only fishing can afford. Gently, very nearly prayerfully, you coax your bait along until a fish strikes your line. You whisper prayers of thanksgiving as you reel in your catch, mesmerized by the silvery scales sparkling under the water, the widening ripples on the surface, the splashes of the tail as the fish submits to you.

You cradle this creature in your hands, and breathe a quiet thanks as its wriggling weight settles into your palms: *Thank you, beautiful creature. Thank you for your majestic flashes and flourishes. May you live a long, healthy, strong life.* And then, you return this wonder of wonders into the water where it lives, moves, and has its being, thanking the God of creation for a moment such as this.

August 17

When I was in college, I had to take a sabbatical for health reasons. During that twelve months off the mountain, I lived and worked in Orlando, and for a brief moment, I adopted a long-haired black kitten who was dubbed Shaq. At the time, Shaquille O'Neal and the Orlando Magic were at the beginning of their rise.

Shaq was a beautiful cat, not too big, not too small, flowy silky hair that didn't seem to tangle, not too much of an undercoat to knot up. His disposition was pretty great for a young male cat. He was housebroken almost immediately, and he learned quickly where he was not supposed to be. The saddest moment of my time in Orlando was surrendering him to a shelter when I had to move, unexpectedly, and my new landlord would not allow him to come with me.

I was heartbroken; I have never apologized to an animal as profoundly as I did to him on that morning when I had to walk away. Asking for forgiveness is almost always difficult; it was so much more difficult asking it of a creature who did not understand and who could not grant me the absolution I needed.

August 18

Oblation is a special kind of offering we make in thanksgiving to God—it indicates a literal pouring out of something we bring to God out of our deep gratitude for all we have been given. We call the bread and wine we bring to the altar and consecrate as part of celebrating Holy Eucharist oblations as well.

Earlier this year, my dog, Brandy, became semi-incontinent from old age. Medication only helped so much, and I became increasingly frustrated with her declining condition...and the condition in which it left my house.

Further diagnosis indicated that Brandy was suffering from congestive heart failure, and the recommended medication—a diuretic—only exacerbated the problem Brandy and my carpet were experiencing. But even in her discomfort, Brandy's eyes remained bright and full of her natural, God-given exuberance about life. She was not in distress, only in need of attention and some extra love.

Caring for Brandy in this new, deeper way became my Lenten discipline—a kind of oblation. Those forty days were magical and miraculous. Instead of feeling frustration over endless puddles, mopping, bathing, washing, and sorting soiled laundry, I made the work into a prayer for my dog's comfort and a labor of love for this creature who had brought me so much joy and such profound companionship. Watching her schedule of household entrances and exits carefully, managing her medications and foods with a sharp eye toward the clock and the ingredients list, making time in the middle of an incredibly busy project to rub her belly and scratch her itchy places all became an offering and an experience of great joy.

August 19

My very best friend in the whole world is a woman named Heather. She has been an important and pivotal part of my life—and has put up with me—since we were in sixth grade and for the next three decades.

Lately, Heather has suffered from some chronic medical issues and so has her beloved Corgi, Mia. Heather and Mia's well-being, comfort, and overall health have occupied a significant portion of my intercessory prayers for the better part of the year. I want my friend to be well, healthy, and happy—to feel confident and peaceful and to be free from distress.

Similarly, I pray for Mia's health. Mia is Heather's constant and longtime companion, and Heather is Mia's. They need each other, and they matter deeply to each other—and to me.

I pray daily for the folks I love and the concerns in their lives, and I invite you to begin (or continue) doing the same. In my prayers for Heather and Mia and folks and furry friends I love, in my prayers for all those in need of relief from pain and suffering or ill health, for all God's creatures who feel cast aside or abandoned, and for all those in any need or trouble, I am reminded that God is at work for this beloved, very good creation and is doing more than we could ask or imagine.

August 20

Frankly, asking for help is not one of my gifts. In fact, I'm terrible at it. I was raised to be a strong and independent person, to fix my own things, to make do with what I had.

So, even though I have a wonderfully attentive and supportive husband, and even though I am close to my parents, and even though I have some truly amazing and loving friends, I am loath to ask for any help.

I am that perfectly imperfect child of God who thinks she can still wallow her way out of or through anything—everything—even though the harsh realities of life have proven this to be otherwise time and time again. Maybe you share this stubborn streak in common with me.

All creatures of this Earth must ask for help at some point or another— whether it is a sheep giving birth to a breeched lamb with a vet's intervention, an elderly pet requiring deepened levels of patience and compassion, or even one of us finding it difficult to ask for help from our Creator. We each and all need help.

August 21

Animals are an important part of my life, and I truly love all living creatures. I have my parents and grandparents to thank for this love of animals. Growing up on a farm was a good start to this relationship, and even when we moved into town, we had cats, fish, hamsters, snakes, rats, and even a baby squirrel. My brother rescued it from the backyard, and after we nursed it back to health, we released it to the wider world.

I try to keep my hummingbird feeder full. There's milkweed growing in my yard for the monarch butterflies to feast upon. Worms in my gutters are relocated to the yard ahead of rainstorms, and I admonish anyone who kills a spider in my presence—those little guys do serious, amazing work eating mosquitos!

I hope that in my small acts of kindness toward the creatures that inhabit my life, an attitude of adoration seeps through. When we show compassion and care toward all the wondrous beauty that God gives us in creation—feeding cats and birds and bugs alike—then maybe the God-given and God-blessed balance of nature will be restored.

August 22

This week's author
Jason Leo

God made the wild animals of the earth of every kind, and the cattle of every kind, and everything that creeps upon the ground of every kind. And God saw that it was good.

Genesis 1:25

When I was young, I never much liked the story of Noah's ark. It seemed to me that a lot of not-so-innocent people drowned, and I was a not-so-innocent kid. The thought of only some of the animals making it through the ordeal was a tough reality for me to swallow. What about all the other animals? What did they do wrong? I never really had a lot of friends when I was a kid, and our family pets were my closest companions. I wondered how they would have fared in the story. Would they have been on the ark or swallowed by the waves?

Several years ago, my bishop assigned me to serve as the priest in a rural farming community. After years in big cities, I was abruptly planted in the midst of farmers, farms, and a whole lot of animals—surrounded, as the psalmist wrote, by "green pastures and still waters." I was apprehensive and skeptical. But over time, I saw a new perspective on God's handiwork. As this new perspective revived my soul, it is perhaps worth sharing with you. And it may encourage you—wherever you may be in your journey—to consider (if only for a brief moment) a new perspective, a change of scenery.

Who knows what God may be ready to reveal to you, what signs God may share with you, what grace may revive your soul?

August 23

The fall stewardship program was at the top of my list of important items to tackle at the small mission church. Members indicated a sincere desire for growth in number and spirit, so this seemed like a good place to start. Commitments of time, talent, and treasure are part and parcel of any Christian community, and I was determined that we would witness this to the whole town.

Personal stories, inspirational letters, and one-on-one visits were all part of our stewardship campaign efforts, culminating with an ingathering of pledges on a specific Sunday. Much to my shock and dismay, the campaign was a total bust. There were maybe three pledge cards in the offering plate. I asked a senior member of the congregation where I had gone wrong. He smiled and said I just needed to be a little more patient. "They're just waiting to see how the corn crop comes in."

The creation story indicates that timeliness was part of the process. Six days. Something different every day. Rest on the seventh day—an orderly process with God setting the schedule. The corn harvest comment reminded me that no matter how much I try to be in charge, try to set the schedule, God's time is the only one that really counts. Lo and behold, the corn came in—and so did our pledge cards. Sure enough, the harvest was indeed more than we could have ever asked for or imagined.

August 24

Friday night football was a really big deal in our farm town. This was a new experience for me, since I had always lived in the city. It seemed everyone in town migrated to the local high school on Friday nights for the big game, so I decided to join them. This was a wonder to behold—pageantry, parades, music, food, dancing, fellowship, and a ton of fun. The games became a weekly ritual for me.

One particular Friday night, a strange thing happened. In the middle of the third quarter, it started to rain. I thought, "Shoot! This is going to ruin everything." Before I could move to find cover, everyone started to cheer—everyone—players, coaches, cheerleaders, even the band dads selling hot dogs. They were *all* cheering. Had I missed something?

The woman next to me noticed my confusion. "Reverend, we need rain! We need it bad. This is a blessing for our whole town." The author of the book of Deuteronomy writes, "He will give the rain for your land in its season, the early rain and the later rain, and you will gather in your grain." In this small town, I learned that there is more to life than a subway train showing up on time or the balance in my bank account. I learned that God really does provide, and people really do give thanks—sincere thanks—and one Friday night in the strangest of places, I was blessed to be among them.

August 25

One day, I drove by the ice cream stand—a hub in our community especially in the warm weather—and I noticed the strangest thing. The wheels of my wife's car were suspended in the air, with the frame resting on a parking block. My wife is prone to creative driving maneuvers; apparently she had pulled forward when she should have reversed. I decided to keep going, wretched man that I am.

There was no mention of the situation that evening at dinner, and no one—not even the car—seemed worse for wear. I finally made a subtle remark that exposed my knowledge of the situation. "Oh that," said my wife, "It was nothing." But she lectured me on my lack of Christian charity.

I asked, "How did you get the car back on the parking lot?" She smiled, "Four big farmers picked it up and put it back down for me. One of them is on our church council."

People who work the land work hard and have the strength to prove it. Many of these same people also have incredible gifts of hospitality and community. The following Sunday, one of my wife's angels handed me a Bible with a page marked—the story of the good Samaritan. He let out a belly laugh and told me if I wanted to stay alive, I should read it.

August 26

A farmer in our church had a lake on his property and invited me to come fishing. We fished for a long time: He caught a lot, and I caught nothing. I was frustrated. He joked about unconfessed sins and that made me more frustrated. Finally, near dusk, I caught a big one. I was so proud—biggest catch of the day. He smiled, saying that it was a fine fish, and it was a crying shame we had to throw it back. *What?*

"Why in God's name would I do that?" The farmer explained, "That fish is pregnant, and she will fill the whole lake with even more fish, and many will come and fish. So in God's name, you are going to throw it back." I was crushed, but I knew he was right.

In the book of Genesis, God says, "Let us make humankind in our image, according to our likeness; and let them have dominion over the fish of the sea, and over the birds of the air, and over the cattle, and over all the wild animals of the earth, and over every creeping thing that creeps upon the earth." Good farmers take good care of their animals—all of them, just as God instructs. And I learned that good farmers take good care of their families and friends too. This is a natural extension of their work and their lives.

August 27

A local famer's mother died. They were not members of a church, so a family friend asked if I would preside at the funeral. I was glad to help. It ended up being a nice ceremony on a really beautiful day. There was a good crowd in attendance—a lot of family, people from the community, and people from our congregation.

Afterward, the farmer whose mother had died tried to pay me for presiding at the service. I explained that payment wasn't necessary. He looked frustrated. I explained that this was part of my calling. He seemed to accept that.

A few days later, my wife called me to inform me that there was a dead turkey in a bag on our front porch. There was a note from the farmer, thanking me for helping with his mother's funeral. I didn't know what to do with the turkey, but I knew I couldn't give it back.

In the Book of Acts, Luke tells us that the early Christians share everything they have with one another. No one goes without. I thought of this passage as the same man who had grieved his mother and shared his bounty attended church the following Sunday.

August 28

A new family joined our congregation. They too came from the city. They had a son who had never lived in the country. His transition was difficult, and he struggled to make friends.

The county fair was approaching and I tried to cheer the city kid up with stories of the fun and excitement that would soon come to town. He would have none of it. A woman in our church asked him if knew how to bake, and he said no. She invited him to join her in making apple pies that afternoon. His mother immediately said yes for him, and the deal was sealed. The next week I learned that the boy was entering his apple pie into competition at the county fair.

To make a long story short, he won first place: blue ribbon, picture in the paper—it was a big deal. He gained rock-star status in the community, and most importantly he discovered a whole new group of friends.

Saint Paul reminds us that there are a variety of gifts, but the same Spirit gives them to each of us. Who would have ever guessed that a generous heart, some apples, sugar, flour, water, and other secret ingredients would transform a young man's life?

August 29

Sometimes, I have a hard time explaining to people how the death of Jesus leads to new life. I never had this problem in our farming community. Death points to new life all the time. Crops and livestock are harvested and processed—and people are fed.

A guy who lived down the road from us had a pig farm. My daughter, who was six at the time, loved to go see the pigs—especially the piglets. These visits became a weekly ritual and slowly she became aware of the reality the pigs would one day face. Sure enough, one day we went to the farm, and the pigs were gone.

What should I say? Six years old is a pretty young age to confront the reality of the food chain. She looked at the pen for a long time, and then she looked at me and asked, "Hey Dad, does this mean we're gonna get some bacon?"

The reality of farming communities is that death is all around—and death is necessary for life. I never found it hard to explain to farmers how Jesus' death leads to new life. They saw this all around them—indeed they help to make it happen—and we should be thankful.

August 30

When I lived in the city and returned from long road trips, the skyline was a beacon welcoming me home. Especially at night, the lights would fill the sky, and I knew that I would soon be back with my family. Life in farming communities is different from life in cities but there are similarities. People work hard, love their families, and try as best they can to be faithful.

Saint Paul reminds us that we are one in Christ, that there is neither Jew nor Greek, slave or free, male or female, that we are one in the Lord. One time, I was driving back to our small farming community with a friend from the city. He asked me if I was bored living in the "middle of nowhere." I told him that I was never bored. There was more going on in our town than he might expect. Off in the distance, I noticed a new beacon drawing me home: grain elevators in the center of town.

August 31

When the bishop assigned me to serve in a small farming community, I followed another priest who had been there for more than thirty years. He left a note on the altar indicating that he used the same prayer every Sunday when people brought the bread and wine forward before Holy Communion. The prayer went something like this:

> *Blessed are you, Lord God of all creation, for through your goodness we have received the bread we offer you, fruit of the earth, and work of human hands. It will become for us the bread of life. Blessed are you, Lord God of all creation, for through your goodness we have received the wine we offer you, fruit of the vine, work of human hands. It will become our spiritual drink.*

I initially decided to use the prayer as a way to ease the congregation's transition to a new priest. Eventually, I thought, I'll switch to something else. But over time, I saw how much this prayer resonated with the congregation—not because it reminded them of their previous priest but because they were *in* the prayer. Their lives were the bread and wine, made in partnership with God each and every day. The God of all creation was relying on them to make food and drink, and they were relying on God to provide the ingredients. It was an amazing partnership to witness, a life abundant and beautiful, and at the same time hard and rough. The prayer was their journey through this side of the kingdom.

September

According to Our Likeness

Then God said, "Let us make humankind in our image, according to our likeness; and let them have dominion over the fish of the sea, and over the birds of the air, and over the cattle, and over all the wild animals of the earth, and over every creeping thing that creeps upon the earth."

Genesis 1:26

Artist's note: Most of the critters in the Creation Series are found in my corner of the world. One of the exceptions is the lion. A few years back, I had the privilege of going on safari in Botswana where we encountered this lion, fondly known by the locals as Old Silver Eye. Being in the presence of these beautiful animals is otherworldly. But there's also something so grounded and primitive about these majestic creatures that they take me to the heart of the Creator.

On the safari, the lions were mostly napping. Nevertheless, seeing the lions in their natural environment was thrilling. And sacred.

A Helper

Then the Lord God said, "It is not good that the man should be alone; I will make him a helper as his partner." So out of the ground the Lord God formed every animal of the field and every bird of the air, and brought them to the man to see what he would call them; and whatever the man called every living creature, that was its name. The man gave names to all cattle, and to the birds of the air, and to every animal of the field; but for the man there was not found a helper as his partner. So the Lord God caused a deep sleep to fall upon the man, and he slept; then he took one of his ribs and closed up its place with flesh. And the rib that the Lord God had taken from the man he made into a woman and brought her to the man.

Genesis 2:18-22

Artist's note: Painting plants, birds, and mammals is one thing, but painting people creates a whole set of challenges. We tend to bring personal associations and projections to paintings of people. If it's a portrait, it must be just right—the slightest difference in the shape of an eye, or any other feature, throws the whole thing off. While we can look at a painting of a bird or mammal and not be particularly interested in details, we tend to relate to people in a more specific way.

I delayed these paintings. I wanted something universal but didn't know who to paint. Finally, my husband suggested the San, also known as the Bushmen (pictured on the previous pages). This was a good suggestion since the San are thought of as the world's oldest civilization. We had spent some time with a couple of San during our time in Africa and learned about their close relationship with nature. Their existence is free from the encumbrances of modern culture or technology. Our guide gave us demonstrations of trapping birds with only a string and a stick and explained how ostrich eggs are used to store water.

I didn't have any good photographs, so I went online and searched for San images. Much to my surprise, I found photos of the very same young San with whom we had spent the afternoon. What wonderful (and God-given) serendipity!

September 1

This week's author
Jonathan Melton

*Then God said, "Let us make humankind in our image, accord-
ing to our likeness; and let them have dominion over the fish of
the sea, and over the birds of the air, and over the cattle, and
over all the wild animals of the earth, and over every creeping
thing that creeps upon the earth."*

Genesis 1:26

I am conflicted as I begin this stretch of the book's journey. The haunting
and beautiful eyes of the lion in this illustration remind me that I have
never seen a lion, except with my kids at the zoo. All too often the things
we consume become divorced from their origins. My family's limited
participation with our local community sustained agriculture (CSA) farm
helps in a small way to offset the grocery-store magic. But I still feel the
disconnect between my life and the rest of the created order that sustains it.

Recent science fiction films, like *Interstellar* and *Passengers*, likewise
break my heart. These movies explore (and assert) the eventual ecological
destruction of the earth and the necessity of space travel. More and more, the
search for extraterrestrial life is revealed to be the search for other planets on
which to live, with critical reflection on why such a possible future has come
to be seen as inevitable. We Christians both struggle to relate well to a word
like dominion and have a hard time remembering that our relationship to
creation is as creatures of God's making.

I wonder if dominion is a word meant to be redeemed from the operative
understandings driving our twenty-first-century ecological crises. Just like
power is a word Christians will never see the same after Jesus' sacrifice
on the cross, maybe understanding and living dominion requires us to
imagine all of the ways Jesus reconnects us to the image of God.

September 2

Love invites us to notice. Just as we appreciate the boss or spouse or parent who notices the details of our lives—the new haircut or the job well done or the unnamed grief—followers of Jesus take steps toward a better exercise of dominion when we notice the details of creation, whether they are the rhythms of the sun and sea and trees or the people around us.

I had been friends with Philip for a couple of years before I noticed there was a lot about Philip I didn't know. Philip was a retired priest living in a retirement community with his wife and their one-eyed chihuahua, Uno. I was a new priest and had leaned on Philip more than a few times through the years, always grateful for his encouragement and observations of my early ministry. But I had never asked about his story until the day I did.

Philip had been a mayor of a small Texas town and a JAG (judge advocate general) officer before becoming a priest. After asking about these unexpected chapters, I asked Philip what changed. He explained that his military service had led him to Japan. There, he met an American cattle farmer who was raising livestock to give away, empowering the poor Japanese farmers in an early version of micro-finance lending. Philip asked his friend why he was spending his life this way—in relative obscurity with the poor. "Because I've discovered a pearl of great price, a treasure in a field, and it's worth everything. I am being given the abundant life of Jesus."

As we go about noticing, let us start close, with a look around at the people right next to us. Who do you already know who is still unknown to you? What would you like to ask them?

September 3

For most of my life, Jesus has been inviting me to explore the connections between gentleness and the presence of God. So when Paul writes in Philippians 4:5, "Let your gentleness be known to everyone. The Lord is near," I do not think the second sentence is a non sequitur. Their proximity names a truth: I am most inclined to violence or harshness (or other kinds of selfishness) when I mistrust or disbelieve that God will remember me and assume that I must take matters into my own hands. But we are in the Lord's hands. "Do not be afraid," sings the resounding chorus of scripture. "Be gentle with one another."

Curiosity is a kind of gentleness because curiosity does not guard itself against the unknown—even when the decision to venture into new waters feels frightening and opens us to change.

I wonder what happens to the image of God in us as well as our understanding of dominion over creation when we aim our curiosity at creation. What happens when I feel curious about *The Book of Common Prayer*'s assertion that "our common life depends upon each other's toil" and make an effort to know the people who grow vegetables and shepherd animals that end up on my table? What are those experiences like? And what happens if I discover unflattering things about the ways my appetites affect others? What will be my gentle response?

My curiosity, too, could be aimed at non-human creatures. Birds and trees. Bears and bugs. What will I notice if I start not from a place of use or consumption but with gratefulness and a gentle posture? Perhaps our relationships with our pets offer an example of this different approach: Knowing more about others almost always elicits a more kindly response.

September 4

One Lent, I decided to walk home each workday for lunch. The walk wasn't far, about a mile from the church. As an added degree of difficulty, I decided to only think about walking while I was walking. Have you tried this before? At first, I was terrible. I found myself resetting my intention every two and a half minutes.

What am I being present to if I am not present to my immediate environment? Usually it is some combination of worry, fear, plans, stories from my past, and speculations about my future. In his worthwhile book *Silence and Honeycakes*, former Archbishop of Canterbury Rowan Williams calls these "the great system of collusive fantasy." He refers to fantasy not as space ships to Mars or sexual adventures afoot but fantasy as in things that aren't real. I have noticed that creation often bears the brunt of our collective, collusive fantasies.

As my Lenten disciple of walking home for lunch evolved, I began talking to myself out loud in order to put a leash on my wandering mind. Speaking my thoughts slowed them down to a speed where I could keep an eye on them. I decided to describe my surroundings. At first, I kept it simple: blue car, unkempt lawn, flag pole, etc. After a few minutes, I began noticing things in greater detail: the house with no cars and the front porch light left on; the boat left out for cleaning after yesterday's fishing expedition; the teachers wrangling children on the playground. I tried not to ascribe motivation or intention. Strangely, if you do this long enough, you end up sounding like storyteller Garrison Keillor. For me, if just for a few minutes each day, I also got my life back.

Be present, Lord Jesus, and keep us present to what is real.

September 5

A rabbi tells a story about a man who told him how much he loved fish. "Nonsense," said the rabbi. The rabbi went on, (and I'm paraphrasing), "You don't love fish. You love to catch, boil, and eat them. What you love is yourself. But loving a fish and loving the taste of fish are two distinct things you would do well to keep straight."

One of the hazards of living in a consumer culture is the way we are wired to confuse our love of a thing with our consumption of it—and not just with fish and fruit but also with people. Of course, we grow (with God's help) into love, but oftentimes God's help brings a recognition that the idea we thought we meant by love has to die in order for us to grow in love.

The thing is, I *want* to love fish. I want the exercise of dominion over the created order to involve a deep and abiding attention to all of creation—an attention that elicits delight. I want to feel the full measure of the giftedness and love God intends when God gives even the fish to our care. I want to feel God's love and not my own strength when I eat and am sustained by plants and animals.

I feel like I am Israel, wandering in the wilderness, claiming God's gifts as the work of my own hands and refusing to be lavished with love. This realization kills me, because there's nothing worse in my mind than giving gifts to people too proud to say, "Thank you, friend." But here I am.

Good and generous God, teach me to love the fish.

299

September 6

When is it too late to turn back? Some years ago, I was walking along the beach with my wife when she remarked about how much trash had accumulated on the dunes. I nodded my agreement, but truthfully I didn't feel much like being an activist that day. We were on vacation. Nevertheless, Rebekah persisted. "Look at that!" she said, pointing over her shoulder, some distance behind us, at a small pile of trash. I nodded again. "If we see more like that ahead, we should pick it up," I offered. It was too late. She was already backtracking to pick up the trash I had dismissed as behind us.

I know Rebekah was modeling the image of God for me that day. Thank God that God does not shrug divine shoulders with an "Oh well, next time" nonchalance. But Jesus "emptied himself, taking the form of a slave, being born in human likeness. And being found in human form, he humbled himself and became obedient to the point of death— even death on a cross" (Philippians 2:7-8). God in Christ stoops down, pours out, turns back.

Whether ecologically, politically, relationally, or otherwise, feelings of inevitability or fatalism can bring a perverse sense of comfort. *Ah well. So it goes. Too bad, but there's nothing to be done.* But there *is* something to be done. With our feet, we can turn and follow Jesus into the messes that grieve our hearts. Indeed, we must. This is part of the image we bear: united to Christ, reconciling, healing, restoring, hearing, and lovingly responding to the groaning of God's good creation.

September 7

A friend of mine and I were talking over coffee about different practices in church. Some people make the sign of the cross; others don't—that sort of thing. I mentioned that as a kid, my parents taught me to genuflect, or kneel on one knee, when I entered or left a pew and when I approached the altar to receive communion. My friend listened kindly before sharing her discomfort with a practice that recalls a royal court. "Frankly," she said, "the whole king language in scripture makes me uncomfortable. The history of kings is not a pretty one." I agreed, and I know she was right.

I also know that God is the first to share my friend's objection, way back in 1 Samuel 8. When Israel asked for a king, God expressed reluctance. Through Samuel, God voices concern that a king would rule harshly, exploit the people, seek out war, and only build himself up. For some people, to call God king is to say that God is the one who does what kings do (things like exploiting, killing, and building themselves up at the expense of their people).

But I hold out hope that calling God king frees us to reimagine things like kingdoms in ways that expose the shortcomings of worldly kings.

To exercise dominion like Jesus does is to wash each other's feet, embody forgiveness, and give rest to the land. Our understanding of dominion comes from the crucified Lamb who rules from a throne on a crystal river with a tree on both sides of it, whose leaves are for the healing of all nations. This Lamb has conquered. Let us follow him.

September 8

This week's author
Mary W. Cox

Then God said, "Let us make humankind in our image, according to our likeness; and let them have dominion over the fish of the sea, and over the birds of the air, and over the cattle, and over all the wild animals of the earth, and over every creeping thing that creeps upon the earth."

Genesis 1:26

I'm looking at the painting of the mouse, a fragile thing. What could this little animal have to say to me about our being made in the image of God, with dominion over all the other creatures?

If you ask my daughter the funniest thing she remembers from her early childhood, she will tell you the story of the mouse in the motel. We were on a road trip around Florida and had taken with us bags of cereal and fruit for quick breakfasts. We had barely checked into our motel room the first night when we saw the mouse, which saw us too, and disappeared. We put the groceries on a high rack and turned out the light, encouraging our daughter to go to sleep. There was the sound of little claws on the wall.

My husband—who had just gotten out of the shower—turned on the light, grabbed a trash can, and on his hands and knees, pursued the mouse around the room. No luck. After all these years, we still laugh at the mental image of "Dad crawling around on the floor, naked, chasing a mouse."

We did not have dominion over that creeping thing and had to move to another room—after my husband got dressed, of course.

We are small things, too, in the vastness of God's whole created universe—how amazing to be told that we're made in the Creator's likeness. I like to think God laughs with us—"a little lower than the angels," as the psalmist says, yet humbled by a mouse. How could we—and our Creator—not laugh at the sheer absurdity and wonder of our being so made and so loved!

September 9

Being made according to the likeness of God means that we are made for relationship, with God and with other human beings. This seemed simple enough when I first remember hearing the concept at a retreat when I was a teenager. Of course—Adam and Eve, made by God, made for each other—relationship.

When you read this on September 9, my husband and I will be celebrating another year of marriage. I remember standing in front of the pastor in the Presbyterian church where I grew up, with John's hand in mine, thinking, for an instant, "Oh—who *is* this man I'm promising to love for the rest of my life?"

But here we are, more than fifty years later, in spite of ourselves: for better, for worse, for richer, for poorer, in sickness and in health, and all the rest. Wedding vows don't say anything about petty arguments and raised voices, or frowns and hurt feelings; about the baby crying all night or the young adult facing difficult decisions; about all the annoying habits we've nagged each other about a thousand times; about counseling when we needed it. But they also don't mention the shared laughter that one word can summon all over again; the music and movies that make us both cry; the encouragement and the pride in each other's accomplishments; and all the months of Sundays we've sung God's praise together in the choir.

God made us for relationship, but marriages—and all our other relationships—are made right here on earth, and *we* have to make them.

"Will you seek and serve Christ in all persons…?"

"I will, with God's help."

That's what we really mean when we say, "I do."

September 10

In a memorable science fiction novel, *The Left Hand of Darkness*, writer Ursula LeGuin creates a planet with people who are like human beings in every way but one: They have no fixed gender. Instead, they are hermaphroditic and move through an estrus cycle in which an individual can be female in one season of fertility and male in another. These transitions are very disconcerting to the male envoy from Earth!

In recent years, our growing awareness of the complexity of human gender and sexuality has made most of us feel at times like LeGuin's protagonist, uneasy on the planet Gethen with its androgynous inhabitants.

At General Convention in 2012, I had a conversation with one of the deputies, a trans-woman, about gender dysphoria. "I guess we just don't quite understand it," I said.

She laughed. "We don't understand it either!" she said. It's a question she plans to take up with Jesus in heaven, she added.

For several thousand years, we have assumed that when God creates human beings in God's image, male and female summed that up neatly. But just talk to a doctor or nurse about chromosomal variations—it's not always as simple as XX or XY. Now we hear of—or know—people who do not identify with the gender assigned at birth or are gender fluid.

So, does God make mistakes with gender? No. I think the mistake is our attempt to simplify God. Our Creator is infinite mystery and infinite love, beyond our comprehension. Why would it be surprising that we—made in that likeness—continue to have our own unfolding and incomprehensible variety?

By whatever attributes we discover to define ourselves, our deepest identity is always as God's beloved children.

September 11

I wasn't going to write about 9/11. Wiser minds and more devout hearts than mine have wrestled with this day and its fallout. Then I remembered that I did dare to write about this shortly after that terrible day.

Do you stand with the prideful who boast of our might,
or the cynics who mock our bright dreams?
Do you think that your answers will always be right
in a world blown apart at the seams?
There is One looking down on the wreck of the city,
and love is the vigil he keeps,
and his heart breaks with ours
for the pain and the pity.
Are you standing with Jesus who weeps?

It's so easy to hate in our hurt and our fear,
and to cry out for vengeance and blood.
Through the dust and the ashes we want to see clear
only struggle of evil with good.
There is freedom at risk, and we know we must save it
from a darkness where rage never sleeps.
You may fight for the flag—
or the right not to wave it;
are you standing with Jesus who weeps?

There's no end to the tears for the pain and the loss;
there's an ache that the tears cannot drown.
There's a world full of anger that's nailed to the cross,
but the hands that are scarred lift it down.
Are there tears for the souls that in fury are waiting
for a harvest brutality reaps?
Can you cry for the hearts that are twisted by hating?
Are you standing with Jesus who weeps?

September 12

Last year an artist friend and I published a book of her paintings, illustrated by my haiku poems. We have sold a few copies, enough to pay another artist who formatted the book for publication and the online publisher who printed the books. We didn't expect to make our fortune; we did it for the joy of making something beautiful.

When I think about being made in God's image, I think about the joy of creation—especially creative collaboration. In a life of making all kinds of things—poems, publications, performances—my greatest joys have been those times when I worked with others to make something none of us could have created alone.

During the years when I made up songs, I had a friend who wrote down the music and invented more complex harmonies than I could play on my ukulele. We wrote a musical revue about environmental concerns for a group of church youth to perform. The first time I heard one of my songs sung by the young people, I wept. It was no longer something I made; it was something we—and God—made.

As diocesan director of communications for the Episcopal Diocese of Southeast Florida, I edited a newspaper. I gathered material from many other writers and photographers and always had gifted layout and design colleagues to put it together. Before the days of sharing files online, I would overnight mail the material to the designer, and in a day or two, I would have a package of page proofs. Again, I would experience a sense of wonder at seeing my own work transformed into part of a greater whole.

Perhaps God too delights in creative collaboration and made us to be makers, to share with our Creator in the continued making of the world.

September 13

Anyone who believes that we have dominion over God's other creatures does not live with a cat.

For most of my adult life, our household has included one or more cats. They are beautiful, entertaining, contrary, exasperating, and more affectionate than their public persona often suggests. But there is something undeniably other about a cat.

My cat is a fine example of humanity's ambiguous relationship with animals. Cats are designed to be carnivores—I watch my cat stalk a lizard on the patio, and reflect that I, too, am no vegetarian. I live my life in the contradiction of feeling great affection for some animals and eating others.

We make animals both pets and prey. When we lived in Florida, our cats lived outdoors and roamed the neighborhood, sometimes bringing us their kill. Our first cat once brought us a cattle egret, bigger than he was.

Human dominion is destroying wildlife habitats and animal species at an alarming rate in all parts of the world. We try desperately to repair this ruination with wildlife refuges and captive breeding programs, but our understanding of the scope of our carelessness has come perilously late. There are so many ways in which, by action or inaction, we continue to damage the intricate web of kinship we share with every other creature on the planet.

How can we fulfill the responsibility our dominion has given us to treat all these other lives with reverence and respect?

September 14

A truth that youth is certain of:
> The antidote for pain is love;
> In turn we learn as seasons wane:
> The side effect of love is pain.

Every day, on every screen in front of us, we are confronted with suffering in the agonized faces of those who are fleeing the horrors of war, are sick, injured, or starving, or have witnessed a loved one gunned down in the street.

Through our own email servers and social media feeds come the heartbreaks of friends and family—illnesses, deaths, broken relationships, money worries. "Pray for me!"

We do pray and offer what help we can, but sometimes this business of being human simply hurts too much, and we're tempted to turn away, asking, "Does the image of God include suffering?" Of course, we know the answer: It absolutely does.

Today is Holy Cross Day, when we "glory in the mystery of our redemption" by Jesus, "lifted high upon the cross to draw the whole world to himself." This is what God does in Jesus: comes right into the midst of a radically free creation, in which every living thing—from the mitochondria in our cells to prelates and presidents—makes choices, often devastatingly damaging ones.

God loves us enough to show us the image of God as Love hanging on the cross, enduring the consequences of all bad choices—degradation, pain, abandonment. Love screams out, as we do, "My God, my God, why have you forsaken me?" Love that is willing to die—and Love that doesn't let death have the last word. We are made in God's image and suffering is part of that package—but so is resurrection. Thanks be to God!

Then the LORD God said, "It is not good that the man should be alone; I will make him a helper as his partner." So out of the ground the LORD God formed every animal of the field and every bird of the air, and brought them to the man to see what he would call them; and whatever the man called every living creature, that was its name. The man gave names to all cattle, and to the birds of the air, and to every animal of the field; but for the man there was not found a helper as his partner. So the LORD God caused a deep sleep to fall upon the man, and he slept; then he took one of his ribs and closed up its place with flesh. And the rib that the LORD God had taken from the man he made into a woman and brought her to the man.

Genesis 2:18-22

I don't know about other priests, but every Sunday as I offer the wafer at the rail, I look closely at each person's hands. Hands tell me a lot about a person. Outstretched hands can be soft and smooth and manicured, or rough and calloused with torn cuticles. I feel more connected with those I am serving just by simply observing their hands.

One pair of hands I especially love are those of a retired medical librarian who lives and works in his garden or greenhouse from early March until October. No matter how much he scrubs, dirt abides under his nails and embeds in the cracks and wrinkles of his hands. He reminds me of Adam, emerging from the ground just like the animals of the field and every bird of the air. My friend wears his deep connection with creation like a badge of honor—the soil on his hands is a reminder to me of our humble beginnings and ends—we came from dust and to dust we shall all return.

It is easy to imagine Adam with leaves in his hair, flecks of mica shining on his cheeks and mud between his toes as he boldly names his fellow creatures. I believe God smiles every time we dirty our hands because they remind us of our beginning in—and our eventual return to—paradise.

September 16

When we were married in 1970, our wedding service came from *The Book of Common Prayer, 1928*. While that liturgy does not mention a wife obeying her husband, there was a great deal of conversation in those days of the feminist movement about the use (or misuse) of the vow of obedience by wives to their husbands.

Budding feminist that I was, I was delighted not to have to pledge to obey my husband. I wanted to be a partner, not a handmaiden. Looking back, I think marriage was recovering its original meaning as described in Genesis. Woman is intended for full partnership in and with creation, not subject to it or to man. God sees that Adam needs a helper—a partner, a companion to be in relationship to him—if humankind is to discover and imitate the creator in the flowering and fruiting of creation.

As the years have gone by, I have come to realize that being a good helper and partner is not about taking turns washing dishes, folding laundry, or taking out the garbage. Being a helper and partner is about holding the light for the other when the way forward seems unclear; it means sharing the path and staying the course no matter how rocky the road. Partnership means carrying the physical, mental, or emotional load when the other is exhausted or weary.

We may demonstrate our willingness to be a good helper in the daily chores of housekeeping, but our best help for our partner comes when we are willing to participate in the refreshment and restoration of our beloved's heart, soul, and spirit.

September 17

Excited to be in the fourth grade with the upper school kids, I was disappointed on the first day of class. It all started when the teacher said my name was a derivative of a proper Christian appellation. Then she announced that she would call me "Sarah."

Knowing I had been named for my beloved great-grandmother, I was devastated. My mother tried to intervene, but the teacher was convicted in her decision. So "Sarah" I would be, at least for the next nine months.

Without enthusiasm, I learn to write my new name on my papers, but often failed to respond when called on in class. My teacher said I was a daydreamer and inattentive, but all I knew was that Sarah was not my name. This teacher taught me early on that names are personal and powerful.

When it was time to name our first child, my husband and I agonized over the choices—a family name for sure, but most definitely nothing trendy or diminutive. Somehow, the personal trauma of having a nickname left a mark on me. We settled on a strong family name, only to realize within a week that our nickname for the baby was unfortunately going to stick tighter than his legal one. Forty-five years later, our oldest son seems to love his name even if it's not a proper Christian appellation.

I can only imagine Adam naming all of the creatures. Does he agonize over cow or butterfly? Do the names roll off his tongue, miraculously inspired by the Creator? All I know is that names matter—what and who we are called is good in God's sight.

September 18

"It's so hard to be alone," said my newly widowed friend. "You just don't understand."

As a person with a living partner, I didn't. Within a few months, my friend began online dating. Her friends, me included, had all been socialized to meet others the old-fashioned way—through friends, family, or, at the most extreme, on a blind date—so we were appalled and a little frightened. We were relentless in our discouraging comments, hoping to keep her from connecting with these surely creepy virtual men. "After all, isn't this kind of thing for the young? "How can you know what they're really like?" And trying to cast doubt, we said, "What if they are not who they say they are?" Our unsolicited advice and lack of support to our friend wasn't helpful—in fact, it was generally hurtful and definitely unappreciated.

As it turns out, our friend has met some really interesting, kind, and delightful men online—some we have even met, and come to know and like. While all of our fears for our friend weren't completely quelled, we finally realized we had completely underestimated the pervasive power of loneliness. We had to be reminded by her courageous example that the need to connect with others is almost always worth the risk.

After years as a priest, I had assumed I understood loneliness and its isolation and sadness. Having spent time with many widows and widowers over the years, I felt sure I knew what being alone was all about. It wasn't until I accompanied my widowed friend on her journey into the wild world of Internet matchmaking that I was able to incarnate God's words for myself: "It is not good that humankind should be alone."

September 19

"Mom," my five-year-old said, "Did you know there's a big difference between boys and girls?" Finally, here was my first chance to discuss God's creation of humankind—male and female—with a tiny creation of my very own!

I was so ready for this conversation. After all, I had read numerous articles about how to have it. So, I took a deep breath and convinced myself I was as prepared for this conversation as any other enlightened, post-1970s mother. I would use the correct anatomical names for all body parts, and I wouldn't hesitate or feel embarrassment about any of it. I was ready to hit the topic square on the head, with supreme confidence.

Several minutes into my well-worded explanation on the wonderful ways of God's creation—how boys and girls, men and women were indeed created to be different but equal—my son said, "Mom, that was *a lot* more than I wanted to know."

Taken aback, I quickly realized my response to his question was all about meeting my own need to be a perfect mother rather than paying attention to the kind of mother my child needed me to be. Forty years later, this pivotal moment in my relationship with my son informs my ministry. My son taught me to listen in order to understand what another person wants and needs before launching into unsolicited advice or information that meets my needs.

God pays good, deep attention to Adam's need before creating a helper and a partner. This kind of attention results in companionship and an antidote to loneliness. Deep listening is a successful, proven model worth adopting for all of us on a daily basis.

September 20

Our Wednesday night Bible study was on Genesis. At chapter two, we read how God took one of Adam's ribs to create a woman. One participant confidently commented, "It's true, you know, that men have one less rib than women."

Without missing a beat, everyone grabbed their smartphones to search for "number of men's ribs." Click, click, tap, tap...and we had the answer. Human beings—whether male or female— have twelve complete pairs of ribs.

The woman who seemed to be in the know grabbed her neighbor's phone to see the answer for herself, asking, "Do you mean that for all these years I've believed a myth?" Our group kindly nodded "yes," and some of us confessed that we too had believed that men had one fewer rib until a biology or anatomy class had provided scientific data that proved otherwise.

Proclaiming her embarrassment, the woman opened up an excellent conversation among us about the power of myth in our lives—how myth can very often shape what we believe, for better or worse. In the case of the rib theory, no theological harm had been done—but when we appropriate the myth of a vengeful, retributive God who is only appeased by blood sacrifice, this kind of mythful thinking can stunt our spiritual growth and block our journey to the heart of God.

When we gather for the communal study of scripture, when we read and discuss theological concepts, we are able to let go of—or even reform— some of our ideas about God and meet our Creator face-to-face.

September 21

Looking at the portraits of the young man and woman, I am struck by their strong features—the healthy shine of their hair, their clear and glowing complexions.

The San live close to nature, and their unadorned beauty seems to reflect this relationship. They have chosen a way of life that nourishes them, body and soul.

I live in the Appalachian epicenter of the opiate addiction crisis in the United States. Addiction rates in my part of the world far exceed the national average. Too often the faces I see every day are not strong, healthy, or beautiful. They are gaunt and gray, held up on fragile necks of dull-eyed men and women, wasted bodies covered in rashes and hungry mouths missing multiple, if not all, teeth. The arms—and sometimes legs and feet—of these suffering ones are marked with needle tracks and oozing sores.

The faces of the men and women I see struggling with substance abuse stand in direct opposition to the well-nourished look of the San. Addiction has taken away the God-given beauty, power, and strength of too many people who snort, swallow, or inject legal or illegal substances into their bodies. Addictions almost always lead to painful, messy deaths. I would offer the idea that addiction may well be the exact opposite of creation. Addiction is an illness that robs its victims of wholeness, growth, renewal, and hope. As the church prays for those suffering and struggling with addiction, my personal prayer would be that one day, each and all of the faces I encounter would be re-created and restored in the very image of the living God.

Then the LORD God said, "It is not good that the man should be alone; I will make him a helper as his partner." So out of the ground the LORD God formed every animal of the field and every bird of the air, and brought them to the man to see what he would call them; and whatever the man called every living creature, that was its name. The man gave names to all cattle, and to the birds of the air, and to every animal of the field; but for the man there was not found a helper as his partner. So the LORD God caused a deep sleep to fall upon the man, and he slept; then he took one of his ribs and closed up its place with flesh. And the rib that the LORD God had taken from the man he made into a woman and brought her to the man.

Genesis 2:18-22

I have a friend who is a rabbi. During a conversation about the different ways Christians and Jews approach scripture, he said something that made an impression on me. He said that he was taught to read the accounts in the Bible as stories about God, not as stories about people. How interesting! This made me wonder how often I read the Old and New Testaments to enlighten me about something earthly rather than something heavenly.

The two accounts of creation in the Bible reveal a great deal about the nature of God. First and foremost, we learn that we are not some accident of nature; we have been created with loving intention and artistry. We are formed out of the dust, and the very breath of God rushes into our lungs so we can live. But just as children often have no appreciation of what happened in history before they were born, it is all too easy to focus only on the part of the creation narrative that happens after humans are created.

Who is this God who created us? What can we learn if we look at this passage as being about God rather than being about us? Perhaps the creation stories are more about the Creator than they are about what was created. Consider the possibilities!

September 23

It is clear from the creation stories in Genesis that God creates us with great intention and care. We have not been created accidentally. There is a plan and even a desire for us. Moreover, we are created specifically. Among a host of other creatures who inhabit the air, water and land, we are created as unique companions for God and one another.

All of this contrasts with what we read in Genesis 1. None of the language used in the first creation story communicates a desire for relationship—either with God or with other creatures. In Genesis 1:28, humankind is commanded to reproduce and rule over all other created beings, but the tone in Genesis 2 is much gentler, more personal. After forming man and a whole host of other creatures, God says, "It is not good that the man should be alone." What makes the Creator realize that man is not yet complete? Is it merely about procreation, or is the absence deeper than that? All we know is that there is a need for a companion, and this need is not apparent until well after Adam has been created.

Today, think about the role of companions in your life. "It is not good to be alone." Where has God blessed you with companions? Do you recognize the gifts of their presence and their importance? None of us are created to live apart from one another. Somehow, God knows this and creates—with intention—counterparts to walk alongside us. How marvelous for the Creator to know us so well that our every need is anticipated before we even know it ourselves.

September 24

Naming something helps us make sense of it; this is a way to wrap our minds around it and lay some sort of claim to it…to recognize it. God asks Adam to name the other creations. God does not say to Adam, "This is a fish. This is a horse." He brings them to Adam "to see what he would call them." What does Adam know of anything at this point? It seems to me that it would make more sense for the Creator to name the creations. After all, God forms them and breathes life into them.

In giving Adam this authority, God bestows the same gift of freedom we enjoy. God is always exceedingly generous with us, giving us free will and permission to live our lives without a precise instruction manual. Aside from a relatively small list of commandments in the Bible, much of life is lived by exercising freedom of choice. So where does this leave us?

The answer, I believe, is in companionship. The closer we are to God, the more our lives begin to align with the One who creates us. We are not merely puppets reacting to every pull on our strings. God has given us creative freedom to live. We have the authority to act and dream in the same way Adam does when presented with God's precious creatures. Such trust is utterly humbling.

September 25

I mentioned a few days ago that Genesis 2 emphasizes relationship in a way that Genesis 1 does not. This is particularly noticeable in the passage selected for this week. After creating a host of other creatures to live alongside man, God invites Adam to participate in the act of naming them. In this way, God essentially gives Adam the privilege of becoming a sort of co-creator. God creates the creatures, but Adam helps establish their identities. In doing this, God bestows upon Adam a sense of ownership and responsibility for all the things around him.

All of this happens before there is any sin in the Garden. All Adam knows at this point is that he is called to live in community with everything around him. All things coexist in perfect harmony. Even after the Fall, the call to remain companions and good stewards of creation continues. If we, like a swarm of locusts, were to wholly consume all of creation, nothing would remain for anything or anyone else. Instead, we must always consider how best to use our resources and to balance our consumption with preservation.

As stewards of creation, we have been called to tend, protect, and reproduce—even as we are also called to use and consume. In order to know the right balance, we must consider the relationship we have with all of creation. Just as in the Garden, we remain part of a community of created beings struggling to fulfill our right purpose in the eyes of the Creator.

God grant us the wisdom to know our role in the world and make right use of the gifts we have been given. Amen.

September 26

What do you see in the paintings for this week? The man and the woman are engulfed by light and surrounded by darkness. They appear to be naked, with nothing to protect them or prepare them for what lies beyond. It's also interesting that there are two images; it is not a single painting with the people in the same space. They are separate, alone.

God sees something in Adam's aloneness that sparks the idea for Eve. Somehow Adam isn't complete, so another creation is made to be his companion. But God doesn't create her out of dust as has been done with Adam. Eve is born when God takes part of Adam's body and forms something new out of it. Part of her is Adam, but part of her is brand new. They are alike and yet distinct in their natures.

It is true that there are biological reasons for these two creations. Man and woman are both necessary in order to create new human life. But scripture does not refer to Eve as a biological counterpart for Adam. God creates her as a companion, a helper. There must be more to their relationship than the physical act of procreation, because God certainly has the capability to create more beings, whether Eve exists or not.

Physical intimacy is one way for two human beings to join together, but mere physical acts are not enough to establish true relationship—true intimacy. Something else is needed, and without that we are like two paintings existing side by side...together but alone. I invite you to reflect on the ways you are connected to and also disconnected from the people you encounter. What makes someone a true companion?

September 27

I continue to think about the nature of true companionship. If not only for procreative purposes, what is God's intent in giving Eve to Adam? Consider the text: "…But for the man there was not found a helper as his partner" (Genesis 2:20b). I like this particular translation, because it includes the word partner. Eve is not merely a helper. Adam and Eve are a team.

There is a traditional type of Native American companion planting arrangement known as a "Three Sisters Garden." Corn, beans, and squash are sown together as three interdependent sisters who grow and nourish one another. Corn provides a natural pole for the beans to climb, and the beans, in return, help make the corn sturdier and wind-resistant. Beans also contribute much-needed nitrogen to the soil. Squash leaves are a natural mulch to help preserve soil moisture and discourage the growth of weeds. Each benefits from the others, and none would do as well alone as they do living within their garden community. Are they aware of this dependence on one another? I wonder.

In the garden of my life, it is important to make room for situations, people, and other things that make me better. Some provide nourishment; others offer shelter or comfort. Still others—because of the challenges they bring—prune me and force me to grow as I should. None of this could happen if I lived solely on my own. I could not thrive—or even exist— without the helpers and partners God has provided. I also know that if I am not nourished and fertilized, my life will not produce a suitable harvest. I will be of no use to God, myself, or anyone I may encounter.

May God give all of us the eyes to recognize our true companions and open our lives to them.

September 28

This week we have reflected on the creative nature of God and the necessity of relationship. We considered our role as co-creators with God and our stewardship of all created things. We wondered together about the mysterious interconnectedness we have with others and the importance of having helpers with whom to share our lives.

Rather than adding more thoughts to these vast ideas, I invite you to close this week with a few prayers from *The Book of Common Prayer* (pages 429-430). These words are taken from the The Celebration and Blessing of a Marriage, but they are not only relevant to marital relationships. These words have broader implications for all of our relationships—particularly those built on intimacy and sacred trust. I believe these relationships are the real gift God bestows on creation when giving Adam and Eve as helpers to one another.

Give them wisdom and devotion in the ordering of their common life, that each may be to the other a strength in need, a counselor in perplexity, a comfort in sorrow, and a companion in joy. Amen.

Give them grace, when they hurt each other, to recognize and acknowledge their fault, and to seek each other's forgiveness and yours. Amen.

Make their life together a sign of Christ's love to this sinful and broken world, that unity may overcome estrangement, forgiveness heal guilt, and joy conquer despair. Amen.

Grant that the bonds of our common humanity, by which all your children are united one to another, and the living to the dead, may be so transformed by your grace, that your will may be done on earth as it is in heaven; where, O Father, with your Son, and the Holy Spirit, you live and reign in perfect unity, now and for ever. Amen.

We teach children to help each other—even when they are very young. We do our best to impart compassion by teaching children to help when another falls down, spills something, or is upset. And we teach them to graciously accept help with a "thank you." Being helpful is one of the most important lessons we teach as we prepare children for the world: With a little love, anyone can be a helper, and everyone needs a helper.

Yet as adults we have so much trouble accepting help. We don't want to ask for directions when we've lost our way. We hesitate to seek out someone to talk to when we're struggling. And we have even more trouble accepting that it is okay for us to need help, and it is okay for others to need help.

We live in an independent and individualistic nation: a DIY (do it yourself) society that expects members to check out self-help books to cope with poverty, institutional racism, mental health, and trauma. We expect people to turn to YouTube videos to figure out how to heal after divorce, abandonment, or loss. We live in a society that has not accepted that we all need help.

God does not mean for us to be alone. God doesn't want Adam to be alone in paradise, and God certainly does not want us to be alone. In giving us each other, God has given us earthly support—a spiritual community to lift us up, a family member to confide in, a friend to laugh with, and professional support in times of need. Let us be gracious in giving help and gracious in accepting it.

September 30

As a young girl, I always wanted a sister. My idealized perception of a sister was a friend who would always be around and would paint my nails and braid my hair. Alas, I was stuck with three brothers.

However, God knew what God was doing with my family. God gave me brothers who looked out for me and took me on their adventures to the creek or to our fort in the woods. God provided a brother who taught me to have fun, a brother who taught me to be caring, and another who taught me to be spontaneous. And very, very occasionally as children, these gifts from God even let me paint their fingernails. Just as God gives Adam a companion, my brothers are my lifelong companions, allies, and best friends.

Although I never received a biological sister, God put a lot of extraordinary women in my life: Women I look up to and confide in and who inspire and amaze me every day. I am in admiration of my peers who have committed their lives to standing up for the rights of others, day in and day out. I am grateful for my compassionate mother who taught me to be kind to every stranger in line at the grocery store and for the other motherly figures in my life. I am empowered by my friends who are excelling at their passions in every field from engineering to nursing to accounting. And yes, I even found a friend to braid my hair.

God has always known exactly what kind of companions I need and has painted them all into my life, in God's good time.

October

God Blessed Them

So God created humankind in his image, in the image of God he created them; male and female he created them. God blessed them, and God said to them, "Be fruitful and multiply, and fill the earth and subdue it; and have dominion over the fish of the sea and over the birds of the air and over every living thing that moves upon the earth."

Genesis 1:27-28

Artist's note: Hummingbirds always seem to be on the move, and only recently have I had the opportunity to see one or two at rest. They are fascinating little creatures and they must think we are pretty interesting as well. More than once, I have looked up from my drawing table to see one hovering outside the window just looking at me. It feels like an annunciation or blessing of sorts, and I can't imagine that even Gabriel could be much more beautiful or holy than these beautiful, tiny birds.

Artist's note: The brush rabbits took up residence on my bluff a few years ago. Their arrival coincided with my decision to plant lettuce in my raised beds. I don't need to tell you what happened to my crop, or why I decided to give up on a vegetable garden. But it was an easy decision to make. I can buy lettuce at the farmers' market or grocery store, but I can't buy the joy I feel from watching these little creatures hop or run across the grass before scurrying into the brush.

Pleasant to the Sight and Good for Food

And the Lord God planted a garden in Eden, in the east; and there he put the man whom he had formed. Out of the ground the Lord God made to grow every tree that is pleasant to the sight and good for food, the tree of life also in the midst of the garden, and the tree of the knowledge of good and evil.

Genesis 2:8-9

Artist's note: The tree of knowledge wasn't really an apple tree (pictured on the next page), but I still wanted an image of this creation in the series. I used to have two pet pygmy goats, Artemis and Aphrodite, who lived in a pen outside of my studio. They preferred herbs and flowers to blackberry vines, and they spent most of their time in the pen waiting for dinner. Goats have an uncanny ability to look you right in the eye, as I learned when I would glance out the studio window.

After a few years, they joined a nearby herd where they had lots of room to browse and roam. This left a well-fertilized fenced-in area that was perfect for an apple orchard. Now I follow the seasons with the trees, and the last of the crop has just been harvested—some by me, and some by the raccoons. Fortunately, the fence keeps the black bear out.

> *So God created humankind in his image, in the image of God he created them; male and female he created them. God blessed them, and God said to them, "Be fruitful and multiply, and fill the earth and subdue it; and have dominion over the fish of the sea and over the birds of the air and over every living thing that moves upon the earth."*
>
> **Genesis 1:27-28**

God creates humanity in God's own image. But let us not hear these words as indicating that humankind is special or better than the rest of God's creation —God projects Godself into and on all that is created.

It is true that an aspect of God in Jesus Christ took on human form in an act of love and that may help us understand God. But God is larger than this and seeing God in only human terms makes God smaller and more manageable to our minds.

As a Native American woman, I see God in many ways that are more descriptive of God's attributes. These lead me into deep relationship with God. This approach works until it limits my experience of God in the world. And then, I have to let go of my limited understanding and allow myself to live into the mystery that is God.

October 2

I spent about half my adult life living out a vocational call as a nurse. I still remember the period of study that was to prepare me for this vocation. It included chemistry, physiology, microbiology, and pharmacy. These studies did not prepare me for the wonder that came with caring for the human body. As I cared for people who needed healing, I began to see the miracle of the human body.

I aw the correlation between the teachings of my elders and the reality of human life. This was one of the only times I could hear myself describing the human body in terms of creation. God uses the same four sacred elements to create all of creation—and this includes us. We are earth. Minerals and elements found in our Mother Earth are also in the human body. We are water—about 60 percent actually. We are fire—we have an internal temperature of almost 100 degrees Fahrenheit. And we are air— breathing God's breath in and out to stay alive.

I also began to realize that humanity is made up of physical, mental, emotional, and spiritual attributes. Balancing these is one of the keys to wellness, wholeness, and holiness. I also began to be see that some physical manifestations of illness might stem from an imbalance of one of the other three attributes of our humanity.

The body and its functions really are miracles. Looking on the surface, we might not ever realize just how miraculous our lives are until we are willing to see what makes us tick. Spend some time today thinking about the miracle that is your body.

October 3

Our elders understand, "male and female he created them," in a way that escaped me for years. I heard it, but I did not understand it fully until I was asked to write for the Anglican Communion's Listening Process. In our traditional ways, before I would write and convey a teaching passed down from our ancestors, I would go to my elders to ask their permission. However, in this case, I was not even sure of how I could relate this teaching in a way that might help people listen to each other. I needed to listen to my elders, and I did.

The moment that I finally heard has transformed my spiritual life. I am aware of the limitations that writing and reading present, and I don't want to minimize what I heard, because I hope you can hear it too. It might transform your own reading of this passage.

The key word in this passage is "and." Really. It seems like a simple word but it holds, at least in my perspective, a great truth. I think I have always heard this passage with the word "or" rather than "and," which makes all the difference. God created humanity as *both* male and female! It may seem like a radical idea to consider, but if we back off the politics of what this statement might evoke, I invite you to hear it in the ways we have been taught since the beginning of time.

God created humanity in God's own image. Attributes we might define as male or female can really best be understood when we see them as complementary to each other.

October 4

What is our fruit? If we take the Bible literally, we might think fruitfulness is referring to having children. But is that all God intends for us? I am not saying that children and grandchildren are not important—we know they are very important. But, I have come to understand that a literal interpretation of fruitfulness can limit our knowing and understanding of God in creation. And this understanding leaves a whole segment of our humanity in a virtual no-man's land.

Relationships are formed in many ways—and they are not only biological in nature. Some of our extended family includes others who are not biologically related to us. I have friends who I refer to as "sister from a different mister" or "brother from a different mother." Growing up, I had uncles and aunts I later realized were not blood relatives but were close enough to our families to have been emotionally adopted. They became a part of our family.

How these relationships came to be extensions of our families stems from the fruit we share with each other. This fruit manifests in the form of love. And love—whether romantic or not—is the relational extension of what is within us toward some other being.

The ability to share what is deep within us—maybe even what is most God-like about us—can only be described as our fruit. The love we share between one another is what God wants for all of us.

October 5

Fill the earth? But how? I have this image of a shopping cart, and I imagine myself going around and picking up things to put in the cart. But that is taking, and not filling. In the context of the creation story, filling the earth requires our participation. Does sharing in creation require us to subdue?

This bit about subduing the earth may only be a segment of our passage this week, but it speaks to us in a very particular way. Some read this as evidence that God intends for humans to rule over creation. This perspective—particularly dangerous in some hands—has created destruction rather than cultivating fruitfulness.

How do we reconcile our consumption of resources with being fruitful and multiplying? Once again, I go back to some of the basic teachings from my ancestors. My ancestors did not go to the grocery store or health food store to get what they needed: They went out into creation and gathered it. When they gathered medicines, they didn't harvest from the youngest plants, and they never harvested the last of any plant. Why? My ancestors wanted to ensure that there would always be medicine plants for generations to come. A young plant needed more time to mature and produce seeds for new plants. Taking the last one could mean the end to that medicine plant. My ancestors apply this principle to plants, animals, and birds—every living thing. How might we fill the earth? Maybe the first step is securing future fruitfulness.

October 6

We can learn a great deal about how to live from our relatives, the birds of the air. Birds gather food from insects and plants and the waters, but they also drop seeds and move pollen from one place to another. They have a constant and circular cycle of life.

Perhaps we can take a cue from the hummingbirds, going from blossom to blossom collecting sweetness and taking it with us as we touch every other blossom we encounter. In the process of collecting and sharing sweetness, hummingbirds are not only nourished, but they also spread pollen and contribute to the propagation of fruit and plants.

Stepping back and seeing ourselves in the image and likeness of God is to see ourselves as creators, not destroyers. Seeking an understanding of what it means to be a creative source of life can be as simple as discerning our words and actions as either life-giving or life-taking. Maybe this is our purpose: To give life with our words and actions as much as we are able. Our words and our actions might be the fruitfulness with which God intends to propagate new life.

October 7

Since the beginning of time, my ancestors have been learning to live in relationship with creation. This relationship begins with birth when the attributes of God come together to form a new life.

Our understanding of the biological miracle that occurs when an egg is fertilized and begins to form a human being cell by cell, limbs, organs, and skin, is amazing. But our wonder and awe grows with the recognition that each new being is unique and yet somehow related.

Have you ever had someone tell you that you look like a relative? I have. I didn't pay much attention until I had someone I had never met before tell me that I did something just like my grandmother. That comment stopped me in my tracks. I had never seen my grandmother in the context of ceremony in our village and yet relatives who had lived beside and loved her saw my grandmother in me. My awe was tuned up to a fever pitch.

As Christians, we often say we are made in the image and likeness of God. But how do we understand this statement? Sometimes we say God is all things and cannot be described—but I wonder how true that really is, if images of God surround us in all of creation.

It has taken me a good part of my life to understand what it means to be blessed. At this moment in my life, being blessed means I am able to see God all the time, just by looking around at creation.

*So God created humankind in his image, in the image of God
he created them; male and female he created them. God blessed
them, and God said to them, "Be fruitful and multiply, and fill
the earth and subdue it; and have dominion over the fish of the
sea and over the birds of the air and over every living thing that
moves upon the earth."*

Genesis 1:27-28

There are no commas in Hebrew, no punctuation marks at all. So what
if this phrase, "God blessed them," stood on its own in English? What
if it didn't lead to, "Be fruitful and multiply," as if procreation were the
blessing but rather followed the phrase, "Male and female he created
them," without any further clarification? What if we read it as: "God
created humankind in God's image, and God was pleased." Or, "and God
was thankful." Or, "God said, 'That is good!'"

When we bless God, we give thanks for God's goodness. When we bless
things in God's name, we praise God for them, give thanks for them, and
ask that they may be used by God. When we bless a marriage, we ask that
God will see it as good and use that couple's union to reveal God's love.
When we ask God to bless us, do we ask God to recognize Godself in us, to
be thankful for having created us, and to use us for good in God's world?

What if "God blessed them" means God is pleased, even delighted with
these last creatures, just as with all that came before them: sun, moon, and
stars, grass and mountains, the sea and the birds, dry land and elephants?

What if God dances and sings with exuberant joy for having found a way
to be present within this marvelous creation newly born? What if God
creates us by the love that God is, out of that same love, for love, and in
blessing humans, and simply says, "That is good!"

October 9

If we believe humans are created in God's image, we imply that every person is like God: male and female, American and Indian, weak and strong, powerful and powerless. Within the Creator are innumerable varieties of good, and every human is born expressing some of those aspects of God's holy Love. Only in Jesus, of course, do we believe the fullness of God abides. But God's likeness dwells in each of us.

I came off the plane and felt the hot Indian sun, smelled the spicy air, and noticed the crowds. When I entered the doors of Ashraya, the children's home where I had lived as an infant, I was surrounded by the Aunties and found myself blessed by those women—and thanking God for them. But when we drove into the courtyard of the tiny house where I had been born and my mother's arms suddenly wrapped me up tight, I knew I really was home. It isn't my only home. But it is my first one, if only for a day.

I am indisputably made in my mother's image—my sisters and I all look like her. And she is made in God's image: gentle, welcoming and full of love for her imperfect child. No expression of shame or embarrassment has ever come from her lips or her eyes, only pride in what I am becoming. She looks at me and blesses me. Even in America, where I have another family, have obtained an advanced education, drive an electric wheelchair, and lead a good life, I am still made in her image. I move like her, smile like her. I am her child.

And even if we deny it, we are God's children, too. We are forever made in God's image. Every single one of us.

October 10

Sparkling white dresses with silky ruffles and Victorian lace tower over me—dozens, hundreds of them. The options are endless. Oh, to know what it feels like to twirl around in one of those elegant dresses, to feel the material cascade around my feet. But I can't.

I wish I were a beautiful size three. Those bodies are beautiful. But instead, I feel intimidated. I enter the bridal shop full of anxiety, on the hunt for a bridesmaid dress for my best friend's wedding. I am miserable and feel out of place. My short waist and wide hips, the wheelchair, and my missing limbs all feel ugly.

"We'll find a perfect dress, Minda," my friend says. So I shove down my rising panic and choke back the fear threatening to strangle me. The sales consultant is kind. This helps ease my anxiety a bit. Pushy people make me even more nervous. We look through racks of dresses and finally settle on three I like.

The next part I hate. I suppress a groan. I am so shy about needing help to try on clothes. But this is the only way I can find out what fits. So I sigh and press forward, reminding myself of who I am, remembering the God in whose image I am created.

Miraculously, the very first dress looks beautiful—makes me beautiful! I am stunned. Delighted. Grateful. With a heart full of joy, I order the lace-covered silk in Sarah's wedding color.

If we are made in God's image, if we have been blessed to be human, then "tall, thin, and blonde," will never be enough of a definition of beauty. Thank God—because I am none of those. Instead, I reveal something different about God's beautiful self, and I bless God for that privilege.

October 11

God creates humans male and female, both in God's image and likeness. Sure, for creation to continue into another generation, toads and antelopes have to reproduce. Humans, too. It's God's method of making more self-images. But this capacity to reproduce represents only a small part of what it means to be human.

Grandpa had beautiful hands, and he made beautiful things with them: award-winning photographs, violins, delicious bread, and lace for my mom's baby clothes. He loved music, and he understood it; he read voraciously and didn't forget what he had read. He could teach anybody anything. He loved math, history, and science. I survived my college algebra and meteorology classes because of his patient tutoring. But he also played dress-up with my young niece. He roasted marshmallows for us and planted seven kinds of sweet potatoes to see which would grow best. He loved this world. What he did reflected who he was; God blessed him, and God said, "That is good!"

Grandmother Marian was a physician, but she has been retired a long time. As she aged, and without complaining, she slowly cut back on work, then gave up her house, and calmly moved into a care center. Eventually she sold her car. Now she doesn't manage long walks alone, either. She knows how to let go, welcoming each change in her life as a gift from the God she trusts. Grandmother Marian prays, loves, still bakes her famous oatmeal raisin cookies, sends notes of encouragement or challenge, and is one of the best listeners I know. Her wisdom has been a gift to me, ever since I was a very little girl—and before that, it was a gift to my mother and to so many other young women. When God created this woman, God breathed, "She is like me!" and said, "That is good!"

October 12

In J.R.R. Tolkien's masterpiece *Lord of the Rings*, death is the gift of the Valar to humans. The race of elves (who do not die) remain bound to the "circles of the world" forever. Death is a blessing. Death is freedom to return to God who created us, the One to whom we belong.

During her last few days of life, I sat by Judy's bed stroking her soft hair, touching her motionless hand, gazing into her beautiful eyes, and listening to her quiet breathing. Again and again I thanked her for her encouragement, for her love, for her friendship despite the difference in our ages. She blessed me with her life. I thanked God for having created Judy, even as she died. She knew her friends were there, was aware of what we murmured, but she was also increasingly withdrawn from participation in this world as she relaxed fearlessly into the next.

She had loved beauty, cultivated gardens and friendships, laughed a lot, mentored young teachers, raised her daughters, loved her husband, and cherished her dogs. How is it possible for such a light to simply extinguish? Was there a moment when God quit blessing her? Did she stop being "God's image?"

This is one of the biggest questions, isn't it: What is the place of death in creation? Where is the blessing in dying? Tolkien, a devout Roman Catholic, suggested in his epic novel that humans are allowed to die, to return to their Creator, where "more than memory" awaits them.

Of course, that is also what the resurrection of Jesus shows us about our own creation: In Christ we are a "new creation" (2 Corinthians 5:17) that, with Jesus, can go into death and yet live forever.

October 13

When I lived in Botswana, the country was already beginning to experience longer dry seasons. People were noticeably concerned about the dropping water level in the Gaborone Dam. My mother visited the following year, and the situation had deteriorated even further.

As global temperatures rise, drought increases all across already dry countries and crops fail, putting even more pressure on precarious ecosystems.

At the other end of the world, Indigenous people in Alaska and farther north in the Canadian Arctic find their winters too short and too warm as the ice melts earlier and earlier. Ocean levels rise, forcing villages to disband communities and abandon ancestral hunting grounds to move farther inland.

The people of our creative God fail to bless God when we think only of ourselves, and not of our future, or when we submit to our selfish demands for goods and services at the expense of other people, animals, and the earth itself.

Is this what God means when God says for us to rule over "every living creature?" How does God intend for us to "have dominion" over this place? God's sovereignty is demonstrated in creation by pouring out love, which became tree frogs and oceans and human beings. It is how God created the world—by blessing all of creation by rejoicing in every single aspect of it. I believe this is what God intends for us to do, too—to cherish every tiny ant, precious little cricket, gorilla, and giant whale whose names are known to God. We have the creative privilege of thanking God for creation, for preserving it, and for protecting "our island home." This is how we receive our blessing.

October 14

In the text of Genesis 1 and 2, the earth is new, empty and waiting to be filled. But fill is an interesting command. Most of us don't dump just any old thing into a crate, simply to fill a crate. We fill our cups with coffee, not shampoo, after all! God wanted humans. Don't you wonder why?

What if we took this idea of filling seriously and understood that we have been asked to co-create with God, tending an ever-green garden, caring for water and air, bamboo, redwoods, and broccoli? What if we imagined our responsibility to be fruitful and multiply as giving birth to children who will take up this vocation to live in God's image as we age and die and return to God?

Perhaps our deepest privilege as humans is to accept this image, to acknowledge our dignity and to enjoy the privilege of bearing God's likeness into the world, delighting in God and each other.

What might happen if we dared for just a moment to see ourselves as mirror images of God's goodness, even if our vision is often distorted?

What if humankind responded to God's urgent hunger for justice and peace on earth and made it a priority to subdue human selfishness, in ourselves and in the systems we create?

What if God really has blessed humankind, male and female, and set us here to be God's presence in the world?

What if this is the truth?

October 15

This week's author
Greg Rickel

*And the Lord God planted a garden in Eden, in the east; and
there he put the man whom he had formed. Out of the ground
the Lord God made to grow every tree that is pleasant to the
sight and good for food, the tree of life also in the midst of the
garden, and the tree of the knowledge of good and evil.*

Genesis 2:8-9

I remember the first garden I really knew as a garden. I was about five
and visiting my grandfather in southern Missouri. He was a carpenter
by trade and a great gardener on the side. He asked me if I wanted to go
with him to harvest some turnips. I could not wait.

We walked along the rows, pulling turnips from the earth—and each
one was like a new surprise. I giggled every time. My grandfather let me
shake the dirt from the roots and throw them in the sack he had slung
around his neck. As we walked back to the house to wash the turnips, I
asked if I could taste one. He had a mischievous grin on his face when he
blurted out, "Of course, as soon as we get back and clean them up!" After
we cleaned them, he handed me a turnip and said, "Okay, have at it."

I bit into that turnip and a big smile came over my face...and then I took
another bite, and another. Then I looked at my grandfather and asked,
"Can I have another turnip?" "Of course," he said, as his face changed. He
could not believe it. He actually told my mother, "You have a weird son.
He loves turnips straight out of the ground!" It is strange, but to this day I
still love raw turnips.

I treasure the experiences and memories of the turnip. Had I simply
taken one from the produce section at the grocery store and tried it,
my love of turnips would be different. When I bite into one today, I
remember vividly that day with my grandfather and the earth and the
surprise I was gifted. Not much in this world could ever taste as good.

October 16

The garden comes first, not us. I think it is very important for us to remember this fact when we contemplate this earth, this garden provided for us by God. Humans come second.

Often, we see the creation story in a way that suggests the garden was made for us, rather than us being made for the garden. This subtle but profound twist has changed the course of our earth and our history in ways that are beyond reckoning.

God wants help in caring for the garden—and that is our role, to be caretakers and stewards of it. If we see the garden as having been made for us, it becomes quite easy to exploit it, use it up, and to see it merely as a resource and not as a gift and a legacy. If we see ourselves as creatures made for the service of the garden, that perception changes things. We become visitors, not rulers.

There is a huge risk in seeing ourselves as completely unattached, disconnected from nature, as though we are merely walking through it and not in a part of it. Luther Standing Bear, member of the Oglala Sioux Nation, once said, "The Old Lakota was wise. He knew that man's heart away from nature becomes hard."

Spend today contemplating the garden—this first-created earth and us late-to-the-party human beings created for the garden—and not the other way around. What does it mean for you to be created as a companion and conservator of the garden?

October 17

I am one of those folks who loves to fly. This is an interest my wife and I do not share. She is a true white-knuckle flyer. I am not sure why I like flying so much, but leaving the earth for a bit and flying over it, seeing it from a different angle and perspective is an exhilarating experience for me every time.

It doesn't matter if I am on a 747 jumbo jet or a tiny Cessna, a floatplane, or a hot air balloon, I love flying. But I have to say, perhaps even as much as the flying itself, I love the joyful and comforting feeling of touching down. Like other ethereal experiences, when I come back down to earth, I have a greater appreciation for the ground—the solidity of the earth, the touch of my feet on the ground I am designed and created to walk upon.

Theologians have used the ground as a metaphor for God, the ground of all being. I used to view my prayer time as a metaphor of flight in this way. I would say the flying part was when I was closest to God. The landing, or coming back to the ground, was when I came back down to plain old ordinary life. Over the years, this understanding has shifted. I sense that praying, for me, is exactly the opposite. The flying part is life and coming back to the ground is finding closeness to God, the present realities of the soil and water and beasts of the field. I love to fly, but the ground—home—is where I am closest to God.

October 18

I am going to state the obvious, a cliché almost: Pain often accompanies growth. In fact, I am not sure any of us can truly grow without a bit of discomfort or downright hurting.

When we grow, we almost always give up something; an old belief, a long-held comforting thought, or a relationship. Maybe we gave up something that was not good for us, but we grieve the loss nonetheless. Sometimes these bereavements are fleeting, momentary, the blink of an eye—but sometimes they last a lifetime. We are not often wise enough—or able enough—to see these losses as blessings. And yet, I have to wonder: Just like plants and trees must be pruned in order to produce fruit and thrive, so must we. We sacrifice love and limb so that we may grow healthy and abundant lives.

Our world spends a lot of time and energy running from this universal truth of the precious ache of growth and the ministry of loss. In fact, much of our life is consumed with trying to make a way where pruning is no longer necessary, where life can be enriched without sorrow or loss or discomfort. This is an understandable desire—and a futile one. Perhaps today we might think about one way we have been pruned and choose to see this as a blessing, giving thanksgiving for the growth that came because of loss.

October 19

I have to admit it: I am a foodie. I plan vacations, layovers, and most of my travels by what culinary adventure I might encounter. Some see food as fuel and others see food as an experience. Put another way: Some eat to live and others live to eat.

The reality is that most people in this world have to eat to live, and must think about it on a minute-by-minute basis because there is so little food and the distribution system is so tragically dysfunctional. The luxury of food so many of us have in the United States should be a basic right for all people in this world.

In fact, there is a wide-ranging debate about food as fuel and how very simplistic this notion is. Some research over the last few years has shown that being social while we eat actually changes how our bodies use the food. An important part of a meal is not just the food itself, but all that is going on around us as we take it in.

Everything we eat has a story. Be prayerful about all you eat today. Be thankful you have food when so many do not. Give thanks for the earth that produced your food, the hands that cared for and nourished it, the precious child of God who placed it before you, and for the living and loving God who created it.

October 20

In my bedroom, placed right where I can see it first thing every morning, is a giant embroidered wall canvas of a tree. This lovely piece of textile artwork comes from Africa. When I first saw it several years ago, I felt like I was looking at the vision I have when I hear or read about the Tree of Life in the Garden of Eden. The canvas is almost covered by a huge tree, with lots of shady branches, giving you the feeling that the tree is old, majestic, and wise.

In the Garden of Eden, we see that there is every tree—those for food and those for other things. One of these trees is the Tree of Life. Much has been written and suggested about this growing thing in the Garden. I find it interesting and good that there is only one Tree of Life in the Garden, not multiple Trees of Life.

For me, this means that life comes from a single source. In this present garden we live in, we all must work together to nourish it. When we water it, we care for everyone. When we till it, we work on behalf of everything that has breath. When we prune branches and vines, we are careful, thoughtful, and hopeful for the growth that tender work will provide.

The Tree of Life represents not just our life, but all lives—everyone and everything that lives and moves and has being. We humans have been placed in this garden, this garden we all share, to care for this tree. Contemplate today how you will do that.

October 21

Good and evil are real concepts. I believe we would not know good unless we also knew evil. I have to think God understands this about us too.

The idea that good and evil are actually part of one single tree in the Garden is a wise metaphor indeed. Good and evil exist together in one tree, not separate trees or separate ideas. And I believe that is how they coexist in reality.

The roots of good and evil are bound together, nourished in the same soil, and part of the same living thing. Good and evil are not separate but forever and always connected, entwined, enmeshed with one another inside your heart and mine. Good and evil are in me, and you, and all things.

We can't really live as if evil is somewhere outside of ourselves. Evil is everywhere and in us. But good is too. Our work in the Garden is to discern the difference, to work to build up the good and keep the evil in check. But, since we have only this one tree, we will never fully eradicate the evil without also eradicating the good. This is inconvenient, to say the very least, and deeply troubling even on our best days, and this is also the reality of our human existence on this side of Eden. Today, practice seeing both good and evil in yourself and see yourself holding them both. Then visualize which fruit of this tree you will consume and which you will leave.

And the Lord God planted a garden in Eden, in the east; and there he put the man whom he had formed. Out of the ground the Lord God made to grow every tree that is pleasant to the sight and good for food, the tree of life also in the midst of the garden, and the tree of the knowledge of good and evil.

Genesis 2:8-9

The first principle of being a spiritual ecologist is recognizing that we are each a part of a mysterious whole. We are part of nature, not separate from her. We are God's creation. This means we are not measured by our output, the schools we've attended, the jobs we've had, or the money we earn. How we conduct our lives is important; but if we measure our lives by the things of economic value alone, we fail to see how God has designed creation.

One of the practices that helps me remember that I am part of nature happened by accident. In the mornings, I like to meticulously prepare Assam black tea with fresh milk. Once prepared, I walk barefoot out in my garden—good thing I live in California and not Alaska!

Holding a mug full of hot tea means I can't water plants or do much of anything except walk and make a mental to-do list of chores. Over time, I've become less interested in creating a task list and being productive during my morning teatime and more compelled to simply notice what is happening in the garden.

I notice the sun's path changing each week around the equinoxes. I notice the worms diving into the soil, making minute tunnels for water absorption. The colors vary in the leaves of my golden raspberries and fall off completely in the winter. The citrusy white buds on the Meyer lemon tree demand a good sniff. This daily practice has become a meditation more than anything else—a walk of praise. I behold life and decay, death and rebirth, and sometimes I see all of it at the same time. And this reminds me that I too am part of the garden.

October 23

Resurrection is a biological fact. Dead matter is constantly being transformed into something that is alive. Think of a compost bin. Leftover carrot tops tossed into the compost bin would never grow if thrown out into the yard. But when we work with the cycle of nature and add them into a healthy compost pile with other tops and tails and yard waste, the intricate, elegant, and unseen microbes and fungi do their work to enliven dead matter, turning it into soil so rich it brings fertility to wherever it's placed.

One summer afternoon I took my boys on a bike ride up Mount Tamalpias, a spot close to our home. For my fourteen-year-old, it's a challenge to ride a bike up a 2,500 foot slope, but it looked overwhelming to his ten-year-old brother. My younger son wasn't five minutes into the ride before he threw down his bike in tears, refusing to continue. His older brother was making the ride look effortless (even though it wasn't), and this didn't help matters.

I decided to tell my younger son a story about my own discouragement, about the time I walked off the track during a race because I was afraid I couldn't finish. As I told my younger son this story, we mounted our bikes and started riding together. I took my time with the details, and by the end of the story we were halfway up the mountain. We stopped to take a drink in the shade. We were sweaty, but renewed confidence welled up in the air. We knew we would all make it to the top.

I have always viewed my track failure with regret and embarrassment—something to be ashamed of. But on this day, my discouraged moment served as a chance to provide encouragement, helping to reveal that even folks who may look older and stronger can also feel overwhelmed by challenges. A point in my life I thought of as shameful helped my son discover his own courage. When nature farms, she recycles everything: Nothing is ever wasted. This seems almost as miraculous and mercy-filled as Jesus' resurrection. And maybe it is.

October 24

We have owned a half-acre of flat, sunny land in Marin County, California for more than twenty years. We purchased the property from the original owners who were horticulturists. They had planted Hachiya persimmon, Gravenstein apple, and French plum trees. There were shrubs too: pink and white camellias, white rhododendrons, and yards of deep green boxwood. My favorite flower, the lavender colored, richly scented lilac, blooms each year—a gift for my March birthday.

Over the years, I grew a half-ton of fruits and vegetables on that land. I gratefully gathered the fruits from those ancient trees and six varieties of tomatoes—and harvested 400 pounds for eating, canning, and giving away. I grew herbs, flowers, and grains. I also raised some hilarious chickens. They would come clucking and running to the gate each time they saw me coming with compost in hand. This land generously fed me and my family, year after year—it nourished us on so many levels.

There is not one inch of soil that I haven't touched and known. Perhaps I should thank the hated, deep-rooted, and plentiful bindweed that drew my time and attention to the soil. Tearing into the flesh of my hands if I wasn't wearing gloves, it took me nearly a decade of weeding to learn that the more I disturbed the bindweed, the fiercer it became.

Returning to our property for the first time in over a year, I bent down and instinctively pulled a dandelion out by its roots. On this hot July day, the earth was cool a few inches down below the top layer of soil. I ran my hand along the warm, dry, familiar surface down to the coolness below. The experience felt so similar to touching the body of a lover, of someone you know inch by inch, freckle by freckle. There was recognition and the feeling of presence: a non-verbal relationship where my hand was wanted, needed, and appreciated.

It's not surprising that when a Roman Catholic priest was asked about God's presence in the world he exclaimed, "That wheat field over there, that is the Body of Christ."

October 25

A piece of land changed my life.

Years ago, I noticed a plot of land that had old greenhouses with broken glass and ancient fruit trees that hadn't been cared for or pruned. An old wooden sign with white lettering announced that this place had once been a plant nursery. The language of the land spoke to my heart, compelling me to stop gazing and take action.

I began to walk around old paths through the property, around dilapidated buildings and rusted-out equipment. I visualized an educational farm school and spoke to people in my community about this idea. People were not only receptive—they wanted to help! I spent two years with many companions by my side, joyfully working to bring it to life.

Intensive pesticides had been used to grow flowers in the old greenhouses and contaminated the soil. I was astounded to learn that soil, even when it's been polluted for decades, can heal itself. The process is called bioremediation. Brassicas—mustard greens and cabbages and other cruciferous vegetables—break down hazardous substances and clean up soil. They are also called bioaccumulators. These wonder plants can literally draw the toxins out of the soil and incorporate them into their bodies. These plants then can be composted and turned into the soil for future fertility. Our soil expert figured it would take us about two years to clean up the soil, naturally, and with little cost involved.

Tragically, a real estate developer I had consulted for advice purchased the property out from under us. After the sale, the contaminated soil in the greenhouses was shipped to another community and labeled toxic waste. It wasn't just me who had been betrayed or the people working alongside me. The developer betrayed the soil itself. Yet Judas' betrayal of Jesus is essential to Jesus' story and to the fulfillment of his vocation.

Thanks be to God.

October 26

Nature is resilient in spite of physical abuse and pollution. The capability of self-restoration or regeneration is inherent in many natural processes. My love of the land persisted even when my heart was broken by the unexpected real estate betrayal at the old plant nursery. After the sale of the property, I began to study sustainable agriculture at a local junior college. I went on a pilgrimage to England where they have been growing food for far longer than we have. A new vision began slowly healing my devastated heart, extracting the pain and uniting me with my deepest calling.

I began to see the connection between what we grow in our fields and what we place on our altars—bread and wine—as being integral and intimate. How we treat the land and how we grow food is made manifest in our sacraments. The idea of bread being life-giving and calling Jesus the bread of heaven was no longer a theological maxim but a biological truth. Organically growing old heirloom grains, stone milling it, and delivering it to churches to be baked into communion bread is a coherent reflection of what Jesus intends when he calls himself the bread of life and asks us to remember him. Contrast this to grain grown with pesticides, then systematically over-processed and sold with the single purpose of profit.

Soil—the dust and dirt from which we are made—is more potent than we can ever imagine. Allowing the land to love us and working to become more skillful in understanding her ways are the most ancient of spiritual practices. The soil has the power to bioremediate almost anything, if we let her. My farming professor once shared, "A compost pile can transform anything. Heck, I've even composted old leather boots!"

October 27

I love Fuyu persimmons but they're only in season for a few short weeks every year, so they aren't viable as a commercial crop. We only enjoy them because small farmers take the time to grow them and bring them to the farmers' market. I start to look forward to them just before Thanksgiving. Once they arrive, I buy them by the dozen. Their cheerful orange orbs stand in contrast to the days that are gray and short.

I remember fondly when cherished friends unexpectedly showed up at our front door with Girl Scout cookies. Seeing our surprised faces, they held out the Thin Mints and blurted out, "Cookies for our new neighbors!" Our friends had quietly purchased the house next door to us and had gone through escrow and the whole works without saying a thing to us.

Between our two families, there were six children—my daughter and two younger brothers and our friends' three boys. Their ages matched up almost identically and our street became an idyllic paradise. The children went to school together, played sports together, and teased each other like siblings. We took care of each other's dogs, car-pooled, texted back and forth, and warmed up hot dogs while drinking Chardonnay together.

One day our friends needed to move back to their family on the East Coast. Our sweet season of living next door to each other ended with a thud. What followed was a season of loss and tears. Like the presence of the Fuyus in November, our time together was a juicy, sweet season. When I bring it to mind, deep gratitude wells up.

Fruits and vegetables without season—the kind that are ever-present in our grocery stores—betray the underlying pattern of nature and life. We take for granted their perennial presence, diminished color and flavor as we eat strawberries and tomatoes in January. This robs us of savoring the brief season of ripeness we have right now—be it a ripe orange Fuyu at Thanksgiving or the presence of a dear and trusted friend.

October 28

I'm not exactly sure when I first started saying thank you to my plants and flowers, but I know it was near the hydrangeas. We inherited an ancient grove of these lovely flowers, and there are almost a dozen plants ranging from deep purple to pink to white. The pink ones are a very old variety called Ayesha. From a distance, they look like a dense version of a traditional hydrangea. Up close, what looks like a single petal is really a complete miniature hydrangea with four petals tightly cupped in a circle; like a hologram, the pattern of each tiny flower looks like the whole when taken together.

Hydrangeas make the most wonderful cut flower. Their thick stems act like soda straws and keep the flower hydrated when placed in water after they've been cut. They are generous in size—a single flower is enough for an entire centerpiece.

More than a dozen years ago, I remember standing in my hydrangea grove, shaded from the heat of the summer sun, surrounded by the grandeur of color and gentle fragrance. It was here that a thank you popped out of my mouth without forethought, after I cut a stem.

Now, even after years of picking Gravenstein apples, pink Mortgage Lifter tomatoes, or Italian parsley, the same words of gratitude emerge. I don't go out to the garden thinking to myself, "I will say thank you to my plants," like a child who is reminded to thank guests for their birthday presents. It's not like that between my garden and me. Thank you is a natural upwelling of my gratitude, as natural as the growth of the blossoms and plants themselves. Mother Nature knows how to restore us to our natural state of gratitude by lavishing us with gifts of color and fragrance and taste and wonder.

October 29

This week's author
Rachel Jones

And the Lord God planted a garden in Eden, in the east; and there he put the man whom he had formed. Out of the ground the Lord God made to grow every tree that is pleasant to the sight and good for food, the tree of life also in the midst of the garden, and the tree of the knowledge of good and evil.

Genesis 2:8-9

The first summer in our garden was magic. I felt like I walked into a brand new world every time I crossed the threshold of the gate. Truth be told, if I could have made a way to be home and outside for most of every single day of the summer, I would have. Just to stand between the rows and smell the perfume of the soil, to hear the birds singing in the hay meadows, to feel the sun beat down on the sunflowers and my own eager, upturned face was enough to bring happy tears every single day.

There were no meals tastier than the ones that included zucchini, carrots, onions, turnips, greens, tomatoes, and peppers from our garden. Even though we struck out with corn and cabbages, we learned about the soil under our feet and nails, discovered where certain plants were happiest, and saw the rise and fall of the seasons.

The chickens have had their way with the last dribs and drabs and dregs in the garden—tilling and fertilizing for the fall on our behalf. In a few short weeks, there will likely be some snow on the ground. The light has already become noticeably shorter. Our seed catalogue will arrive soon, and my beloved and I will start planning and planting seeds for spring. But first, we'll go over our lists of what grew well and what languished, what we enjoyed and what we did not. And we'll talk about what all we wish we had more of, what we'd like to have more of to can and store, what we would do just as well to purchase at the store, all that kind of business. But in the meantime, we'll relish the memories of squash blossoms, tomato soup, and all the blooming things that are beautiful and delicious.

October 30

My pie pumpkins came in a bit ago. I roasted the flesh, toasted the seeds, and set about making my own pumpkin puree for Thanksgiving and Christmas baking. I've already made a loaf of our family's favorite pumpkin bread. But for the life of me, I can't make it taste like my Grammy's. I've run into this same issue when I make my Aunt Lu's piecrust. I follow the recipe to the letter, and it sure looks pretty. And the folks I've shared the bread and pie with have assured me that they are delicious. But they don't taste right to me. I've tried everything— switching out my baking soda and powder, freezing my butter, using lard, trying milk instead of water, putting everything in the freezer, leaving everything on the counter to reach room temperature. You name it, I've tried it. And I've missed the mark every time.

I imagine there might be some alchemical magic in my grandmother's mixing bowls and wooden spoons. I'm all but convinced that Aunt Lu's hands were entirely magic, because not only did she make the most amazing piecrusts ever, she could also cut her own dress patterns out of newsprint. Then again, I'm reminded that we aren't masters of an activity until we've sunk at least 10,000 hours into practicing. I imagine Grammy and Aunt Lu's hour counters are pretty close to that 10,000-hour mark in the piecrust and pumpkin bread departments.

I remember family dinners—usually on Thanksgiving or Christmas—when pies and fruit breads and all manner of baked goods were in high supply. My brother only had eyes for Aunt Lu's pie. He still maintains Aunt Lu made the greatest pies of all time because she made them with so much love.

I have a lot of practicing to do—mixing, making, loving, and baking.

October 31

I think my mom, grandmother, and fiancé thought I was having a total break with reality when I told them I didn't want to order any decorations to go on our wedding cake.

You mean you just want a plain cake? Are you sure? Aren't you worried it's going to look kind of...well, boring?

I didn't want sugar flowers on this cake. I wanted real flowers, the kind you can eat. I had a plan.

On the night before my wedding, I ran down the main aisle of a slightly fancier-than-normal grocery store like my hair was on fire. I finally found the aisle I mentally named Strange Herbs and Fancy Edible Decorations. I found packages of pansies, marigolds, and some blue and pink borage and had to force myself not to dance all the way back to the register. I had to bite my lips to keep from singing out loud: Tomorrow is my wedding day, and we are going to live happily ever after!

I arrived back at the kitchen where we were prepping the cake and other items. My mother and Aunt Nea were curious to see what I had found at the grocery store and still pretty skeptical about my crazy plan for decorating my own wedding cake. But there we stood for the next twenty minutes, sniffing and giggling and crying happy tears while we scattered edible flowers all over the top of my cake, just like I wanted. They agreed, along with my grandmother, that it was prettier this way than sugar flowers. Pleasant to the sight and good for food, indeed.

November

The Face of All the Earth

God said, "See, I have given you every plant yielding seed that is upon the face of all the earth, and every tree with seed in its fruit; you shall have them for food. And to every beast of the earth, and to every bird of the air, and to everything that creeps on the earth, everything that has the breath of life, I have given every green plant for food." And it was so.

Genesis 1:29-30

Artist's note: Many of the animals I find to be so beautiful also eat my garden. It's challenging to not focus on this, even though the deer love my lettuce, sugar snap peas, and roses! I'm glad they feel comfortable enough to spend time in such close proximity to the house. They capture a moment better than just about any other animal, (except perhaps a brush rabbit). They freeze and stand perfectly still when they become aware of someone watching. The deer look right at you, and that momentary connection is worth all the roses they eat. Then they bound away weightlessly and disappear into the forest, breaking the spell.

Artist's note: I've never seen a bear in my yard, but I know they've been there. I've heard commotion at night and in the morning will discover that a bear has walked through my fence. Yes, walked right through it as if it weren't even there. Or a bear has decided to get a few apples off the tree, and pretty much takes the tree down in the process. Bears are powerful and opportunistic. It's remarkable that such a large, lumbering animal can be so elusive and mysterious.

Indeed It Was Very Good

God saw everything that he had made, and indeed, it was very good. And there was evening and there was morning, the sixth day.

Genesis 1:31

Artist's note: I have only seen a cougar (pictured on the next page) once. It was late at night and I was already asleep when my husband came and woke me up. We looked out our second story window and saw a very large mountain lion—about 160 pounds—lying just outside the gate of our goat pen. He looked like a huge house cat, lying there grooming himself before he roused up and lumbered off into the darkness. After I went back to bed and started to doze off, I woke in a start, wondering if that had really just happened.

**November 1**

This week's author
Miriam Willard McKenney

God said, "See, I have given you every plant yielding seed that is upon the face of all the earth, and every tree with seed in its fruit; you shall have them for food. And to every beast of the earth, and to every bird of the air, and to everything that creeps on the earth, everything that has the breath of life, I have given every green plant for food." And it was so.

Genesis 1:29-30

Visiting Portland, I had a few hours' break from my conference, so I sought a place to walk. That's how I found the Hoyt Arboretum, which was founded in 1928 to conserve endangered tree species. The Hoyt Arboretum not only provided a beautiful place to walk, but it is also a tree museum. You can walk on a trail and see twenty different kinds of trees. I saw trees I had never seen before and may never see again. Until I sought a place to walk, I'd never heard of the Hoyt Arboretum.

How many people, items, or wonders of creation do we come across in our lives because we need to run across them, and how many times do we find those things because we want to find them? How many more everyday miracles do we find through sheer happenstance? God opens us to receive bounty when we are ready, because God is always ready.

Before I visited the Hoyt, I never considered the beauty of the bark of the black cherry tree. Now, the fact that I can close my eyes and see it means I have gone deeper into my connection and communion with God's creation.

November 2

When we moved to Cincinnati for my dad's first job as rector of a parish, my parents chose a house on a quiet street that fulfilled my mom's main requirement: room for a garden. After a few years, she decided to plant three fruit trees. My brothers and I were skeptical, but sure enough, after a couple of years we had green apples and peaches growing in our backyard. Mom would have us pick apples for her to fry. She made applesauce and jam. And the neighborhood animals enjoyed the overripe fruit that fell from the trees.

When we are children, we sometimes think things will forever stay the way we see them through our childhood eyes. I thought we would always have those trees. After I went to college, the trees became sick, and my dad had them cut down. I came home several times before I realized they were gone.

These trees, and the memories they evoke, remind me that God provides all we need, and always when we need it. My parents may have decided to plant those trees and to remove them—but God always has a hand in our hearts, when we let God in. When you cut a tree down, plant two in its place. Contribute to organizations committed to reforestation. Where the Spirit calls you to help creation, your heart and hands should always follow.

November 3

One day I was walking one of my favorite trails, one that traverses up and down hilly woodland, and I was on a downhill portion headed toward a creek. As I nonchalantly—and not very quietly—made my way around a bend along a dry streambed, I heard a loud crashing sound. I glanced to my right and saw a huge whitetail buck. I did not stop to count his points—I took off running, only going slowly enough to not fall down the steep hill. I didn't look back.

Later, when someone asked me why I ran, I explained, "I'm in that deer's house. I'm a visitor. I don't want to wear out my welcome." I realized that I hadn't been respectful of the woods and the creatures who make their home there.

As we carve out the paths in our life, are we respectful of others around us—including animals? Do we think of the earth as ours, or are we caretakers of this beautiful place? Does the earth provide for us, or do we provide for it—or both?

In my mind, that buck couldn't imagine what I had to teach or offer him. But he certainly had plenty to teach me. That buck's gift to me was to remember my place in God's creation: to be of it and in it, but not to overtake it.

Now, when I hike, I'm much more quiet. I know whose house I'm in, and I don't want to be an unwelcome guest.

November 4

Bird watching for me is like watching a soap opera—each character has a part to play in a perpetually unfolding saga. Today I watched a bird fly haltingly to an unseen nest with a huge stalk of ornamental grass in its beak. Another bird bobbed up and down on a stalk of the same grass until it bent so far he fell off, like a one-bird seesaw. I couldn't help but smile as he bounced higher and higher, and then tumbled to the ground. He flew up and around and landed on the same stalk and did it again. Then, his playtime spent, he picked up a fallen stalk and carried it to the nest.

The little bird created his own fun while he attended to the job at hand. He enjoyed God's creation and used it in his own joy-filled way. The same thing that created a nest gave the bird a fun experience. I pray that God will call each of us to the same joyful work and play today.

By the time I stopped watching my little friend, four more birds were playing in the grass.

November 5

Daaaad, there's a spider. Come get it!

Oh no, there are ants in the kitchen again!

It's acceptable for us to appreciate rabbits but not moles. We love bees, but not flies. I'll post a cute cat video, but please get those raccoons out of my yard. We pick and choose which creatures we like and which ones are pests or unattractive inconveniences. What does God think about that, I wonder?

God has created everything that creeps on the earth, and God makes sure they all have food to eat. This proves that God cares about all of God's creation, even the scorpions and lantern fish. Beauty is in the eye of the beholder—and in the eye of the Creator we are each and all beheld as beautiful.

As I spend more and more time in nature, I commit myself to caring for all of God's creatures, even the ones I don't appreciate or understand. God wants us to care for all of creation, not just the parts we think are worthy or nice or useful to us personally. Imagine the consequences of our society if we decided that some of us were worth taking care of, and some of us weren't.

> *Q. What does it mean to be created in the image of God?*
> *A. It means that we are free to make choices: to love, to create,*
> *to reason, and to live in harmony with creation and with*
> *God.*
> **The Book of Common Prayer**

November 6

The Ugly Food Movement has blossomed in response to the widening understanding of food waste generated by supermarkets and restaurants. An extra root on a carrot or a misshapen apple doesn't make them inedible, but thousands of pounds of food are wasted each day because they're not magazine-cover perfect in appearance. Thankfully, more and more attention has been brought to this problem, particularly the need to connect food waste with organizations that feed the poor.

God has brought us into being and promised us food. The thing is, God makes that promise by putting us in charge of cultivating and caring for the land. God has given us the intelligence and the propensity to grow and share food. I don't think that some of the food usage and farming practices we employ now are what God has in mind for how we should treat the food the earth offers us in exchange for our sweat and effort. But I believe that God believes in us, in our ability to do better by this garden and each other. God has made us in love, and for love, and that love lives in and animates us as we accept our God-given role in the work of creation. Part of the work, however we choose to do it, is making sure all living creatures have access to nutritious food.

For a blessing upon all human labor, and for the right use
of the riches of creation, that the world may be freed from
poverty, famine, and disaster, we pray to you, O Lord.
The Book of Common Prayer

November 7

My daughters had an amazing Montessori teacher during their preschool and kindergarten years. Of the many, many lessons they learned from her, one continues to permeate our lives: *Make it better—or more beautiful—than when you found it.* Whether it's their desk or the playground at the end of recess, the cafeteria table, or the trail around the harbor, make it more beautiful than when you found it.

Ms. Margaret constantly demonstrated her understanding that everything is connected. She introduced the girls to animals, plants, planets—and helped them understand the ways we are all connected to those things. And always, she would remind them that *we must make it better than when we found it.*

When I contemplate my life, I often wonder what legacy I'll leave behind. But the more connected to nature I become, the less I worry about my individual legacy and focus more on my commitment to taking better care of the earth in this present moment. The stronger my connection is to nature, the stronger my connection is to God. The scriptures have different meanings to me when I read them now because I think much further beyond myself than I used to, and consider how I can be a better steward of the gift of creation.

November 8

*God said, "See, I have given you every plant yielding seed that
is upon the face of all the earth, and every tree with seed in its
fruit; you shall have them for food. And to every beast of the
earth, and to every bird of the air, and to everything that creeps
on the earth, everything that has the breath of life, I have given
every green plant for food." And it was so.*

Genesis 1:29-30

This passage from Genesis seems to imply something countercultural.
What God seems to say is that there is enough. There's not only enough to
feed humans, there is enough in creation to feed every living thing. God
has provided the gifts we need to live in harmony with all of creation.

How can this be? Every time I turn on the television or open the
newspaper, I am told that I need more. Usually, having more is tied to
my happiness. I need more food, more medicine, a better car, a better
beer. If only I had these things, I would be happy. Newspaper stories are
not written from places of gratitude for what we have but tend to point
out our deficits and needs: We have fewer graduates studying the hard
sciences; not nearly enough resources are available to fix aging roads and
bridges; religious life and practice in America are in decline. So, how can
it be that we have enough?

What if, instead of building an awareness of our needs, we started with a
celebration of the many gifts God has given us? The presiding bishop of
The Episcopal Church, Michael B. Curry, preaches that as Christians, we
should not be satisfied with the way things are but should strive to realize
God's dream for us.

Perhaps part of that dream is to recognize the gifts God has given us
to live in harmony with creation. They are here. And celebrating them
means putting away the idea of scarcity and living into the deep joy of
gratitude for all the abundant gifts God has placed at our feet.

November 9

Baruch Atah Adonai,
Eloheinu Melech haolam,
Hamotzi lechem min haaretz.

Blessed are you, Eternal our God,
Sovereign of the Universe,
Who brings forth bread from the earth.
—a Hebrew blessing over bread

In his recent book, *Harvesting Abundance*, Brian Sellers-Petersen shares stories of church-folk participating in cultivating food. I am grateful for the movement afoot to grow food on church-owned land, but I am also in awe of people like Sellers-Petersen who are passionately drawn to the beautiful intersection between food and faith.

The evangelism these folks proclaim is holistic nourishment: body and soul, because these two are profoundly related. Body and soul come together to dig and plant, to weed and water. They pray as they do these things, and the doing of these things is prayer. Body and soul are connected to creation in the doing, and they are joined with the rest of God's children in the feeding of all creation.

God has planted a garden in the center of creation. Then God places people in the garden to tend it. Jesus talks of sowers of seeds and owners of vineyards. And he blesses those who feed the hungry.

And they, and we, and all our sisters and brothers from across the ages, bless God for bringing forth bread from the earth.

November 10

I'm a fan of singer/songwriter Sturgill Simpson. He is young and his songs are raw, providing a view straight into his soul. He wrestles with God, faith, and sin. A product of coal mining roots in eastern Kentucky, Simpson was raised by a loving family. I can tell all of this about him simply by listening to his songs.

In "Panbowl," a song named for an oddly shaped lake filled with bass and pan fish, Simpson remembers the innocence of his Kentucky childhood. He shows us a clear view of love and loss and a child's connection to the earth. I've never been to Panbowl Lake, but if I close my eyes, the song connects me to the sacred place of my childhood.

My personal Panbowl was on a mountaintop in Arkansas. On top of Petit Jean Mountain, overlooking a long bend in the Arkansas River, is Camp Mitchell. There, I learned to pray and to praise; I fell in love for the first time and first felt my heart break. Camp Mitchell was where I learned to be loved and cared for in community, all while surrounded by the beauty of God's creation.

On top of that mountain, I imagined God and knew Christ in community. It was a beautiful place, yes. And like my friend Sturgill Simpson sings, the love I knew in that place made it sacred.

November 11

I loved living in Richmond, California—although most folks in the state don't have the highest opinion of this working-class city. At times, it has been known for its crime rate and also for its level of environmental pollution. Richmond is an industrial city, and during World War II, it was the home of Kaiser Shipyards.

Richmond also makes a good claim as the birthplace of the Rosie the Riveter persona, a cultural icon from World War II that honored and encouraged women in the workplace. Rosie had many faces in Richmond. After the war, many Rosies stayed in Richmond. You can still meet some of them today.

One heir of the Rosie spirit is a woman named Rebecca Newburn. She is one of the co-founders of Richmond Grows Seed Lending Library. This library is a place to check out seeds. People come to the library for seeds, promise to grow a portion for future seed stock, and return seeds to the library after their harvest. They don't fine you if you don't return seeds, but the record of seed returns is remarkable.

In her own garden, Newburn grows plants for three reasons—face, place, and story. The connection to a person, place, or captivating narrative inspires her to plant particular seeds and certain varieties of plants. She is a keeper of stories and cultivates them as plants in her garden. Newburn is not only tending God's garden, she is making sure that everyone in her urban food desert has healthy food and that they have enough.

November 12

Sacramentals are objects that are the visible signs of grace. My dad, a priest, noticed that many things were sacramentals (yes, I do mean that as a noun). If a sacrament is an outward and visible sign of an inward and spiritual grace, then what might be a beautiful piece of art or a song that conveys a particular and potent sense of God's grace?

In baptism, the sacramentals are water and the oil of chrism. In Holy Eucharist, the sacramentals are bread and wine. In matrimony, the sacramentals are wedding rings. My father, a bit of an Anglophile, wondered if coronation might not be a kind of sacrament as well—with the crown and scepter being the outward and visible signs.

My friend Elizabeth DeRuff is a priest and a farmer, as well as a fellow author in this book. She is a farmer of wheat and the founder of Honoré Farm and Mill, a nonprofit "focused on restoring vitality to wheat and the land upon which it grows." The way she writes and talks about wheat makes me imagine that it is sacramental for her. Every activity that goes into the process of transforming wheat into bread is her ritual, which makes baking her sacrament.

When we bless God for bringing forth bread from the earth, we bless Elizabeth and all of God's farmers who are revealing God's grace through the growing and milling of wheat, the processing and baking of flour into bread, which is for us nothing less than the Body of Christ.

November 13

I have had two professors named Jay. When I was an undergraduate, I attended a small liberal arts school called Hendrix College where I had the privilege to study with process theologian Jay McDaniel. As a practitioner of process thought, McDaniel invited his students to have "fat souls." To have a fat soul means "to widen out in love, compassion, inclusivity, and full-bodied joy." Fat soul theologians live out this love and compassion with a joyful connection to all of creation.

In seminary at the Church Divinity School of the Pacific, it was my honor to study systematic theology with Jay E. Johnson. Johnson is a theologian, an ethicist, and historian. I also got to know him as a dog person. As long as I have known Jay Johnson, he has rarely been without a dog as a spiritual companion. He is filled with joy when witnessing a dog being a dog.

Both of the Jays have a deep sense of connection to humanity. It's almost as if their ties to humanity are deepened by a divine connection through all other living things. For them, every beast of the earth, every bird of the air, everything that creeps on the earth, and everything that has breath is a revelation of God's grace pulling them into a deeper sense of being human. The Jays still teach and lead by example that the love of God can be found in happy dogs and purring cats and by cultivating fat souls.

November 14

The account of creation presents us with humans, birds, fish, creepy-crawly things—all fitting together in harmony. Recently, we have grown more attuned to the complexity and fragility of this harmony in creation. We have been given all that is necessary to maintain balance in this garden. But we humans also hold the power of destruction.

In his recent book, *I Contain Multitudes*, Ed Yong offers a view of the microbial level of creation. Once considered only for their role in causing disease, microbes are now recognized as necessary components of the fabric of all life. The complexity of the created order calls us to be stewards of life forms—even those we are still discovering and understanding.

Chinese-Canadian theologian Wee-Chong Tan, in his book *Dialectica Reconciliae*, takes this idea a step further. He suggests that the Greek word *logos*, which we translate in John's Gospel as word, is best translated to the Chinese word *tao*. Westerners probably imagine *yin* and *yang* when we hear the word *tao*, but it more precisely refers to balance in creation.

If God the *Logos* is the balance that sustains creation, and if it is this divine balance that takes on human form and dwells among us in the person of Jesus, how are we—the image bearers of God—called to live?

November 15

This week's author
Julianne Day

*God saw everything that he had made, and indeed, it was
very good. And there was evening and there was morning,
the sixth day.*

Genesis 1:31

Have you ever stopped to consider what is meant by the phrase, "God
saw?" Certainly we know what is meant when we hear the phrase, "I
saw..." or "You saw..." Thanks to science, we even have a pretty good idea
of what we mean when we say, "Rover saw...." or "Felix saw..." We know
dogs see pretty much the same thing we see, except blurrier and without
the greens and reds that human eyes perceive.

But how can a being who exists outside of space and time, without a
physical body, be said to see? When Genesis tells us that, "God saw
everything," what does this mean?

In my mind, seeing is a verb that signifies the broadest and most
intimate kind of awareness. This bit from Genesis might easily read,
God understood everything or *God heard everything, God felt everything*
and *God experienced everything.* Since God is God, God experiences
this broad and intimate awareness of every created thing—all at once.
God knows, penetrates, and is penetrated by all aspects of creation
simultaneously. All of creation is fully known by God, and it fully knows
the Creator.

November 16

Genesis makes no mention of God having helpers or advisors during creation. However, according to the Nicene Creed, Jesus Christ is understood to be present during creation. This is a rather curious point in Christian doctrine. It's certainly a radical reimagining of the way generations of devout Jewish believers understood the creation story handed to us in Genesis. And given that Genesis 1:31 clearly states that God (singular) made all things, how, exactly, is Jesus a part of this story?

A cynical interpretation is that Christians' insistence on Jesus being the means by which God's creative vision was manifested in the beginning is at best, wishful thinking—and at worst, willful blindness. I actually have some sympathy for this view. After all, for me, any effort to place Jesus at the center of the creation story seems like a stretch when he's not directly mentioned. But, every so often in human history, a total reimagining of an old story becomes possible. The old information no longer makes sense, and a paradigm shift is required.

One can tell the earth is flat simply by looking at it. Likewise, anyone with eyes can see that the sun circles the earth. Yet we no longer believe these once-deeply held "facts," because evidence beyond ourselves has revealed a more mysterious, provably accurate, and beautiful truth. Every once in a while, all the same facts can be true—and our understanding and interpretation of them can diverge wildly. When we are dealing with a living God who calls order out of chaos, who separates dark from light, nothing is impossible for God.

In just this way, the creator of mankind can be both God and Son of Man.

November 17

Genesis 1:31 proclaims creation "very good." God sees at various points along the way that creation is good, but now for the first time, the word "very" is added to the evaluation. Why are things very good now? What has changed at this point in the story?

On the sixth day, God creates wild animals, livestock, and people. Do wild animals make the difference? Humankind? Many biblical commentators see the creation of humankind as the climax of the creation story. Are we Homo sapiens sapiens the extra something special?

My suspicion is that, as climactic as the creation of human beings is, and as unique as we are as God's image bearers, the word "very" in Genesis 1:31 has more to do with a word that appears nine words before it—"everything."

There is a concept in systems theory—and it can be difficult for our analytical, reductive minds to grasp—of a whole being greater than the sum of its parts. Known as synergism, this concept is tied to the idea that traits or features can arise in a system with the introduction of additional complexity that was not present at lower levels of development.

Through this lens—and the introduction of animals and human beings —creation becomes greater than the sum of its parts. What makes everything "very good" isn't wild animals, livestock, or human beings, but rather the way in which the addition of these creatures impacts the rest of creation, causing all that was created earlier to relate to themselves and each other in slightly different, deeper ways. In other words, there is no one single secret ingredient. Creation itself is the extra something special.

November 18

What does "very good" mean to you? How many of us hear "very good" and think, "needs improvement"? In our perfectionistic, hyper-competitive modern-day America, very good can seem like code for underwhelming. However, in Genesis, very good is as good as good can get.

Imagine how the entire creation story might be changed if Genesis 1:31 said excellent, glorious, stupendous, amazing, terrific, or perfect instead of very good. Go ahead and try it out: *God saw everything that he had made, and indeed, it was stupendous…God saw everything that he had made, and indeed, it was terrific…God saw everything that he had made, and indeed, it was just flat-out incredible.*

If you're anything like me, you may be seized by the desire to laugh at this exercise. For some reason, the fancy versions ring a bit hollow, don't they? The better words seem to come up short.

There is dignity in the phrase very good. To me, it feels more forthright and forgiving than perfect or amazing. Who would want to live in an amazing, stupendous, terrific world all the time, anyway? Such a world would be exhausting and overwhelming. Thank goodness God knows better than to dial things all the way up to eleven.

In Genesis, goodness is an absolute—something that cannot be improved upon. Goodness is something that cannot become better or worse but just is—it may increase or decrease in scope but never in quality. The modifier very emphasizes the fact of creation being good, not a qualifier of how good it is. In the end, can anything truly be better than very good?

November 19

In Genesis, we see God working with total freedom and without interference. There is no sense of pressure or struggle. No conflict. No constraints or limits. And no editing. Six times in all we read, "God saw that it was good." Just once, wouldn't it have been interesting if *God saw that it could use some improvement* or *God saw that creating ticks and malaria may not have been the best ideas?*

We learn later in scripture that God is capable of judging creation and striking out (or striking down) those parts that fail to live up to their potential. But these decisions are occasioned by human sin, not a failure of God's creativity or agency.

At no point in the creation story does God edit, qualify, or tweak things. Since later chapters of Genesis show God is capable of making modifications, we must conclude that changes simply aren't necessary at this point in creation. If sin is described as missing the mark, then God's activity over the six days of creation might be described as sin's antithesis: hitting the mark. Every. Single. Time.

Genesis isn't a Greek myth—God isn't some foil for Zeus, constantly making mistakes, becoming jealous, and taking sides in arguments or wars, nor is God an action hero. Unlike the creation myths of other ancient Middle Eastern cultures, God has not salvaged creation from some wreckage. There are no villains in the creation story, no missteps. And this is a deeply comforting thought: The world we live in has been created by a God not subject to sin, disorder, or any kind of constraint. Indeed, it is very good.

November 20

We hear the cosmic question at the heart of the creation story, a question that remains an intriguing mystery despite all the information in Genesis. Why does God create?

What is the original impetus for making light and sky, earth and sea? What purpose is being served? Where do all of God's ideas come from anyway? Would you in your wildest dreams imagine a platypus or a giraffe? Does God have a plan? Is there a blueprint for creation? The Gospel of John begins with the same first three words as Genesis: "In the beginning." John continues: "was the Word, and the Word was with God, and the Word was God. He was with God in the beginning."

The word in John's Gospel that is translated as word is *logos* in the original Greek and might more accurately be rendered as blueprint, plan, knowledge, or reason. John's Gospel implies that God definitely has a plan. There is a blueprint for creation, and this plan is both a reflection of and an extension of God's very self. It is not an overstatement to say that creation exists because God exists.

Why God creates platypuses and giraffes may always remain a mystery to you and me. Genesis leaves us no doubt that what God has created is good—and God is good.

November 21

Many people living in post-modern societies don't spend much time interacting with God's creation. We are far more adept at identifying a product by a logo than various species of plants and birds by their blooms or feathers. We are more likely to be found driving in cars than walking on our own two feet. We spend more time staring at screens than the sky. The only stars we see regularly are the ones in Yelp reviews.

Have your actual feet touched actual soil today? Or have the soles of your feet come in direct contact with just the insides of your shoes, the bottom of your bathtub, and the floorboards or carpet in your home? If you are feeling blue or disconnected—like your life contains no good or growing things—try getting in touch with those things that Genesis tells us have been created by God: light, sky, earth, seas, plants and trees, seeds and fruit, the sun, the moon, the stars, fish and birds, animals and people. Turn off the TV, close the computer, silence the phone. No matter how amazing that five-star app or movie is, it will never measure up to the actual stars in the sky. God has some very high, very good standards for creation.

Scientists have determined that merely looking at photographs of natural spaces can reduce levels of specific stress hormones and produce positive cognitive benefits. There is something profoundly special about that which God has made.

November 22

*God saw everything that he had made, and indeed, it was
very good. And there was evening and there was morning,
the sixth day.*

Genesis 1:31

Many of us turn to the outdoor world when we're stressed. Maybe you
are someone who does this, too. Even though nature isn't always peaceful
or quiet, it isn't crowded with physical or mental clutter. In the outdoor
air, my breath seems to flow easier and deeper, and my thoughts become
more settled.

It's not as though I only enjoy the outdoors during difficult times, but the
space and light outside have healed me over and over again. When I first
heard about the planes on 9/11, I walked away from the houses in my
neighborhood toward the hills. I was in a state of disbelief and needed
to walk to regain my bearings—to feel solid ground. As I walked, Psalm
121 began to speak in me, "I lift up my eyes to the hills, from where is my
help to come? My help comes from the LORD, the maker of heaven and
earth."

These ancient words of prayer soothed me on that difficult day, and they
have been a balm to my soul on other hard days as well. But the words
also accompany me in times of gratitude. What a joy it is to be a part of
this amazing world, with hills and trees reaching skyward, fog snaking
through valleys, a dependable sun shining down on me, and even the
wind to remind me of the Spirit's leading and meandering. When I go
outside, feel the ground beneath my feet, and allow my thoughts to melt
away and be replaced by pure gratitude—even if only for the briefest of
moments—I am made new and whole again.

*Thank you, Creator God, for this most amazing world and for this moment
to enjoy it.*

November 23

As a child I was more likely to be found outdoors than inside the house. Maybe it was because of the freedom I felt under the sun in our big backyard, or maybe I just liked the kind of playing I could do outdoors. I made a lot of mud pies, rode my tricycle (and later my bike), and climbed trees.

I am still drawn to the outdoors. I go outside to read, play, work, walk, observe, photograph, write, think things over, exercise, rest, and on and on. More than anything I go outside to be renewed and to feel in closer contact with the energy of creation and our Creator.

I tried to describe this is in a poem I wrote when I was recovering from an illness and feeling stress from political turmoil:

> *Take It In*
>
> *Fill the cup with riversong,*
> *clear breezes from the mountains,*
> *pine-sprinkled sunlight,*
> *fill it and drink it down.*
>
> *It's time to leave despair behind,*
> *to restore body, mind, and soul*
> *left dull by any number of things.*
>
> *Take in what the earth has been doing—*
> *take it in like a tonic,*
> *like medicine, like faith.*

November 24

Years ago, I presented a workshop for women in our diocese who were interested in exploring stress reduction and relaxation through a spiritual lens. I began our presentation with the notion that we often feel scattered and separated from our own selves, from God, and from the wholeness of creation.

Over the course of the workshop, I used words and phrases that have been touchstones for me over the years, talismans that draw me back to God and creation. Each word or phrase came in its own way, is rooted in simplicity, and brings my intention back to the basic things I know—we are God's creatures, our lives are gifts from God, and we are part of God's creation. Three of my touchstone phrases were, "Be still," "Just breathe," and "Be here now".

Being still is far easier said than done for many of us. One helpful practice I have learned from Franciscan monk Richard Rohr is repeating a line from Psalm 46, shortening the line with each repetition. "Be still and know that I am God." "Be still and know that I am." "Be still and know." "Be still." "Be."

"Just breathe." We do it automatically. Just breathe and pay attention to your breath moving in and out. Imagine the breath of God breathing in us and on us—this is the breath present since the first moment of creation.

"Be here now," in this place, in your body with all its sensations, with its chattering, and with your spirit longing for God. When I tell myself, "Be here now," I am reminded to come back home to myself—to God. Be here now.

November 25

Our church has a fairly new courtyard between the sanctuary and another building that houses the parish hall and several other rooms. The main feature of the courtyard is a labyrinth laid out in intricately cut stone tiles and brick. At the center of the labyrinth is a black metal bench encircling a tree whose upraised arms are bare this time of year.

Beyond the labyrinth are wooden benches, stones, and plantings of many colors and shapes. Tall, waving grasses and columnar evergreens stand alongside the smaller plants that tolerate winter's harshness. Near the sanctuary, water flows softly in a fountain, joined on one side to a brick and wrought iron columbarium. People often pause in the courtyard before entering or leaving the sanctuary. Children run and walk the labyrinth pathway, or dart across it toward the flowing water. This corner of creation is alive with God's presence.

Our older home sits on a large lot in town. Dozens of rhododendrons I planted more than thirty years ago grow under tall white oaks. Deer often rest in the backyard and wander through the front. I treasure the respite and refreshment of the setting, and yet so often I head out the door without paying it any attention.

A little while ago, I built a small slate patio in our front yard and placed a curved, concrete bench out there. I purchased a small statue of Saint Francis, who now looks out between my rhodie branches toward the bench. It's a little retreat spot—I love being out there and looking around our corner of creation. This place to sit and linger was just what I needed to remind me to wholeheartedly say, "Thank you. Amen."

November 26

Participating in a book group is one of my weekly joys. Members take turns hosting the group, generally in our homes. Everyone involved attends the same church, and many of us offer our time and efforts in addressing the needs of others in our community and in the world through direct service or advocacy.

We only read three or four books a year because we read them aloud to one another. Each person reads a couple of paragraphs at a time. We typically choose books that help us explore our faith—how and when we experience God in the world and the intersections between belief and trends in society and politics.

We read, discuss, eat snacks, and support one another. We pray for one another and for the world. This is a Sabbath time for many of us—a time when we put other busyness aside. Sometimes we guiltily wonder if the refreshing time we spend like this—reading, discussing and having another cup of coffee together—makes a difference in the world.

What we know is that we experience God's love in and through community when we come together. Perhaps this is a bit of the unity God dreams for all of creation. Faith and doubt are laid bare before one another and God, and the breath of God that breathes through all creation blows away the weariness of the past week, leaving us with greater energy and focus. In our time together, we are renewed, blessed and reminded that God uses our hands, feet and voices—and maybe even a book and some coffee—in the ongoing dream of creation.

November 27

Cardinals are not native to Oregon. I first saw one in Tucson, Arizona, at Tohono Chul Park more than twenty-five years ago. I was astounded at the male's brilliant red crest and body. The female's red-tinged golden-brown was more subtle but still striking. Their song was a crystal-clear whistle. I fell in love with them, just like I did when I first heard sandhill cranes calling through fog in Central Oregon. There was something so mysterious about the sound these birds made.

As a child, I could identify robins, crows, owls, and a general category of "other birds." This list seemed to be enough birding information for me. My interest in watching, listening for birds, and identifying them may have started with the cardinals and cranes. Some curiosity opened my eyes to distinctions between species and to the amazing detail in the coloring and plumage of some birds.

I can imagine the tiny black and white stripes on a loon's throat painted with the finest, most precise brush. The creative design of the wood duck's feathers and the exactness of pattern on the ring-necked duck astound me. And I love to watch the way light plays on hummingbird feathers, making them seem to change colors.

I could go on and on about the wonders of creation, some big and dramatic like the Grand Canyon, Bryce Canyon, or the blue whale. Or I could mention things like fingerprints, glints of mica in granite, or the wagging tail of a happy dog. Right now, as winter approaches, bright green moss grows thick again on rocks and tree trunks. I imagine God saying, "It is very good."

November 28

I wonder what inspires the authors of hymns of praise. These songs seem to burst off the page, exalting all of creation. Some days, I can barely keep myself from singing when I'm out for a walk, especially when I'm surprised by something unexpectedly beautiful. I think of these songs when I experience the wonder of creation—double rainbows and the way sunbeams stream through the clouds, making what I call a "God sky."

A hymn by Joachim Neander starts, "Praise to the Lord, the Almighty, the King of Creation." Another by Folliot Sandford Pierpoint begins, "For the beauty of the earth, for the beauty of the skies," which inspired the title of this book.

What a gift to be able to put into words what we see and feel deep inside ourselves! I remember a hymn from childhood that begins, "All things bright and beautiful…" As an adult, I've loved the more modern hymn by Herbert F. Brokering that proclaims, "Earth and all stars, loud rushing planets, sing to the Lord a new song."

We have been gifted with many hymns singing praise to God for beauty, and we can read countless essays on the natural world and its impact on our health and well-being. Nature is also featured in many fine poems. Some years ago I discovered the poems of Mary Oliver. I was stunned by the living pictures she created through her words. I read about the "rumpled sea" and "the clear pebbles of rain." If I turn to one of her poems, it is as though I am out in nature, even if I am tucked away, inside my house.

November 29

In early summer I make several trips to plant nurseries and to home and garden stores to choose from the wide array of flowering annuals. I fill my cart with two-inch and four-inch plants. Coleus and impatiens are planted in the shady bed next to the house. For full sun and partial sun plots, I get a little wild and select plants for their color and the way they grow. These plants will go into an assortment of larger pots we will place around the yard.

I most often come home from my shopping expedition with deep purple petunias, hot pink and peach geraniums, golden-yellow marigolds with large heads, purple or white bacopa, fuchsia, and lots of bright blue lobelia. If I see fluttering ornamental grasses, I bring some of those home, too. What fun to arrange these plants into little communities of contrasting colors, and what great joy there is in the months that follow as I gaze at the celebration of color surrounding the tall, graceful grass! Hummingbirds sip nectar from the offerings, as do bees and butterflies. Deer and gray squirrels are attracted to these tender plants as well, so I experiment with numerous sprays designed to discourage nibbling and digging.

In the Northwest, most flowering plants look fairly scraggly this time of year. Yet even in November I've seen a few blossoms on brave geraniums, hardy fuchsias and aging bacopa, even outlasting the leaves slipping off the maple and sweetgum trees. All of this feels like a miracle—the growth and colors. Birds and insects are attracted even to the fading blossoms, as are the voracious and curious deer and squirrels. The bigger miracle is that this world of great diversity was created in the first place: We are each and all a part of it, and somewhere, something is blooming.

November 30

I am not sure where my favorite place is. It would be hard for me to name just one, because I love so many.

I grew up in a town with a river. I didn't pay a lot of attention to the river as a child, but once I was grown I wanted to know the river's source. I found it flowing from the side of a high mountain lake. I've gone back there each of the last twenty-five years to walk the riverside trail through lodgepole pine, just to see the flow of water, watch osprey winging overhead, and spy on the occasional mallards and mergansers near the river's edge.

As a child, my favorite place was likely a small lake where I fished from a boat with my parents and discovered frog eggs and tadpoles on the shallow shoreline. My favorite place might also have been my own backyard, with water skippers in a small irrigation ditch running along the back of the property.

Now I might say my favorite place is just outside Sedona, Arizona, on a red sandstone trail. But this thought would lead my heart to other redrock areas I love, where I feel similarly transfixed and enlivened by the landscape.

But I have come to realize something. Any place can become a favorite if I allow it to be. I can see God's hand at work anywhere if my eyes and heart are open. There is beauty to be found everywhere, even right here where I am sitting, right now.

December

All Their Multitude

*Thus the heavens and the earth were finished, and all
their multitude.*

Genesis 2:1

Artist's note: I have completed about fifty paintings in the Creation
Series, and I don't see an end in sight. Exploring scripture and creation
one element at a time is both exciting and challenging. Most of my work
is reductive—I try to express the essence of something in the simplest
way possible. This is particularly challenging when you are dealing with
"multitude." I couldn't get away from a literal approach, and there was
no way I could really paint a multitude in a fairly small format, so I was
stuck. The context is at least as important as the multitude—after all,
the heavens and the earth, in this moment, are finished, and all their
multitude. Perhaps this speaks less about numbers and more about the
interrelatedness of all of creation and our role in that.

Artist's note: When I was going through paintings to include in the Creation Series, this one jumped off the shelf. I tried to put it back, since it was painted years ago as part of a different project, but it kept insisting. My older brother Bill was an alcoholic and drug addict who died a few months before I painted this. Like so many people who struggle with substance abuse, Bill was intelligent and sensitive, and his tortured life and early demise were tragic.

There are stories of elephants traveling long distances just to be with the remains of one of their own, often standing in silence over the remains. Biologists are hesitant to say that elephants grieve, but I think they do.

All Their Multitude

And on the seventh day God finished the work that he had done, and he rested on the seventh day from all the work that he had done. So God blessed the seventh day and hallowed it, because on it God rested from all the work that he had done in creation.

Genesis 2:2-3

Artist's note: Every Memorial Day, folks from our small church gather to honor those who have given their lives for our country and share memories of loved ones we have lost. A few years ago, Kathleen, a recent widow, was sharing a bit about her husband, an Army veteran who had served in two wars. Love and comfort flowed to her from our little group.

After a few moments, we heard a soft cooing coming from the top of the house, three stories up. We all looked up to see a dove. Time seemed to stand still—the moment was infused with meaning and divine presence. We all felt it. Then, the dove flew away. I wish I could say that the dove has graced our lives often, but this was the first and only time we have ever seen a dove in our community.

Noah sends a dove (pictured on the next page) out to see if the waters have subsided. Artists represent the Holy Spirit as a dove at the Annunciation. Luke tells us that the Holy Spirit descends like a dove at Jesus' baptism. Just maybe the Holy Spirit made a similar appearance here on the north coast. Our dove certainly felt like the whisper of God.

December 1

This week's author
Cory Reinisch

Thus the heavens and the earth were finished, and all their multitude.

Genesis 2:1

As I approach the end of any year, it's important for me to take a moment to reflect on the wide expanse of scenarios, situations, and possibilities that presented themselves in the last year. Taking a fearless inventory of all that has happened to and around me is an exercise in fulfillment—an opportunity to give myself some meaningful perspective, especially when examining losses or hurts, joys and successes.

Each moment is an integral part of the intricately woven fabric of my life—and yours. Any time we complete a task and feel that fulfilling sense of accomplishment, we connect deeply with God's sense of goodness and satisfaction—a feeling intentionally woven into us by the creation story. We must consider ourselves and how we live our lives with this in mind.

We are more than just our jobs, bank accounts, or hobbies. We are more than our prized possessions, community status, or our physical bodies. Our totality is impossible to contain in what we have done and what we have left undone. How we choose to spend our time, how we offer our talents and abilities, and how often we extend help, compassion, and love to all of creation are reasonable measures of who and how we really are, in our deepest hearts.

The sum total weight of our minds, bodies, and souls outweighs even the relationships we have with those we love. Make no mistake, we are all these things, and in this immeasurable, unfathomable abundance lives God's intended plan and dream for each of us and for all of creation. Everything—the sacred and the profane and the uncategorized—is touched and completed by God's hand, and within that, we are complete through God's grace and mercy. God leaves nothing undone.

December 2

Born and raised in the country, I spent as many of my childhood waking hours as my parents would allow outdoors. I was fascinated with the natural wonders that surrounded me on every side; truth be told, I still am.

Exploring every inch of it was never a far-fetched idea to me. I spent innumerable daydreams thinking about the creation story. I wondered why a fox looked and behaved like a fox. Or how a fish was able to live, breathe, eat, move, and make babies just like people, only all of their lives are lived underwater. And exactly how did God decide that the sky would be blue, my favorite color? In my little boy way, I wondered about the omnipotent power of decisions that lead to such fantastic and wonderful forms and functions.

As I've grown older, I have only become more awestruck and wonder-filled by the diversity in creation, right down to our very own human consciousness. I still can't comprehend the complexities and intricacies of the natural world—even with the scientific discoveries that allow us broader and deeper understandings of our ecosystems, of both the gift and necessity of biodiversity. Of all that I know, I truly believe that when God is creating, God applies humor and wit (even among the natural order) and is playful. I am so thankful for that.

December 3

My entire life has been scored by the most beautiful music—sometimes it swells and demands, and other times it murmurs and hums, but it is always there. I am intimately and intricately connected to music—regardless of form or genre—and even when I've tried my hardest to set my passion for it aside, the notes always come drifting back toward me, heavier in their specific and demanding gravity than they were the last time I escaped their tug and pull.

To deny music and the fact that it is a required element in my life is a study in absurdity at this point. Most likely, this compulsion has something to do with having a musical family who passed this desire and drive to me in their genes, or perhaps because my family provided an environment for the love and making of music to flourish. Either way, music truly is a considerable part of my life and cuts such a large swath through the middle of it, I could say that music comes close to helping me define exactly who and how I am.

As a songwriter who acknowledges that I will never fully understand or comprehend God's creation story, composing a song gives me a sneak peek into creation as I work through writing music and words for a new song. My creations are not steeped in divinity, but they are part and parcel of my own individual, God-given nature. Never do I feel more complete or whole as when I have successfully crafted a song. On the flip side of that coin, when I deny or neglect this creative impulse, I feel anxious and unfulfilled until I start writing and playing—picking up the thread of music and weaving something beautiful out of time and tone.

Of all God's creations—and I'm not trying to keep score—music is surely one of the most reassuring of God's nature. The ability of sound, harmony, and poetry to connect us to each other, to the world around us, and ultimately to God's great goodness, is supernatural and mysterious. Music is another language God has given us, and we are invited to use it to sing praise and thanksgiving as we marvel over the wonders of creation.

December 4

My father and I took many fishing trips when I was a child. I suppose these trips were designed to teach me the importance of silence: You can't catch fish while you're talking up a storm. I imagine my father wanted to teach me the importance of patience, as well. Fish are seldom found at the end of a line unless you've offered the fish some silence and time to swallow your bait.

Dad offered up sage advice I didn't appreciate or fully understand for a long time. As I've grown older, his words come back to me, and I have come to understand and apply them to the best of my abilities. I remember one day when we talked about people we admired, and Dad told me that he'd always admired woodworkers. The patience and skill, the characteristically reflective and unassuming quiet confidence, the reluctance to self-congratulate, the willingness to let their work speak for itself—he remains amazed by people who work with wood. I remain amazed by him.

In so many ways, the way my father thinks of woodworkers is how I think of him. And ultimately it's how I think of creation and God as a creator. The beauty in the completeness of creation, even as it continues to unfold before our eyes, is easily seen when we are willing to quiet our hearts, mouths, and minds long enough to study it—running our imaginations and laughter and tears over the grain of it, the way we run our hands over a polished piece of furniture or a hand-turned bowl—to be still and come to understand in our hearts and minds what it means to be a part of God's creation. Even the simple act of thinking about creation and recognizing the beauty of each part brings us closer to understanding and acceptance that we are each and all integral parts of the whole.

December 5

My mother was an elementary school teacher—and to the end of her days and in whatever life comes after this one—she will always be a teacher. As a teacher's son, I came to understand a couple of things. Learning anything is useless unless you are willing and open to hearing someone else's thoughts and opinions. Pride and privilege must be checked at the door to every classroom. Secondly, once you engage any idea or task, you must complete it. Failing to complete the tasks—even if they blow up in your face miserably—teaches us something, every single time.

Mom put this into practice with my sister and me. Openness and tenacity have guided us throughout a life of learning, trying, failing, trying again, and sometimes getting things all the way right. Completion of a task and the corresponding satisfaction that comes along with it are parts of who we are, because this same drive to do and finish are parts of who God is and continues to be. Throughout the Bible, we witness miraculous acts of completion and miracles of wholeness over and over again. Jesus is Alpha and Omega, existing outside of time and throughout it, present before and in and all over creation.

I believe God means us to see things through to completion—even when we make missteps and mistakes along the way. Only the best teachers are able to help us learn by showing us where we have gone wrong—and still have the forgiveness and patience to put us back on track, facing the right direction.

December 6

The heavens and the earth have always been interesting concepts to me. When I think of the creation story, I mostly have a conceptual understanding of what the Bible means by "earth." But I haven't yet experienced the "heavens"—at least not from anything more than an observable study in airplanes or with weather satellites. On top of that, what of our "heavenly home?" What will our surroundings look and feel like when we have finished this present life?

If you're anything like me, the creation story absolutely boggles your mind—every intricate detail from the molecular weight of helium to the massive gravity displaced by a black hole can make your head spin. What new knowledge will be gleaned from each scientific discovery we make? How will our discoveries allow us to more fully understand God and God's intentions for creation? What do they mean for us? What will the afterlife feel like?

I believe God is revealed to us in ways we can sometimes understand, especially if we're willing to remember the infinitude of those things which we can neither ask nor imagine—the power of a God who, even now, is making all things new.

December 7

As this calendar year comes to an end, I hope that we are able to take a fearless, unblinking, and compassion-filled inventory of ourselves and our lives and see that some of what we have made together with God is very good, indeed.

On top of that, I hope we are able to be proud of what we have accomplished and completed alongside our friends, families, and communities. Just as God has made each of us special, sacred, and unique creatures, we are all gifted with opportunities to shape the lives God has given us.

When we look back on what we have done and left undone, how well have we responded to and cared for what has been given us? How well are we using the time God grants us? How well do we take care of the resources and the stunning abundance of beauty and inspiration and creativity that God has given to us in each other and in the world?

We think of the creation stories in Genesis as the beginning of everything—and rightfully so. And yet, the story of creation is still carrying us through our lives as we come to know and understand God and the divine purpose intended for each and every one of us. God leaves nothing undone.

December 8

*Thus the heavens and the earth were finished, and all
their multitude.*

Genesis 2:1

Sometimes just the right atmospheric conditions take place in just the
right geographic location, and an optical phenomenon called the green
flash occurs, usually around ten minutes before sunset. Seeing the green
flash takes flawless timing. You have to be looking kind-of-but-not-
really at the sun as it hits the horizon but not so closely that you fry
your eyeballs. It's kind of like falling in love, I guess. A green flash was
observed by Admiral Byrd's 1934 Antarctic expedition for more than
thirty-five minutes, but most of the time the phenomenon lasts for less
than two seconds.

I have never seen the green flash at sunset. But I have seen the green
that rises up after the first warm rains at the end of March in northern
Kentucky—this hovering glow of new grass and leaves on once-barren
branches and honeysuckle that seems to leap out of dead stumps and
undergrowth. It's a sneaky kind of green, one you hardly notice at first,
but for which my winter eyes ache each year. Green—maybe God's
favorite color—flashes and explodes over the hills, into the tree canopy,
and across the face of my backyard garden.

On our little farm, the last of the leaves have been added to the compost
pile, along with a healthy dose of horse manure. There isn't much green
in my part of the world right now—it's colored brown, gray, black, and
filigreed with the white lace of frost in the mornings. I know it's not
nearly time to begin my watching and waiting for spring, but I know the
green is coming.

December 9

The summer I was nine, my parents took my brother and me to Audubon Park, the world-class zoo in New Orleans. We rode a paddle boat from City Park down to the zoo—a feat of locomotion that would have seemed miraculous to the peoples who lived along the banks of the river for millennia before my father's great-great-great-grandthings came over on boats from the Canary Islands, France, and Prussia to settle in an odd corner of creation renamed Louisiana.

We zipped from enclosure to enclosure, smelling the strange smells of creation and summertime. When we stopped for ice cream, my brother began squealing with delight. Just beyond the kiosk, two Dominican nuns in their habits were enjoying a rest and a snack, too.

"Mama! Daddy!! Sissy!! Look!! Nuns!! They have nuns here!!" His five-year-old excitement was too much to contain, and he began running toward the sisters. Dad snagged him just before he launched himself into their laps. The ladies took his wonder and wild greeting in stride and wished us all a happy afternoon. I don't think my parents attempted to explain to the sisters that they looked just as exotic and exciting to a kindergartner from small-town Texas as did the scarlet ibis and lions.

We are all so rare and lovely, whether we are plumed or veiled or merely in our own skin. God has made such an amazing and delightful variety of life in this world. And it is a blessing that we are all here together, learning to love and live alongside each other in this beautiful garden.

December 10

There's an old, old story about how the world is balanced on the backs of eight pairs of elephants, who are balanced on the shell of an enormous turtle—who holds up pretty much everything else in the universe, including the universe. Like I said—it is an old story, and the telling and retelling of it has made it a little fuzzy and worn in places. This story makes me think about my great-grandparents.

Velma and Paul; Bessie and Fred; Vannie and Charlie; Mickey and Beryl. I see bits of all of them in me and my family members. This brings me no end of delight and consternation—how my sweet tooth comes from Vannie, and my foul mouth comes from Bessie; how I think of Charlie every time we build a fence, and of Mickey when I drink a Coke. I think about Paul's hands and Velma's biscuits with sour cream and honey. My inclination to offer unsolicited advice comes from Fred, and my love of old bobbin lace and handwork comes from Beryl. Parts of their faces rest in my face—Beryl's cheekbones, Fred's complexion, Bessie's chin, Mickey's square face, the way my eyes crinkle up like Charlie's when I stare off at something in the distance.

Their lives and the legacies of the families they formed are the nearest history I can reach out and touch. They are the elephants upon which my world rests. Underneath them are all the men and women who made them—the big turtle holding up all the rest of everything that I am and will become. Such a tapestry of love, such a multitude of blessing.

December 11

My affinity for elephants is most likely deeply rooted in the Muppet known as Aloysius Snuffleupagus. With his long, droopy eyelashes and penchant for adventures with Big Bird, I found Snuffy endlessly fascinating. Because of Snuffy, I have always been willing to believe that elephants are a little bit mysterious, mischievous, and miraculous.

The older I've grown and the more I've learned about elephants, the more my original conceptions of Snuffy and elephants have been shown to be true. Elephants do have an air of mystery—their memories and their culture of community are different from so many other animals, so much like us in many ways. Among the animals, elephants are one of only a handful of species to use tools, which can encourage them to mischief and occasional mayhem. The largest of all land mammals, elephants offer the miracle of elephant gestation and a birthing process that is truly awe-inspiring. The way a herd rallies around a new mother and baby will make your heart swell and eyes well up.

Most beautiful of all is the way elephants always remember—sonorously calling across miles of savannah to tell their companions the correct directions to watering holes, directing safe passage through dense and lion-filled bushes, taking their final walks before lying down next to the bones of those who have gone before them. I love the poetry of having this painting for the artist's brother as one of our final pieces in this book. This lovely painting and the creature it encapsulates remind us of the creativity and care God has taken in making this amazing world, and it encourages us to celebrate the glorious multitude of all that is in it.

December 12

My little brother was almost two years old before he ever saw rain falling from the sky. We were raised in a rural farming community in Texas that was hard-hit by a long drought in the early 1980s.

I remember waiting for the rain at my grandmother's house. Thunder started up first, and I kept my fingers crossed hoping lightning wouldn't follow. I knew lightning meant there was no way I would be allowed outside, and I had already changed into my purple bathing suit in preparation for the rain. In my almost six-year-old mind, cavorting in the front yard like a tiny maniac was the only option I was willing to accept.

The air stopped. I could smell hot tar seeping out of the streets. Maybe this was like that time last week, or the week before that, when the clouds gathered up and thundered and then nothing—just a sweaty trip to Mr. Stewart's snow cone stand after another swimming lesson in a lukewarm public pool. Then, a breeze lifted the branches of the pecan trees, and the music of raindrops began to tap itself out on the sidewalk and windowpanes. I was out of the front door like a shot.

My grandmother followed me out, and so did my mother with my brother in her arms. I remember his blue, blue eyes staring up in wonder at the sky, asking her, "What is this, Mama?" "Oh! It's rain, baby! Do you want to play?"

She put my brother down in the grass, and we danced until his diaper was soaked through and the sugar high from my snow cone had worn off. And it was very good.

December 13

"The waiting," says Tom Petty, "is the hardest part." That's a real mouthful—and heartful—of truth. I am terrible at waiting. But I've come to realize that no one is good at waiting. I wonder if this has anything to do with our beginning? There's nothing to wait for in the Garden—by the time we arrive on the scene, God has already made everything we need. Our only job is to name things, to learn about what is around us, and to accept the companionship of the counterpart God gives us. But we draw our first breaths and lay freshly opened eyes on a world that is already in motion and filled to the brim with life. Somehow, on this side of Eden, we can't imagine how or why things should be any different. But they are. Make no mistake, we live in the very good reality of what God has made in creation. But we are not finished—creation is not finished.

We live in the midst of the already-and-the-not-yet, and that posture can be excruciating. Communities that seem to be knit together with love can be torn apart in a matter of hours by hateful words, flaming torches, and racist displays. Rivers can run clean and clear one minute, and then a pipeline ruptures and what has taken millennia to develop and grow can be ruined in mere minutes. Dance parties can turn into shooting galleries between heartbeats.

And yet, forgotten animal companions are rehomed every day. Homeless heroin addicts are treated with humanity and offered meaningful assistance in beginning recovery. Babies are baptized into communities that love and celebrate them as whole and holy people of God. And in vacant lots and church plots and backyards and container gardens, people are partnering with God to grow creation. Waiting is not the mindless, minute-counting exploit we so often imagine it to be. Waiting is the hardest part, but it may also be the most important. In those waiting moments, we find ourselves holding our hopes and wishes up to the light of the Spirit, and praying for the will to keep growing. And the will to keep growing—that's what makes the waiting bearable and beautiful.

December 14

Gene Cernan was the last person to walk on the moon. One of only twelve people to do so, Cernan's final stroll across the lunar surface took place over forty years ago. From the relative ease and comfort of our place in time and history, we may wonder over our parents' and grandparents' choice to go to the moon when we still hadn't eradicated smallpox or been to the bottom of the Marianas Trench. But we went to the moon—more than once. And those trips changed every single life on Earth.

When we think of the whole multitude of creation—all the birds and bees and flowers and fruits—the scope is stunning. We don't even have an accurate list of the life that currently exists, much less a list of everything that has died out. We can't begin to imagine the ways life will change and adapt and evolve in whatever time is still left on God's clock. But twelve people stood on the face of the moon and looked back to Earth and saw us in all our collected glory, fury, fear, hope, hate, and love. Knowing everything they knew about us, they still chose to come home. God knows every rotten and awful thing we do to each other and still comes to be among us in the person of Jesus. Faith and love like that leave me breathless.

You and I stand at the edge of another year, looking back over our shoulders at the year in review. Like Cernan and the other moon-walkers, we see a whole panorama laid before us. The whole scope of what we have done and left undone stretches out before us, and we can look with the unaided eye to see the deepest scars and brightest colors. From this point, it is impossible not to love the bravery and boldness of life, sneaking green into every corner possible and making the blue of the ocean seem even bluer. Cernan pondered the wonder of creation from the surface of the moon; you and I ponder the wonder of our own lives and corner of creation from the vantage point of this waning year. What we see before us is loved and lovely; indeed, this multitude is very good.

And on the seventh day God finished the work that he had done, and he rested on the seventh day from all the work that he had done. So God blessed the seventh day and hallowed it, because on it God rested from all the work that he had done in creation.

Genesis 2:2-3

Our text says that God stops working and is finished. But could it be that God actually creates something essential on this seventh and final day? That "something" is time itself. God creates time to rest: Time to kill, not fill; time to waste, not work. In the words of author Matthew Sleeth, "Up to this point, everything has been created out of nothing, but on the morning of the seventh day, God makes nothing out of something. Rest is brought into being."

We often talk about stewardship in the church. Sometimes, stewardship is narrowly understood as financial pledges and tithes made to fund the ministry of a congregation. But most Christians recognize that we are called to be good stewards of all that God has given us, not merely our financial resources. Stewardship is a year-round, whole-person practice. We are stewards of our bodies, our gifts and talents, our children, and our relationships, for all our lives.

And God has called us—made us—to be stewards of the earth itself. As we stand in awe and celebrate the intricate workings and sheer beauty of creation, we are reminded that God has given us the job of taking care of it. Conserving energy, polluting less, living simply, recycling, and walking gently on the earth are all part of our God-given responsibility as residents of this place.

But we are also called to be stewards of that which God created on the seventh day—our time of rest. Whether we observe a weekly sabbath or treasure sabbath moments and hours throughout the week, this time is a gift from God. It is holy.

December 16

I wonder how God spent that first sabbath. How did God rest? My husband says God played tennis. I say God mowed the lawn. My husband says, "No. That would be work!" Well, I insist, at least God surely puttered around in the garden, maybe pulling a weed here, planting a seed there. Certainly the Bible says more about yardwork than it does about tennis.

One of the great challenges in sabbath observance is our individual set of unique needs for this day of rest. One person's sabbath activity could well be another person's hard work. After sitting at a computer screen all week, for some folks the most relaxing way to spend a day off is to plunge into a household project. Whether building a cabinet or clearing out the tool shed, these folks can lose themselves in a task and emerge feeling satisfied and refreshed. For others that same project would be torturous labor. Yardplay (not yardwork) is one of those relaxing, sabbath-honoring activities in my family. For me, yardplay is contemplative and refreshing; for the rest of my family, it is torturous labor.

When Jesus and his disciples are confronted for plucking heads of grain on the sabbath, Jesus says, "The sabbath was made for humankind, and not humankind for the sabbath" (Mark 2:27). I suppose this provides a good rationale for a custom-made sabbath. But, however we choose to spend our sabbath days or sabbath moments, we would do well this time of year to set aside our holiday to-do lists, our busy minds and full agendas in order to live in this present moment, resting in the awareness of God's presence.

December 17

A friend of mine gave me a mug that reads, "I really need another day between Saturday and Sunday."

"Yes," I thought, "that pretty much says it all." An extra day of the week? That sounds like pure luxury. I would finally catch up. This is especially true in my life during the month of December. There is always too much to do.

But in reality, if I had another day between Saturday and Sunday, I would probably just fill it with more plans, more projects, more worries, more things to do, more things left undone. I suppose the desire for more time is a form of greed. We think of greed as a desire for more wealth or power or material goods, but we can be greedy for more time too.

We never seem to have enough...of so many things in our lives. Even if our physical and material needs are met, we want more: more gadgets, love, security, more likes on Facebook. Old Testament scholar Walter Brueggemann calls this desire the myth of scarcity: Our human propensity to believe that there is never enough. The conviction of the Bible is that God gives in abundance, provides all we need—and more.

On this seventh day, God stops and says, "Enough!" We are reminded here that God has given us all we need. God has even given us enough time. A popular mantra says it well: "I have enough, I do enough, I am enough." May we rest in this awareness and abundance today.

December 18

Here in Genesis, God rests. Later, in Exodus (20:8-11), God commands the children of Israel to do the same: "Remember the sabbath day, and keep it holy. For six days you shall labor and do all your work. But the seventh day is a sabbath to the Lord your God; you shall not do any work...For in six days, the Lord made heaven and earth, the sea, and all that is in them, but rested the seventh day; therefore the Lord blessed the sabbath day and consecrated it."

The creation story in the first chapter of Genesis shares similarities with creation myths from other religions and cultures in the ancient Middle Eastern world. The story of the flood also has several parallels. But the setting apart of every seventh day and the call to observe sabbath is distinctive—something that set the children of Israel apart from other peoples.

Why is sabbath so important? Why is it still important today? Maybe it is because God knows how easily we humans can fall into the trap of playing God ourselves. We become so caught up in endless activity and endless anxiety, the many ways we try to control our lives and the lives of others, that we forget God is God. This weekly observance reorients us to our humanity and God's divinity. As we take a break from the constant doing, we are reminded that we are creatures, fallible and vulnerable, and that God alone gives us all we have and truly need.

Without our day of rest, we forget that the planets will keep spinning, the grass will keep growing, the trees will keep producing oxygen—without our constant toil. It is not up to us. God is God.

December 19

Throughout this first chapter of Genesis, we hear, "God saw that it was good." God sees. It is as if every day, God works hard forming this, shaping that, and only comes around to look at all that has been made at the end of each day. And finally pausing, God affirms beauty and goodness in what has been created.

Slowing down enough to see the world around us is a challenge and an invitation for many of us. I can take a run or a walk in the morning and be so immersed in my thoughts that I miss the wonder all around me: a colorful sunrise, flowering trees, a cardinal on freshly fallen snow, the neighbor who calls out my name as I move past. I simply don't see any of it.

One day, I was determined to take a contemplative walk on a neighborhood trail. I saw everything: Two gray squirrels chasing each other around a tree trunk, a group of white-tailed deer eating acorns. There was a hawk soaring high in the sky, a flock of geese honking overhead, runners passing by me in stylish spandex. An elderly man came into sight. Walking stick in hand, he wore Birkenstock sandals with calf-length white socks, hiking shorts, and a tie-dyed shirt. Instead of the standard good morning nod, our eyes met, and he gave me the peace sign. This made me smile. I was so glad my eyes were open.

There is a line in one of our eucharistic prayers where the celebrant asks God to "Open our eyes to see your hand at work in the world about us" (*The Book of Common Prayer*). Sabbath time is often just that: Time to slow down and open our eyes to see the diversity and beauty in creation—including other human beings.

December 20

A deer darted in front of my car on my way to work. Thankfully, I swerved just in time, but I came within inches of hitting it. Sometimes we collide with creation—our human activities and agendas running against nature's. Whether it is the destruction of the rainforest or mountaintop removal, roadkill or mole traps, our interests sometimes clash. But we were created not to collide but to cooperate with all of creation.

As God stopped work on this seventh day, I hope God was able to see and savor how well it all fit together, this work of creation. I hope God was able to stand in awe of what God had made: the planets set in motion, trees providing homes for birds, predators and prey in delicate balance, oxygen and carbon doing their dance, inhaled and exhaled.

In his book *God has a Dream*, Archbishop Desmond Tutu writes: "The first law of our being is that we are set in a delicate network of interdependence with our fellow human beings and with the rest of God's creation." This interdependence can be abused or ignored. What one of us does or doesn't do has a ripple effect, making a mark on all of creation.

As humans, we long for wholeness. And, in its intricacies, its balances, and interconnections, creation models wholeness for us. We not only need to cooperate with creation, but we also need to cooperate—not collide—with ourselves, our bodies, minds, and souls. A restful sabbath reminds us that everything has been created to be balanced, whole, and very good—including us.

December 21

I am sure you've seen the slogan on t-shirts and bumper stickers: "Be patient. God isn't finished with me yet." I suppose this is a good reminder for all of us who have high expectations for ourselves and others. We can often be too quick to judge each other, too impatient for change in ourselves and those we love. Yet the reality is that we are all works in progress.

The text in Genesis says that God finishes the work that God had been doing. But is God really finished? I kind of doubt it. Yes, God has had a very busy week, what with setting the planets in motion, dividing night from day, land from water, creating all living beings and growing things. The Spirit moving over the deep in the beginning has breathed life into so many places. Genesis will soon be moving on to the story of Adam and Eve. But I'm guessing God goes right back to work on the eighth day.

This is good news for us. God the Creator hasn't checked out but has kept on working. The Bible tells us about how God goes on to create a people, deliver them from slavery, sustain them in the wilderness, and give them a home. As Christians, we believe this same Creator God sends Jesus, the Word incarnate. And, as Paul says, "If anyone is in Christ, there is a new creation: everything old has passed away; see, everything has become new!" (2 Corinthians 5:17). We ourselves are being created anew. Every new idea, every work of art, every medical breakthrough, every new day is a gift from God. God continues the work of creation within us and throughout all the earth, creating new paths and possibilities.

We are all works in progress. God the Creator is patient, and God is not finished with us yet.

December 22

This week's author
Barry Beisner

> *And on the seventh day God finished the work that he had done, and he rested on the seventh day from all the work that he had done. So God blessed the seventh day and hallowed it, because on it God rested from all the work that he had done in creation.*
>
> **Genesis 2:2-3**

One of the wonders of God's creation, the winter solstice, is here. We are passing from the constant lengthening of nights into a relentless brightening of days.

As Advent draws to its conclusion, nature points us more emphatically toward our preparations to welcome the Light that enlightens the life of every human being. These last remaining days of Advent are probably as busy as can be imagined. It is a great challenge, then—and all the more important—to pause and recall that which is not only the climax of the creation story but also the great truth at its core: God rested.

God rests on the seventh day, not because the work of the previous six has been so exhausting but rather, God's rest is an affirmational and celebratory pause in which God delights over all that has been created and set in motion. It is all "very good," and God is confident in creation's ability to be the beautiful, blessed world that God has made it to be. This is, of course, the basis for the sabbath, the biblical day of rest.

We are busy with many things (especially on the 22nd of December!), but we live in a world of time that has been structured by the creation story, divided into weeks of seven days, each culminating in the reminder that on the seventh day God rested. This is both an example and commandment to us to participate with God in affirming and celebrating all that God has made—embracing with love and confidence God's abiding sovereign presence in the world and in our lives.

December 23

God rests.

We are given the image of a dove, hovering just as the Spirit hovers at the beginning over the chaos of the waters. Now God creates all things, sets them in motion, empowers and provides for them. The Spirit hovers still.

The last thing God creates is a day of rest, a sabbath time in which we are helped by the Spirit to become aware of God's constant, pervasive presence and providence. The Spirit hovers; it is God at work to bring all things—to bring us—into the fullness of what God intends. It is the power of God to renew and transform the world.

Soon we will celebrate the birth of Jesus, in whose story the holy dove of the Spirit also appears. The work the Spirit empowers Jesus to do continues, as the new creation begun in him continues. We have a part to play in this great unfolding. We have work to do. And so the dove appears above the birth-waters and baptismal waters of our lives. The Spirit empowers us, brings order and life out of our chaos and confusion, and guides us into the restful fullness of life God intends for us.

Our Advent waiting is drawing to a close. Soon we will celebrate the coming of Christ, whom we have promised to follow and obey as Lord and Savior. The Spirit helps us live faithfully into that promise, empowers us for the journey, guides us along the way. The Spirit hovers over us. Our souls find rest in this assurance, helping us to know and trust that the God who made us is not finished with us. We are becoming what we are, what we have always been: Beloved of God, God's new creation in Christ.

December 24

In our time and culture, well-meaning, decent people have lost interest in efforts to connect with other well-meaning, decent people who happen to think differently from themselves. Sociologists call this an "empathy wall." We have seen plenty of evidence of that wall in our lives, along with other walls that divide us. You and I have seen—and likely felt—the depth of such divisions and felt the disappointment, anger, anxiety, and confusion that walls so often stir up.

Tonight is a night for us to remember our essential unity in and with the Creator. We are all part of the one creation, which God has called "very good." This creation has a divine purpose, recognizable in its order, beauty, fragility, and power—and in the way that all things are profoundly interconnected and dependent upon one another for their well-being.

Christmas teaches us that God has not only wonderfully created—but now has yet more wonderfully restored—the dignity of human nature. Every human being, made in the image of the Creator, is endowed with that dignity. Can we be restored to that understanding, that way of being in the world, this very day? Are we actually willing to live the promise of our Baptismal Covenant: To respect the dignity of every human being?

Could our congregations become laboratories where people can learn to see and value—to communicate and even love—other-minded folks in that transformative and transfiguring way that comes with respecting the dignity of the other, seeing in them the image of the Creator?

What can we do to help make this Christmas like that?

December 25

We cannot fully comprehend our Creator, but we can experience what God is like, so as to speak of God with real authority. We can live in response to God, live God-ward, live in a way that participates in the divine life of God and the creation.

We can do this because of Christmas—the Mystery of the Word made flesh. And in choosing to follow Jesus and to walk in the way of his love, we are choosing a new way of being in the world, and this includes a new way of being in and with creation.

The story of God resting and the image of the hovering dove speak to us of this new way. They are invitations to enter sabbath—a time holy and set apart. I recommend to you two books on sabbath, from two important teachers and guides. One is Abraham Joshua Heschel's *The Sabbath*; the other is *Sabbath As Resistance: Saying No to the Culture of Now* by Walter Brueggemann. Herschel weaves traditional Jewish views of the sabbath into a mystical, lyrical, timeless meditation inviting all of us who live time-determined lives into the timeless realm of the Creator. Brueggemann honors the sabbath invitation and draws from it a practical agenda for an urgently necessary transformation of our lives and our world. Both writers are emphatic in reminding us of the most essential fact of our lives: That God—and God alone—is God.

This God is our Creator. God is with us. All creation is full of God's glory. And we are part—the most beloved part—of that creation. May this Christmas help us begin again to walk in the way of the Child, the way of his sabbath.

December 26

Today, the church remembers the life and ministry of Saint Stephen, the first Christian martyr. We are told in the Book of Acts that, like his Lord, Stephen dies praying that God will forgive his murderers. In this, he is truly a witness—a literal translation of martyr—to the reconciling power of Jesus.

God so loved the world, scripture tells us, that Jesus is sent to us. Christmastide celebrates God with us, God who has come to reconcile us and all of creation to Godself.

One of those present and complicit in Stephen's death is Saul—later to be converted to The Way and known as the Apostle Paul. Here is further evidence of the power of Christ's ministry of reconciliation to transform lives. That reconciling power is at work in all the world to restore all things to unity with God. The whole of creation is being transformed.

Saint Stephen is also one of the first deacons in the early church. This servant ministry helps the church remember that our relationship to creation—including, but not at all limited to, our fellow humans—is one of servanthood. Humanity is charged in the moment of our own creation with shepherding and stewarding the earth and its inhabitants. God expects us to share God's love for creation—to delight in it, to see the great and beautiful goodness of it, and to be God's partners in caring for it.

We are blessed to have deacons lead the people of God in addressing the needs, hopes, and concerns of the world, and in continuing Christ's ministry of reconciliation. Our deacons help us work for justice and peace in our communities and in the wider world. In these times, we must also be especially careful not to neglect our need for reconciliation with the earth itself and the work we must do for our species to live justly and peaceably in creation.

December 27

"In the Beginning was the Word." These opening words of Saint John's Gospel (on this, his Feast Day) remind us of a profound theological truth: the divine *logos* (word/expression/self-communication) is involved in creation because the nature of the creation is that it is an expression of God, a divine intention to be in relationship. Where humans are concerned, God communicates and reveals Godself to us, expecting us to do the same in return. This implies that the relationship between Creator and creature is one of love and trust, requiring of us all a full measure of effort toward the kind of communication that all relationships need in order to grow, thrive, and flourish.

"He was in the beginning with God". John points to the eternal Word as what Christians later come to call the second person of the Trinity—the Son. "And the Word became flesh, and dwelt among us". The creation story we have been reflecting on all year has taken on a new dimension: God, revealed in and through creation, present and active in it, becomes part of it in a unique and wonderful way. Human and divine come together in the incarnation, and creation is transformed. The entire scope of creation is always a revelation of the mind of God, always a place of encounter with God. Now, as the Word takes form, God takes on the fullness of our humanity.

The universe has always been gloriously revelatory; now it is truly sacramental.

God in Christ reconciles, restores, and renews the entire face of creation, including us. We now can have the kind of relationship with God that God intended from the beginning—one of love and trust, in synch with God's plan and purpose for us. We can enter into God's rest.

December 28

God rests, trusting that creation will unfold according to its nature, which is a reflection of God. God trusts that humanity, made in God's image, will live a relationship of love and trust and care for God and creation.

God's rest is an invitation to us to participate with God in this work, to participate in the life of God. The tragic side of the freedom bestowed upon us by God is seen again and again in our individual and collective choices to not live in right relationship to the Creator but as selfish servants of other gods—power, ignorance, fear, and greed prominent among them.

Today is the Feast of the Holy Innocents. In this story, Herod shows how devoutly he serves false gods. In his determination to eliminate a perceived threat to his rule, he orders the murder of numerous young children.

The logic of creation indicates a relationship between our Creator and us, such that we can only truly be who we truly are—the people the Creator intends us to be—by being in harmony with creation. That is where our true happiness is found, and nowhere else, because it simply does not exist anywhere else.

The story, in its countless variations, is all too familiar. Herod's horrible attack on creation—on children, the first fruits of our hearts—is only a more dramatic version of a dynamic each of us sees in and around us every day.

December 29

Today is the Feast of Thomas Becket, twelfth-century Archbishop of Canterbury. Becket has long been venerated as a saint and martyr, whose death came, at least indirectly, as a result of a protracted power struggle between church and crown, the archbishop and king.

Whether Becket died as a result of politics or because of his faithful defense of the integrity of the church is a matter of debate. Perhaps it was both: Unambiguous martyrdoms are scarce in our histories. Certainly, it is as a martyr that Becket has held a special place in the imagination of the church and has been given this day on its calendar.

American representative democracy rightly celebrates the benefits of living in a system that separates church and state, both guaranteeing free exercise of religion and preventing governmental preferences for any particular religion. Yet such separation was not intended to keep religion out of civic life or to silence religious voices in debates or matters of public policy.

You and I have a responsibility as servants of the Creator to make use of civil government as an instrument that furthers the well-being of creation and all its multitude. We who have so recently come together to adore Christ the newborn king must not fail to measure public policy by the standards of Jesus' kingdom.

December 30

Today the Church recalls the witness of Frances Joseph Gaudet, who until her death in 1934 dedicated herself to prison reform and the education of poor black children in Louisiana. That she did so from a place of faith puts her on the church's calendar of feasts and fasts and calls her to our attention today.

Certainly more, much more, needs to be done to address these issues, further compounded by generational racism, poverty, violence, and systematic injustice. None of these things—nor any of the things that corrupt and destroy the creatures of God—are part of God's intention for creation.

God does not want to see such evil in creation. Saint Augustine, writing in the early fifth century, tells us that since evil was not created by God, it has no being in itself but is really only the distortion and perversion of good—as all things made by God are originally good.

Evil has no power, then, except that which we give to it. God has made a good and beautiful world—you and me included—and has placed this world in our care. In God's love, we have been created with the innate ability and desire to respond in love and therefore to make our own choices.

God rests, trusting us to do our part for the well-being of the world. But in the familiar words of the eucharist prayer, we turn against God and betray God's trust, and we turn against one another. That power of sin and death, which Christ came to overcome, has no place in creation.

Gaudet worked with Christ to overcome evil in her context. Likewise, we must work with Christ in ours, to reconcile, restore and, renew God's good creation, that all might enjoy true rest—relationship—with the Creator.

December 31

The old year ends and the new one begins. Arriving at this point could simply be a matter of riding along as our planet makes its regular orbit around the sun. That in itself is a wonder—one of many wonders of a creation that includes countless planets, suns, and more. The universe is God's handiwork, wonderfully expressing God's own self.

All the universe is filled with the glory of God; God resting means God affirming and celebrating the great goodness of it all, trusting it to move along the trajectory of God's purpose.

Certainly we have not come to this day simply by riding along. Even if it has held great joy for us, chances are it has not been easy arriving at the doorstep of this year. Perhaps the year now ending hasn't seemed to unfold along the divine trajectory. Perhaps in our small part of creation, chaos and confusion have been more evident than God's purpose; loss more prevalent than providence. Maybe there has been real suffering.

And yet, the Spirit, like the dove, hovers over God's creation.

Can you see it?

As you look back over this year that is about to end—and further back—over all the moments that have brought you to this present moment, can you see the signs of the hovering dove? The Spirit has been at work in you, bringing you to this threshold. The invitation is not only to cross into the new year in hope—but also it is to enter God's rest now, to be in a relationship of love and trust with the Creator who loves the creation, and to trust creation to continue to become the blessing that it is.

The most real thing about the world—about us—is that God loves us.

May that love abide with you always.

About the Artist

Kathrin Burleson

Kathrin Burleson is an artist and writer living in Northern California. Her work explores the interconnectedness of all of creation. The recipient of numerous awards, Burleson has exhibited her work in museums, galleries, and churches throughout the United States.

Kathrin is founding member of Saints Martha and Mary Episcopal Mission in Trinidad, California, and is an associate of the Community of the Transfiguration, a religious community for women in The Episcopal Church.

You can see more of Kathrin's artwork and writing by visiting www.kathrinburleson.com. Her previous book with Forward Movement, *The Soul's Journey: An Artist's Approach to the Stations of the Cross,* is available by visiting www.forwardmovement.org.

About the Authors

Barry Beisner serves as the seventh bishop of the Episcopal Diocese of Northern California. Ordained a priest in the Diocese of California in 1979, Beisner served at parishes throughout California and Ohio before being named canon to the ordinary in the Diocese of Northern California in 2002 and consecrated as their diocesan bishop in 2007. He received his master of divinity degree from the Church Divinity School of the Pacific in Berkeley and was awarded master of sacred theology and doctor of divinity degrees from the General Theological Seminary in New York.

Mary W. Cox retired in 2012 as director of communications for the Episcopal Diocese of Southeast Florida. She now lives in Charlotte, North Carolina, where she and her husband enjoy singing in the choir at Church of the Holy Comforter. She takes walks and photographs, writes haiku and light verse, is part of the parish's Outreach Ministry Support Team, and reads (in English only) to children in the bilingual preschool. She posts her photos and haiku on Facebook at www.facebook.com/mary.w.cox.

Minda Cox is an energetic and engaged Episcopalian living in Bolivar, Missouri. Born in India without arms or legs and adopted as a toddler, she loves to travel and to encourage others. Cox is an artist, speaker, and writer, having discovered that these are ideal gifts for a happy introvert. She enjoys losing herself in a pencil drawing or a watercolor painting, and she spends hours reflecting on her journey, scripture, and the situation of the world around her, and knitting together words to create something that may open the love of God to others.

Julianne Day graduated from Kenyon College in 2006 with a bachelor's degree in English and environmental studies. Upon graduation, she served as a disaster relief worker with the Episcopal Diocese of Louisiana in post-Katrina New Orleans. She has served as a youth leader and vestry member in her home parish of St. Andrew's Episcopal Church in Grand Rapids, Michigan. Day enjoys reading, writing, making art, and spending time outdoors, especially at her family's cabin in the woods and in Michigan's Upper Peninsula.

James Derkits lives in Port Aransas, Texas, with his wife and young son, where he serves as the rector of Trinity by the Sea Episcopal Church. He surfs, runs, writes, paints, and enjoys the wonderful community of his island. Besides his ministry in the church, he is also one of the leaders of the Inner Journey Retreat, a spiritual retreat based on Jungian psychology. His favorite form of prayer is writing and playing music; he released his first musical album, *Buffalo Roam*, in 2016. He blogs at James-Derkits. blogspot.com, writes a monthly column for the South Jetty newspaper, and writes for the magazine of the Diocese of West Texas, *Reflections*.

The Rev. Elizabeth DeRuff is an Episcopal priest, agricultural chaplain, businesswoman, and farmer who makes her home in Marin County, California. She is a pioneer in exploring the intersection of food, land, and faith. She founded the non-profit Honoré Farm and Mill where she conducts research, writes, teaches, preaches, and consults with congregations around the country. The Honoré Growers Guild is a national CSA (Community Supported Agriculture) that supports churches and landowners in growing heirloom wheat for communion bread or wafers. Honoré's goal is for every Episcopal altar in the United States to have the opportunity to serve bread baked from local and sustainably sourced wheat. DeRuff has a bachelor's degree in business administration from the University of Southern California, a master of divinity degree from the Church Divinity School of the Pacific in Berkeley, and a certificate in bread baking from the San Francisco Baking Institute. She is married with three children and grew a half ton of fruit and vegetables in her home garden last year.

The Rev. Sister Diana Doncaster, C.T., is a member of the Community of the Transfiguration in Cincinnati, Ohio, and a priest of the Episcopal Church. She is the first sister in her community to become a priest and prays for others to follow. Writing is one of her greatest pleasures and privileges, followed by making beaded jewelry that she sells to raise money for micro-loans, which she believes is one of the most effective ways of helping people help themselves and their community.

Alyssa Finke spends her time writing, hiking, and cooking. She also enjoys a nice adventure and will cross oceans or city limit signs to have one. A graduate of the University of Cincinnati, Finke is the marketing coordinator for Forward Movement. Currently raising a tomato plant, a cactus, and several geraniums, her green-thumb aspirations are a work in progress.

Linda Gelbrich is an active lay person at the Church of the Good Samaritan in Corvallis, Oregon. She is retired from working as a clinical social worker in mind-body health care and continues to teach and encourage others in the value of creative expression and stress reduction. If she's not outside, she's probably near a window. She and her husband are grandparents to four delightful young grandchildren.

Jayce Hafner is a writer and environmental advocate based in Washington, D.C. Hafner represents the domestic policy priorities of the Episcopal Church to U.S. Congress and mobilizes faith advocates across the United States. A Virginian born and raised, she grew up on a cattle farm in the Shenandoah Valley and graduated from Hendrix College in 2011 with a major in sustainable communities.

Susan Hanson is a longtime member of the English faculty at Texas State University in San Marcos, Texas. She teaches a variety of writing courses, including environmental writing and an honors course in nature writing. She also worked for almost twenty years as a newspaper journalist and for thirteen as the lay Episcopal chaplain at Texas State University. Hanson is the author of *Icons of Loss and Grace: Moments from the Natural World*, a collection of personal essays, and co-editor of *What Wildness Is This: Women Write about the Southwest*. She has written critical essays on Barbara Kingsolver and Loren Eiseley and has had work published in numerous publications, including *Texas Parks & Wildlife* and *Northern Lights*. Hanson is married and has a grown daughter living in Austin. In her free time, she enjoys native plant gardening, snorkeling and canoeing, doing photography, and traveling.

Nancy Hopkins-Greene is an Episcopal priest serving as associate rector at Church of the Redeemer in Cincinnati, Ohio. She and her husband Roger are empty nesters, with two children in their twenties. She spends her free time outdoors when possible, running, hiking, and gardening. Nancy served as an assistant editor at Forward Movement from 2009 to 2016.

Rachel Jones loves Jesus, her husband, their respective families, barbecue, breakfast tacos, Bob Dylan, baseball, the Book of Jeremiah, trips to the beach, finding money in a jacket pocket, and snagging the shadiest parking spot in the lot—in that exact order. Rachel and Mr. Jones live on a farm in Northern Kentucky with dogs, cats, chickens, and other critters. Rachel is the associate editor for Forward Movement. When she's not working on *Forward Day by Day*, she's usually looking for her car keys or putting up preserves, but should probably be updating her blog at makeshiftfarms.wordpress.com.

Douglas Knight was raised in central Arkansas to love the woods and all life he could find there. He studied creative writing at the University of Central Arkansas, married the love of his life, and moved to Japan for a year to work humbly on an organic farm in the name of the Episcopal Church under a program called the Young Adult Service Corps. Knight and his wife serve at Camp Mitchell in Arkansas, where they grow a garden and allow it to teach anyone who enters.

Nicholas Knisely serves as the thirteenth bishop of the Episcopal Diocese of Rhode Island. He is a member of the Society of Ordained Scientists and prior to ordination studied physics and astronomy. Knisely previously served as a priest in Delaware, Western and Eastern Pennsylvania, and as dean of the cathedral in Phoenix, Arizona. He has been active in a number of ministries with particular focus in the areas of homelessness, communications, college and youth, finance, and ecumenical relations. He and his wife, Karen, have been married for thirty years and have an adult daughter. Knisely blogs at entangledstates.org and is active on Twitter and Instagram.

Jason Leo is an Episcopal priest and serves as missioner for congregational vitality for the Diocese of Southern Ohio. His vocational career has carried him across oceans, up mountainsides, and all the way back home to the Ohio Valley, where he makes his home with his wife and their three children. Jason is an enthusiastic contributor for Forward Movement.

Sean McConnell has served the church as a lay professional since 2000 when he became program producer at GraceCom, the media ministry of San Francisco's Grace Cathedral. In 2006, he was named canon for communications in the Diocese of California. He has served on the board of Episcopal Communicators; as chair of the Standing Commission on Episcopal Church Communications and Information Technology; and as technology coordinator for the House of Deputies of the Episcopal Church. In 2013, McConnell landed his dream job as director of engagement for Episcopal Relief & Development.

Miriam Willard McKenney is a child of God who finds extreme joy parenting her three girls: Nia, Kaia, and Jaiya. She and her husband, David, met at the Union of Black Episcopalians conference in 1981. Miriam works as Forward Movement's development director and also writes and edits *Daily Devo: Devotions for Families*. She was a children's librarian and school media specialist for twenty years before joining Forward Movement's staff. She has recently discovered a love of outdoor fitness in extreme temperatures, as there is no bad weather, just incorrect clothing choices.

Jonathan Melton is a husband, dad, Episcopal priest, and friend. He develops ministry at St. Francis House, the Episcopal faith community at the University of Wisconsin-Madison and has previously served parishes in South Texas. He is a longtime blogger, avid reader, novice hiker, commuter-type cyclist, and occasional knitter. His prayer is for a life determined by prayer and centered in the waters of baptism.

Jason Merritt is an old millennial, marketing director at Forward Movement, an avid soccer fan, fisherman, and dog lover. He currently lives in Cincinnati, Ohio, with his fiancé Kristen, and their two rescue dogs.

Cory Reinisch is a native Texan and a singer-songwriter living in Austin, Texas. He enjoys fishing, tinkering with guitars, selling records, making music, and playing gigs with his band, The Harvest Thieves.

Greg Rickel is the eighth bishop of the Episcopal Diocese of Olympia, consecrated to the role in 2007. Prior to his election as bishop, he served as a priest in Arkansas and Texas, where he also worked as a hospital administrator before his ordination. Rickel embraces a radical hospitality that welcomes all, no matter where they find themselves on their journey of faith. He envisions the church as a safe and authentic community in which to explore God's infinite goodness and grace as revealed in the life and continuing revelation of Jesus Christ.

Debbie Royals is Pascua Yaqui from Tucson, Arizona. She is an Episcopal priest, author, retreat leader and educator. She received her undergraduate degrees from the University of Arizona College Of Nursing, a specialized degree in Native American theology from Prescott College, and her master of divinity and master of fine arts degrees from the Church Divinity School of the Pacific and the Graduate Theological Union. Royals serves as the canon for Native American ministry in the Diocese of Arizona, a consultant for the Indigenous Theological Training Institute, and a faculty member for the Church Pension Group. She has served in numerous roles in Native American ministry throughout the Episcopal Church. She has published in several journals, as well as written for books on prayer and meditations. She lives out her passion as a Native American woman in her home community of Old Pascua.

Sallie Schisler is a lifelong Episcopalian and answered her calling to the ordained ministry when she was sixty. She currently serves in an historic Ohio River church among amazing people. She and her husband of forty-six years, a retired judge, are the proud parents of two grown sons, and they delight in their four marvelous grandchildren.

Jeremiah Sierra is managing editor for Trinity Church Wall Street in New York City. He has a master of fine arts degree from the New School and has written for the Episcopal Church Foundation, the Huffington Post, and other publications. He volunteers regularly with social justice and climate change organizations. He lives in Brooklyn with his wife and their daughter, Joana.

Lauren Wilkes Stubblefield is a native of Vicksburg, Mississippi, a lifelong member of the Church of the Holy Trinity, and a proud graduate of the University of the South at Sewanee. She served as the diocesan communicator for the Episcopal Diocese of Mississippi during and after Hurricane Katrina. Most recently, she worked with the Society of Saint John the Evangelist as their project manager for www.ThyKingdomCome. global, the Archbishop of Canterbury's eleven-day call to prayer. She posts on Twitter and Instagram @EVNTHZN.

Richelle Thompson is a mother of two teenagers, the wife of a priest, and the deputy director and managing editor of Forward Movement. She loves camping trips and long afternoons looking at the canopy of trees from the perch of a hammock, and she's often reading novels at light speed. She has served on the board of Episcopal Communicators and on the Standing Commission on Episcopal Church Communications and Information Technology. She is also a regular blogger for Episcopal Church Foundation. Prior to serving at Forward Movement, she was the director of communications for the Episcopal Diocese of Southern Ohio and a reporter for *The Cincinnati Enquirer*. She lives in Northern Kentucky with her family and animal menagerie, including two dogs, three cats, and a horse.

Jennifer S.T. Wickham works for the Episcopal Church in Haiti as development coordinator for Saint Vincent's Centre for Handicapped Children in Port-au-Prince. She is married to an Episcopal priest and is the mother of two adult sons. She enjoys the additional role of being a longtime mentor trainer and mentor for Education for Ministry program housed in Sewanee, Tennessee. In her spare time, she enjoys cooking, gardening, pottery, and weaving rag rugs on her floor loom. She lives in Corpus Christi, Texas, with her husband and attends All Saints' Episcopal Church.

About Forward Movement

Forward Movement is committed to inspiring disciples and empowering evangelists. While we produce great resources like this book, Forward Movement is more than a publishing company. We are a ministry.

We live out this ministry through publishing books, daily reflections, studies for small groups, and online resources. More than a half million people read our daily devotions through *Forward Day by Day*, which is also available in Spanish (*Adelante Día a Día*) and Braille, online, as a podcast, and as an app for your smartphones or tablets. It is mailed to more than fifty countries, and we donate nearly 30,000 copies each quarter to prisons, hospitals, and nursing homes. We actively seek partners across the church and look for ways to provide resources that inspire and challenge. A ministry of the Episcopal Church for eighty years, Forward Movement is a nonprofit organization funded by sales of resources and gifts from generous donors.

To learn more about Forward Movement and our resources, visit www.ForwardMovement.org or www.VenAdelante.org. We are delighted to be doing this work and invite your prayers and support.